Essential Guide to the Psychedelic Renaissance

Essential Guide to the Psychedelic Renaissance

Antón Gómez-Escolar

PSYCHONAUTGUIDES.COM

Idea, business project and coordination: Santos Rodríguez
Direction and management: Eva Huici
Corporate counsel: Sunny Bates
Editing: Martín Rasskin
Marketing and social networks:
Gabriel García and Jhoselin Moudallal
Book series: Psychonaut Guides - www.psychonautguides.com
Category: Psychedelic Science
Title: Essential Guide to the
Psychedelic Renaissance. Color edition 2022
Author: © 2022 Antón Gómez-Escolar
Translation: Vanessa Benavente and Sergio Lanza
Series Director: Antón Gómez-Escolar
Scientific advisor: José Carlos Bouso
Legal advisor: Francisco Azorín
Cover design: RodilHerraiz.com
Copyright of this edition: © 2022 Argonowta Digital SLL, Madrid, Spain. All rights reserved
"PsychonautGuides.com" is an Argonowt project.

ARGONOWT: We are adventurers engaged in a quest.
www.argonowt.com
Follow us:
https://psychonautguides.news/
https://www.instagram.com/psychonautguides/
https://twitter.com/PsychonautGuide

This work may not be reproduced in whole or in part, or incorporated into a computer system, or transmitted in any form or by any means (electronic, mechanical, photocopying, recording or otherwise) without the prior written permission of the copyright holders. Infringement of such rights may constitute an intellectual property crime. Any form of reproduction, distribution, public communication or transformation of this work may only be made with the authorization of the copyright holders, unless otherwise provided by law.

Standard ISBN: 978-84-1894-327-0
Release date: May 2022
Printed in Spain

Printed by: Podiprint
Mandatory Deposit: M-10256-2022

*To so many brave and unprejudiced people,
who prefer to listen and research before speaking,
who question dogmas and make the world move forward.*

*To family and good friends,
to love and other miracles of life.
Thank you for always being there for me.*

This work has a purely informative and general dissemination function under article 19 of the International Declaration of Human Rights, which recognises and protects the right to information. However, the information contained in this work is intended exclusively for persons of legal age.

In no case is the content of this work intended to promote, propose or provoke the possession, trafficking, production or consumption of psychoactive substances or any other crime, whether related or not. The lack of criminal significance regarding the mere personal consumption of psychedelic drugs in most Western countries also means that these figures cannot be found in a work that only contains informative, bibliographical and scientific information on a topical subject of medical-scientific interest which has a regular presence in the mass media, such as research and therapeutic use of psychedelic drugs and other psychoactive substances, whether legal, controlled or illegalised.

The publisher and authors disclaim any inappropriate, risky, dangerous or illicit use that the reader of this work may make of the data and knowledge contained herein. The content of this work, whether of a scientific, medical, legal or risk-related nature, while seeking to be as rigorous and up-to-date as possible, does not represent a guarantee in any field.

This collection of books is relevant and necessary at a time when psychedelic medicines are already available for use in psychiatry, as is the case with ketamine, and as the arsenal available will grow over time: psilocybin, MDMA, DMT, etc. The collection fills a necessary gap in this new medical and social panorama. The authors responsible for the texts are the best Spanish specialists in their field and the collection can only be a publishing success. It will also serve to provide the media with objective and accessible information on a subject that, although still unknown, will be the near future of mental health treatment, at a time of pandemic when it is more necessary than ever.

José Carlos Bouso, PhD,
Scientific Director, ICEERS.
(International Center for
Ethnobotanical Education,
Research and Service)

Index

Foreword 19

Introduction to the Collection 23

Chapter 1. Basic Concepts
of Neuroscience and Neuropharmacology 27
    Brain and Central Nervous System 28
    Neurons, Synapses, Neurotransmitters
    and Neuroreceptors 29
    Neuropharmacology 37

Chapter 2. Introduction to Psychoactive Substances 41
    Psychoactive… drugs? 41
    Types of Psychoactive Substances 44
        Stimulants 50
            Main Uses 51
            Main Risks 51
        Depressants 53
            Main Uses 54
            Main Risks 54
        Opioids 55
            Main Uses 56

Duration 207
Specific Risks.. 208
5-MeO-DMT ("Toad")... 209
   Definition, Composition and Origin 209
   Applications 210
   Forms and Routes of Administration................ 210
   Pharmacology and Effects 211
   Dosage... 211
   Duration 212
   Specific Risks.. 212
Mescaline ("Cactus") 213
   Definition, Composition and Origin 213
   Applications 213
   Forms and Routes of Administration................ 214
   Pharmacology and Effects 215
   Dosage... 217
   Duration 218
   Specific Risks.. 218
Ibogaine 219
   Definition, Composition and Origin 220
   Applications 220
   Forms and Routes of Administration................ 220
   Pharmacology and Effects 221
   Dosage 222
   Duration 223
   Specific Risks.. 223
MDMA ("Ecstasy") 224
   Definition, Composition and Origin 224
   Applications 224
   Forms and Routes of Administration................ 225
   Pharmacology and Effects 226
   Dosage 227
   Duration 228
   Specific Risks and Risk Reduction Strategies..... 229
Ketamine.. 233
   Definition and Origin 234
   Applications 234

Forms and Routes of Administration 235
Pharmacology and Effects 236
Dosage 236
Duration 237
Specific Risks... 237

Chapter 8. Psychedelic Risks & Harm
Reduction Strategies.. 241
   Risks and Harm Reduction................................ 241
   Person & Context (*Set & Setting*) 248
      Set 250
      Setting 251
   Tripsitting for Managing "Bad Trips"
   and other Psychedelic Emergencies...................... 253
   Substance 257
      Dosage, Frequency of Consumption
      and Tolerance 257
      Purity and Adulterations.................................. 260
      Routes of Administration 264
      Mixtures and Combinations 265

Chapter 9. Conclusions: Looking to the Future 269
Psychedelic Resources 277
   Information on Psychedelics
   and Risk Reduction 277
   Psychedelic Research 278
   Psychedelic Societies and Others 279
   Risk Reduction Organizations 280
   Dug checking / Testing / Analysis........................ 280
   Activism... 281
   Forums.. 281
   Youtube Channels 282
   Podcasts... 283
   Phone Numbers 283
   Apps.. 283
   Documentaries about Psychedelics 284
   Manuals and Other Publications 285

Books 285
Legal Information 286
Other Resources 287

Glossary 289

Appendix: The Legal Status of
Psychedelic Drugs Psychedelics Around the World 295

Foreword

Throughout the 1970s and 1980s, most psychedelic substances, as well as research with them, were banned nationally and internationally despite millennia of traditional use, decades of Western scientific studies, having facilitated key discoveries in neuroscience and obtaining promising results in mental health treatments (as you will learn in this book). But the Western sociopolitical context at that time was different from the current one, with very limited scientific and social knowledge about these substances. There was little accurate harm reduction information to effectively minimize the risks of widespread recreational use, and because research and clinical use were blocked by massive "war on drugs" propaganda, it was impossible to counteract the misinformation that circulated. Stronger scientific understanding of psychedelics was lacking and, because humans tend to fear what they don't know, can't control or don't fully understand, these substances were left in a difficult stalemate. In 1986, just after MDMA was classified in 1985, I founded MAPS to unlock that situation with new research and scientific insights. MAPS is a nonprofit educational and scientific research organization that develops medical, legal, and cultural contexts for people to benefit from the controlled use of psychedelics.

For more than 30 years, despite all the difficulties, knowledge about these powerful tools was maintained and expanded both underground and in clinical research for therapeutic applications, which has seen a comeback in the new millennium. All this thanks to the conviction of many brave therapists, activists, scientists and organizations who, like MAPS, believed that psychedelics were "as valuable to the mind as the telescope is to astronomy or the microscope to biology" (quoting the Dr. Stanislav Grof) and had immense therapeutic potential. With the new millennium, research began to bear fruit, and finally all this important knowledge began to sprout everywhere in modern science. It did so in the context of the great mental health epidemic that has been developing in Western societies in recent decades, an epidemic that current treatments are struggling unsuccessfully to contain. The enormous potential of psychedelics, for neuroscience and for therapy, attracted the interest of many great scientists and highly regarded institutions around the world who joined the field, further accelerating both its research and push for its accepted medical use, which is fast approaching.

Right now, in the midst of a psychedelic renaissance capable of forever transforming mental health treatments and our understanding of the mind, esketamine is already approved for depression, Phase III clinical trials with MDMA for post-traumatic stress disorder (PTSD) are showing great results, and psilocybin and other psychedelics are being investigated for many different mental health indications. Every day we have more and more scientific knowledge about psychedelics, and a great opportunity to make all this new knowledge accessible to everyone, so that everyone can understand how and why psychedelic-assisted psychotherapy works, and why all this scientific research is such great news for public health in this century. Finally, we will be able to bring these treatments to those who need them, in a context in which society understands what, why and how. This is the goal of these pages.

In this book and this collection, you will learn the basics of psychedelic drugs, the history of their renaissance, the new neuroscience discoveries made through them, and the highly promising uses of psychedelic-assisted psychotherapies to treat many difficult conditions, such as depression, anxiety, post-traumatic stress disorder, and addiction. You will also learn about potential risks and practical approaches to their reduction and prevention, inside and outside the laboratory. Because, if psychedelic substances are currently in the process of demonstrating their full safety and efficacy, it is because we now know more about how to better manage the variables of *set and setting* (subject and context) to maximize the chances of a good therapeutic result and minimize potential risks when used in a controlled context, with the right mindset and preparation.

Knowledge is power. For this psychedelic revolution to become a lasting clinical reality, for millions of patients and for humanity, we need our societies to be well educated on this matter, to avoid the mistakes of the past and to understand both the potential risks and benefits, as many other cultures around the world have done for millennia. After decades of propaganda and misinformation, well-informed public opinion, through books like this one, is the safe path to science, public health, and preventing the prohibitionist approaches to drugs that we still face in many places. Despite the amazing results and safety that psychedelics are showing in clinical studies so far, much understanding, work, and legal developments are still needed in most countries and societies to further research, optimize, and ultimately bring these powerful and beneficial therapeutic tools to those who need them, now and in the future. We need both the administration and the public to have good knowledge to do more research and lay a solid foundation for an informed debate on how best to use the incredible opportunities that this "psychedelic renaissance" brings us.

An unfortunately enduring legacy of this COVID-19 pandemic will likely be a worsening mental health epidemic that will require better therapeutic tools, including safer and more effective prevention and mental health treatments, along with the importance of trusting science. As you will read in these pages, science is showing that psychedelics can be a powerful tool for treating mental health, so further development of psychedelic-assisted psychotherapy is needed more than ever.

Psychedelic research has the potential to change our approach to mental health forever, if we can continue to educate society and minimize the sometimes uninformed and risky use of these substances. After a very long and strange trip, psychedelics may finally be back to stay.

Rick Doblin, Ph.D.
Founder and CEO of MAPS
(Multidisciplinary Association for Psychedelic Studies).

INTRODUCTION TO THE COLLECTION

This is the first of a series of books that will be published within the Psychonaut Guides collection and one that will allow you to learn many things about psychoactive substances in general and psychedelics in particular, as well as the current status of their promising therapeutic uses for a variety of mental health disorders, so unfortunately widespread in our days.

This collection will provide a closer look at these issues, in a simple and didactic way, seeking to bring the subject within reach of anyone with an interest in learning about it, but without neglecting scientific rigor and objectivity, avoiding delving into moral or philosophical questions, and focusing on science, rational knowledge, pragmatism and public health.

In this first volume, which serves as an introduction to the collection, we will begin by introducing the topic of drugs and some of their generalities, seeking to provide the reader with a basic understanding of their types, mechanisms of action, uses and risks, in order to focus then on the specific topic of psychedelic drugs, their recent history, their mechanisms of action, their growing scientific and clinical interest, its legal status, its risks at different levels and how to reduce them as much as possible.

As you will discover in these pages, we are at a key moment to learn about these issues. Not only are there growing movements clamoring for the failure of the "war on drugs" and calling for a revision of the policies in this regard (mainly aimed at decriminalization and even regulation), but there is an important research current that proposes the therapeutic use of some of these psychoactive substances, particularly cannabis (a compound on which we will not focus), and those with psychedelic properties, since they can become very effective treatments for some of the most difficult illnesses we face in mental health today. These substances can be both pure psychedelics (psilocybin, LSD, mescaline or ayahuasca) and empathogenic-entactogenic (MDMA) or dissociative[1] (ketamine).

Disorders such as depression, anxiety, addictions or post-traumatic stress, very widespread fundamentally in modern Western societies and very difficult to treat effectively or efficiently, are being treated experimentally, even achieving complete remissions[2] in a safe and effective manner through the use of psychotherapies assisted by psychedelic substances (or semi-psychedelic[3]) in controlled therapeutic contexts. These results have earned recognition from the most important regulatory agencies in the world, such as the U.S. Food and Drug Administration (FDA) and the European Union's EMA (European Medicines Agency), designating psychedelic-assisted psychotherapies as of great innovative importance and facilitating their research and accelerating their clinical development.

---

[1] Defined in the "Types of Drugs" section.
[2] In mental health, the word "cure" is not used much, preferring the concept of complete or partial "remission."
[3] Substances with psychedelic properties, even if these are not their main effect; also known as atypical psychedelics.

The return of these substances, which decades ago (and in a very different sociopolitical context) were classified internationally as having "a high potential for abuse and no recognized medical value," classification which led to their illegalization, means that we are now rediscovering these powerful molecules that have been used for millennia by many other cultures outside the Western world. For us, this means a real *psychedelic renaissance*, the beginning of a revolution in neuroscience and mental health that could change our societies forever.

BASIC CONCEPTS OF NEUROSCIENCE AND NEUROPHARMACOLOGY

Before addressing issues of drugs in general and those with psychedelic properties in particular, it is necessary to be clear about some basic notions of neuroscience[1] that will allow us to understand both their most basic mechanisms of action and the elementary terminology necessary to be able to speak about them properly. Although you can find some key definitions in the glossary, and in this collection, there are specific publications in the field of neuroscience and neuropharmacology you can examine[2]. Let's start by briefly exploring the terrain.

---

[1] Science that studies the nervous system and all its aspects (such as structure, function, biochemistry, pharmacology and pathology), and how its different elements interact, giving rise to the biological bases of cognition and behavior.

[2] Definitions are detailed later and in the glossary.

Brain and Central Nervous System

In the human body, our thoughts, emotions, behaviors, etc., originate in the most complex and unknown organ we have: the brain.

Arrangement of the parts of the nervous system (both central and peripheral) in the human body. *(Medium69, Jmarchn, CC BY-SA 4.0 <https://creativecommons.org/licenses/by-sa/4.0>, via Wikimedia Commons).*

This organ is located inside our head and is part of what is known as the nervous system, a system that runs throughout our body and performs numerous functions for our survival, such as regulating and maintaining each vital function, controlling voluntary movements, speech, intelligence, memory, emotions and processing the information received through the senses, being the organ where the mind and consciousness of the individual reside.

The brain is the directing part of this complex nerve network that extends throughout the body and allows it to carry out its important functions. Based on these functions and the anatomical structure, human beings divide our nervous system into: Central nervous system or CNS (which includes the brain and spinal cord) and peripheral nervous system or SNP (consisting of all the peripheral nerves that are outside the CNS but connect to it).

Both the central nervous system (CNS) and the peripheral nervous system (PNS) are made up of many different elements and subunits, but the most famous and important are highly specialized cells known as neurons.

Neurons, Synapses, Neurotransmitters and Neuroreceptors

The neuron is the specialized cell that makes up the tissue of the nervous system. In the human brain there are some 80,000 million neurons interconnected through a huge tangle of physical "wires" that extend from their bodies and link them together to form a network. These wires, called axons (which are long and send messages) and dendrites (which are short and receive messages), allow communication between the cells, through chemical and electrical signals that we will see below.

Neural Tissue

Morphological structure of a neuron.
(Blausen.com staff (2014). "Medical gallery of Blausen Medical 2014". WikiJournal of Medicine 1 (2). CC BY 3.0
<https://creativecommons.org/licenses
by/3.0>, via Wikimedia Commons).

These electrical impulses that travel through the neuron as if it were a wire, are known as action potentials, and could be compared to telegraph messages in Morse code. They are electrical impulses that can propagate within the neuronal "wiring" of the brain and travel long distances through the nerves of the body at very high speeds.

In any cable network there must be "connectors" that link them to each other and to other devices. In the nervous system, those connectors that link the axon of a sending neuron with the dendrites of a receiving neuron are known as synapses, and they are the points where neurons almost touch. But, as they do not really touch each other most of the times, upon reaching these points, the electricity that traveled through the axons (wires) makes some chemical signals "jump": these are the neurotransmitters. So, although neurons use electricity to send messages within the different parts of their elongated body, when it comes to passing that message

Simplified drawing of a synapse, "connectors" where the axon of a neuron almost touches the dendrite of another neuron, and communication between the two is carried out by the release of chemical signals (neurotransmitters). *(Nrets, CC BY-SA 3.0 <http://creativecommons.org/licenses/by-sa/3.0/>, via Wikimedia Commons).*

to other neurons they do so mostly by "splashing" each other with chemicals, called neurotransmitters, which are released when that message in the form of an electrical impulse reaches the end of the axon and must pass on to the next neuron. Although it seems impossible, this process that can seem so complex occurs in intervals of milliseconds, and each neuron can be connected to 10,000 others.

These chemical signals between neurons (neurotransmitters) are quite varied and can send very different messages to the next neuron. We could say that they act as different "keys" that are released by the sending neuron (presynaptic neuron) to the synapse (the connector), and will only fit in some specific "locks" (called neuronal receptors or neuroreceptors) of the receiving neuron (the postsynaptic neuron). Depending on the type of "doors" the receiving neuron wants to open or close, the sending neuron will release one type of key or another.

The substances used by the body to send "non-nerve" messages over long distances or throughout the body are known as hormones[3], while neurotransmitters are substances that also send messages but only between neurons and over very short distances, in those synapses we have discussed, producing effects that can be immediate and very localized, or propagate throughout the entire neural network. Some hormones that are generally used by the body can also be neurotransmitters, and some neurotransmitters behave like hormones. However, the key is that the electricity we generally associate with neurons and the nervous system, in reality only occurs within each neuron, the communication between

---

[3] For example, testosterone, adrenaline, insulin, cortisol or melatonin.

different neurons being fundamentally chemical and based on neurotransmitters, and these are involved in various processes. For example, some of the most famous neurotransmitters are serotonin, known to many as the "hormone of happiness" (although this is only partially true), or dopamine.

Just as there are multiple neurotransmitters that perform different functions, there are several types of neuroreceptors in the membranes of neurons, which are protein structures that act as locks for these keys, and that are activated or not depending on the specific neurotransmitter (key) that comes close to them. For the same neurotransmitter there can be several subtypes of neuroreceptor, so it can even be said that some of them are "master keys" insofar as, sometimes, they can not only open a single lock, but several of the same type, although they do not always turn equally well in all locks. In neuronal communication, what is ultimately important is not so much the neurotransmitter but what happens at the level of the receptors in the postsynaptic neuron, the locks that are being open, and how they do it.

These neurotransmitters and neuroreceptors can serve many different functions both inside and outside the brain, and, depending on the specific region of the brain or neuronal circuit on which they act, they can even be involved in completely opposite processes; so the generalization that a neurotransmitter only has a specific effect is overly simplistic and not always accurate. To give an idea of their diversity and the multiple processes in which they are involved, these are some neurotransmitters with their neuroreceptors and some of their main brain functions:

Neurotransmitter	Involved in processes of...	Neuroreceptors on which it acts
Serotonin (5-HT)	Mood, sleep, hunger, anxiety, emotions, social behavior...	5-HT1A, 5-HT1B, 5-HT1D, 5-HT1E, 5-HT1F, 5-HT2A, 5-HT2B, 5-HT2C, 5-HT4, 5-HT5A, 5-HT5B, 5-HT6, 5-HT7...
Dopamine	Motivation, concentration, reward, pleasure, humor, euphoria...	D1, D2, D3, D4, D5
GABA	Related to inhibition, relaxation, sleep...	GABA-A, GABA-B
Norepinephrine (or epinephrine)	Related to action, concentration, fight or flight response...	α1, α2, β1, β2, β3
Glutamate	Related to activation, learning, pain, memory, neuroplasticity...	NMDA, Kainate, AMPA, mGluR1, mGluR5, mGluR2, mGluR3, mGluR4, mGluR6, mGluR7, mGluR8
Acetylcholine	Related to memory, motor skills, attention...	Nicotinics (Nm, Nn), Muscarinics (M1, M2, M3)

Molecular structure

Serotonin (5-HT).

Dopamine.

Norepinephrine (or epinephrine).

Glutamate.

GABA.

Acetylcholine.

There are many other neurotransmitters and neuroreceptors, as well as other types of molecules that can act as neurotransmitters, although they are not released in the same way, such as oxytocin (related to emotional bonding, childbirth and breastfeeding) or endorphins (related to analgesia and acting on opioid receptors).

As we can see, all this is not as simple as saying that serotonin is the hormone of happiness, but rather that it acts as a modulator with various functions depending on which of its 14 different receptors it is activating and in which brain region, or neural network, it is found. Other neurotransmitters with fewer receptors can fulfill functions that are easier to explain, such as glutamate, which activates neurons and increases their electrical excitability, or GABA, which "turns them off" or reduces their electrical excitability. But these effects at the

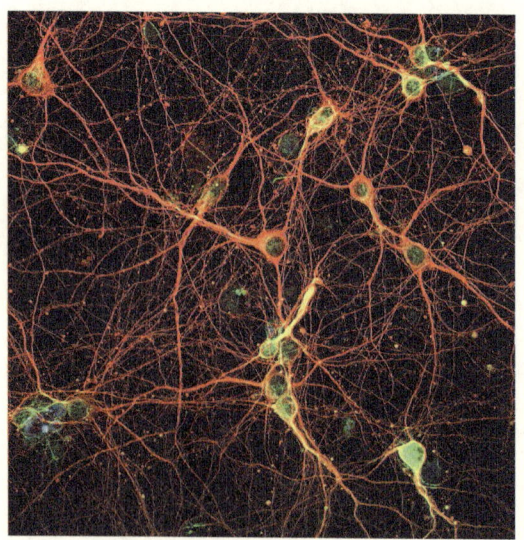

Network of neurons seen under the microscope. *(ALol88, CC BY 4.0 <https://creativecommons.org/licenses/by/4.0>, via Wikimedia Commons).*

neuronal level do not always translate to the entire brain, and it will also depend on the specific networks that are being activated or deactivated.

Why is it so important to talk about how neurons communicate in this book introduction? Because it is this chemical communication between neurons that allows the brain and the other parts of the nervous system to carry out all their functions. Just as it happens inside a computer, the operation of which does not depend only on the work of one of its parts but on the interaction (communication) between many of them, a neuron in our brain does not "think;" the neuronal network does. It is at this point that we can start talking about how exogenous molecules[4], like psychoactive substances, influence these processes.

Neuropharmacology

A drug is a molecule that is considered "bioactive" because, due to its structure and chemical configuration, it can interact with protein macromolecules, generally called receptors (locks), located in the membrane, cytoplasm or nucleus of a cell (such as neurons, for example), giving rise to an action and a noticeable effect. For example, when we take ibuprofen, it reduces pain and inflammation. For this reason, pharmacology is the branch of science that studies how the drug (be it a medicine bought in a pharmacy, a medicinal plant or a beer served at a bar) interacts with the body – its actions, effects and properties.

Neuropharmacology in particular studies how some drugs act specifically on neurons and the nervous system. Drugs with the ability to interact with our neurons and nervous tissues are called "psychoactive substances" or "psychoactive drugs," and sometimes simply "drugs", and they cover a wide range

---

[4] Produced outside the body.

A lock and its key – an analogy of the interaction between drug-receptor or neurotransmitter-neuroreceptor. (*ItalianLocksmith, CC BY-SA 3.0 <https://creativecommons.org/licenses/by-sa/3.0>, via Wikimedia Commons*).

of molecules such as alcohol, anxiolytics, analgesics, tobacco, cocaine, coffee, LSD, MDMA, etc.

Based on this definition we can begin to understand why the concept of neurotransmitter (key) and neuroreceptor (lock) is so important to understand, since psychoactive substances (both legal and illegal) act precisely there, on those locks in our neurons. They affect the interaction between our internal keys and our locks, sometimes acting as if they were the keys themselves and opening those locks (agonistic effect), like a pick or false key opens a lock in the absence of the original key; and other times blocking them, as if they were broken keys which fit but do not turn, and not letting other keys in (antagonistic effect). Also, sometimes, they simply make the neurons unable to withdraw those keys after releasing them (reuptake inhibitors), or even "release" more keys than expected (transporter reversals). All these possible actions of drugs in the synapse are what give us such a wide range of possible effects, causing neuronal activations or preventing them, in a way that is different from the normal functioning of the system. They are said to have a certain "affinity" (or fit) for one or more neuroreceptors at a time and can bind to them with lesser or even greater affinity (strength) than our own neurotransmitters.

In essence, it could be said that psychoactive substances act as if they were our own neurotransmitters, but instead of being generated within our own body (endogenous), they enter our body from the outside (exogenous), and their way of interacting with neuroreceptors is different from that of our own neurotransmitters. They are like picks or false keys that can open our locks, even if they are not our own keys.

This happens at the neuronal level, but if we see what happens at the brain level, these changes in the locks of our neurons have a global impact that temporarily changes the way the brain works, and may affect the way different brain regions communicate with each other: overactivating some regions, turning off others, causing incoordination in others. This is what produces the changes in consciousness that we

Temporary decrease in blood flow/activation in certain brain regions after psilocybin. Image shows regions where there was a significant decrease after psilocybin compared to placebo. (Taken from Robin L. Carhart-Harris et al., "Neural correlates of the psychedelic state as determined by fMRI studies with psilocybin," Proceedings of the National Academy of Sciences of the United States of America 109, 6 (February 7, 2012): 2138-43). With permission from RCH, first author)

notice, for example, when we drink a beer, drink coffee or consume any other substance with psychoactive properties.

Although much remains to be discovered about the neurochemical processes that form the basis of our consciousness, every day we know more about the basic neurochemistry of our brain functioning, the one that lays the biological foundations of our thoughts, feelings and behaviors. Therefore, every day we have a better understanding of how drugs influence them, and how we can use them to advance science and therapies.

Introduction to Psychoactive Substances

Psychoactive... drugs?

In the previous chapter, we saw that psychoactive substances are those that, upon entering the body (via any route: oral, nasal, intramuscular, intravenous), exert a direct effect on the central nervous system, causing specific changes to its functions (pain, state of mood, perceptions, etc.). Examples of these substances may include: alcohol, caffeine, anxiolytics, antidepressants, painkillers...and other psychoactive drugs, including some of the illicit kind.

When we speak of illicit psychoactive drugs we are referring, of course, to those whose production, trafficking or sale has been illegalized. If we were to ask about them on the street, the first thing people would comment on would be their addictive, harmful and, in certain circumstances, even deadly nature. Yet, these characteristics are not intrinsic to these substances, but rather depend to a large extent on the use that is made of them.

So, when talking about psychoactve substances: if they are not all illegal, not all addictive, not all harmful, what do they have in common? What identifies them as a family and differentiates them from all other drugs or any other existing substance?

As we began to see in the previous chapter, it all comes down to where they act and what effects they produce.

What all the molecules mentioned above have in common is their ability to directly influence neuronal activity in the central nervous system. Psychoactive substances act on the neuroreceptors of these neurons (or on the neurotransmitters that allow them to communicate with each other), resulting in psychoactive effects of various kinds, like modifying our consciousness, mood, level of alertness, etc. Drugs, whether legal, restricted for medical use, or illegalized[1], are those keys that, like our internal neurotransmitters, fit into the locks of our neurons (or act on our internal keys).

Therefore, if we want to be more precise when referring to substances such as alcohol, cannabis (marijuana), cocaine or LSD ("acid"), ideally, we would not just talk about drugs, which is a very broad term, but "psychoactive substances" or "psychoactive drugs." These terms are essentially synonyms. In

---

[1] Instead of talking about legal and illegal drugs, the author prefers to talk about legal drugs, drugs restricted for medical use or "illegalized" drugs. This distinction between illegal and illegalized is made because the legal status of a drug is not an intrinsic characteristic, but rather derives from a social construction, such as laws, which are subject to constant change. Drugs, like any other natural element, is "legal" in principle until society, through its governments and legislators, decides otherwise. Drugs were not created illegal, nor did they exist being illegal and then legalized, quite the opposite: they existed and were legal (in the natural world or when they were created by the hand of man) and later, rulers and legislators decided to restrict some of them for medical use and others were directly illegalized.

addition to being synonyms, they would be the most precise terms to use. However, to make it easier for the reader and keeping with the usual social lexicon, throughout this book we will use the word "drug" as an abbreviated form of "psychoactive drug" or "psychoactive substance."

Far from technical definitions, drugs, whether legal, illegalized or restricted for medical use, are fundamentally known for their effects on the mind and behavior, since they are tools that not only stimulate or relax us, they allow us to access other altered or non-ordinary states of consciousness.

The science that studies the effects of these substances on the mind – cognition, emotions, thoughts, sensations, motivations and behaviors – is known as "psychopharmacology."

Fortunately, psychoactive substances are not the only tool we have to access these altered states of consciousness.

Sensory isolation tank, where you float in body-temperature salt water in the dark, in silence, to deprive the brain of any sensory *input* and achieve altered states of consciousness. *(Floatguru, CC BY-SA 3.0 <https://creativecommons.org/licenses/by-sa/3.0>, via Wikimedia Commons).*

There are various ancient and modern practices that allow us to achieve states that can resemble those obtained through psychoactive substances, such as: meditation, breathing, fasting, extreme sports, sleep deprivation, sensory isolation chambers[2], or lucid dreams[3]. People who enjoy exploring altered states of consciousness, through these various pharmacological or non-pharmacological tools, are known as "psychonauts" and the discipline they practice as "psychonautics."

Types of Psychoactive Substances

What do a boat, a car, a plane and a bicycle have in common? Not all of them have wheels, or motors, or move on the same surface, or at the same speed, or work the same... However, we can say that, in essence, they are all vehicles whose function is to move people, other living beings, or things. However, if we wanted to go beyond a generic description, we would be making a mistake by referring to all vehicles in the same terms, without distinguishing their different functions and characteristics and without taking into account the different security measures that we must employ prior to using them.

The same goes for drugs. When we hear about them as a whole, one of the first things we should keep in mind is that we are talking about a group of very heterogeneous chemical substances and, although all of them act on the nervous system and can alter our perception, emotions, mental processes,

---

[2] Sensory isolation chambers or tanks seek to minimize the information provided by the senses to the brain, through a combination of darkness, silence, absence of odors and body comfort. They were very popular in the 1960s and 1970s thanks to the work of neuropsychiatrist John C. Lilly and the movie *Altered States*.

[3] Lucid dreams are those in which the person is aware of dreaming and takes control.

behavior, etc., they not all do it in the same way, nor in the same intensity, nor in the same direction nor, of course, carry the same risks.

Moreover, as it is not possible (nor functional) to carefully test or study each drug and their effects, one by one, in order to talk about them, we inevitably need "classification models" to arrange what they have in common and what differentiates them; a way of systematically grouping psychoactive substances that allows us to know their main effects and risks, and thus be able to speak, properly this time, of types of drugs.

Currently, it is very common for the general population to be guided by the classification system dictated by the legal status of substances, something that is not very informative, is susceptible to change and has no scientific basis. This very basic approach to drugs basically tells us that substances are divided into a small group of "legal drugs", such as alcohol, coffee and tobacco (which many people do not even consider drugs), and another enormous group of "illegal drugs[4]" (or simply "drugs" for most), such as cocaine and cannabis. If we were to ask on the street about how we can somehow classify illegal drugs, many people would apply a subdivision based on their own subjective perception of the risk they pose, dividing them into "soft drugs" and "hard drugs", which is another arbitrary classification based on press headlines, rumors or the more or less well-founded opinion of each individual.

Also, you may be surprised to discover that many of the "drugs" you probably think are hard or totally illegal today turn out to have authorized medical use. In fact, drugs with such gloomy and stigmatized names as "liquid ecstasy" (GHB), "speed" (amphetamine), "heroin" (diamorphine), "crystal meth" (methamphetamine), ketamine, etc. are authorized for medical use and currently marketed under names such as Xyrem®, Adderall®, Desoxyn®, Ketalar® and are dispensed

---

[4] People don't usually say "illegalized drugs."

in pharmacies or hospitals on a daily basis, just as cocaine, opium, LSD and many others once were.

Probably, some people would also allude to the usual classification between natural or synthetic drugs that, contrary to popular belief, tells us very little about their effects and their risks. In fact, many substances that were believed to be synthetic are not, such as GHB (liquid ecstasy), which later turned out to be naturally occurring not only in wine, vermouth or berries, but also in our brains and the brains of other mammals.

On the other hand, if we go to a more academic field, we can find more technical answers generally related to the different chemical structures of substances, such as tryptamines, phenylethylamines or cathinones, which are tremendously complex classifications to handle for practical or informative purposes.

Luckily, for those people who are really interested in learning the main intrinsic characteristics of psychoactive substances, in a rigorous yet simplified and useful way, classifications based on their effects have existed since ancient times, the richness and complexity of which are advancing led by science and experimentation.

Until the end of the last century, the classification based on their main effects was very simple, and it was limited to dividing drugs into: stimulants, sedatives and hallucinogens, which could be represented graphically in a triangle, square or star, depending on whether some combined categories were added, such as stimulant-psychedelic or depressant-psychedelic drugs. In this regard, a very good and very complete graphic layout is the one created by Derek Sneider with its four spheres; or the version by David McCandles named "*Drugs World*[5]", which allows us to clearly see the different profiles of effects that sometimes occur in the same molecule; or the

---

[5] Information is Beautiful, "Drugs World — Information is Beautiful," https://informationisbeautiful.net/visualizations/drugs-world/.

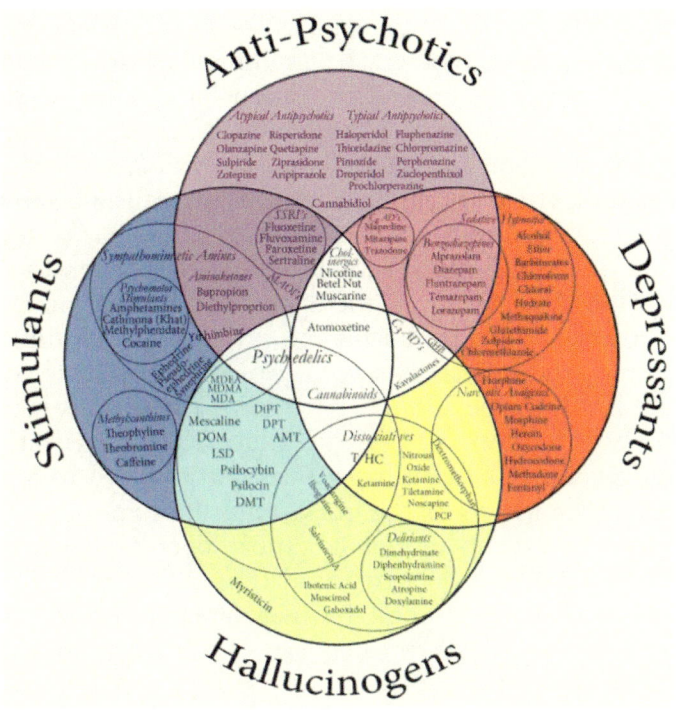

Venn diagram with psychoactive substances divided into 4 overlapping categories: stimulants, hallucinogens, depressants, and antipsychotics. *Derek Snider, 2005.*

version prepared by the NGO Espolea (Mexico), baptized as *El Universo de las Drogas*[6] ("The Universe of Drugs"), using a four-pointed star.

As some parts of these graphs were confusing, over time some of these basic categories were added and subdivided (for example, the group of sedatives became divided into depressants and analgesics). However, starting in the year 2010, the limitations of such a rudimentary classification began to be

---

[6] *What is the Universe of Drugs?*", https://idpc.net/es/alerts/2016/01/que-es-el-universo-de-las-drogas.

seen very clearly with the explosion of the market of *research chemicals*, new illegal synthetic drugs inspired by already banned molecules, some even described as far back as the 1980s in books such as the *PiHKAL*[7] and the *TiHKAL*[8], and that were sold freely on the internet and in *smartshops* during the time it took them to be illegalized. Many of these substances were assigned to the "miscellaneous" or "other" category, or were placed in mixed sections, as has always been the case with MDMA or "ecstasy" (the effects of which were located at the intersection of stimulants and psychedelics), or cannabis, which used to be placed between depressant and psychedelic.

In 2012, in the United Kingdom, a new classification model was developed by Mark Aldey, UK Drugwatch and several psychonaut forums that managed to solve, to a great extent, the limitations of the old systems through the creation of three new categories such as: empathogenic-entactogenic, cannabinoids and dissociative, updating the term hallucinogens to psychedelics, and the term analgesics to opioids. They decided to place all seven categories of substances in a circle, and "The Drugs Wheel" was born[9] – probably the best effects-based drug classification model that we have today, and one that combines simplicity and rigor by classifying most of the established drugs and many of the new synthetic substances (or new psychoactive substances, NPS)[10] in these seven categories of effects.

---

[7] Alexander Theodore Shulgin and Ann Shulgin, *Pihkal: A Chemical Love Story* (1991).

[8] Alexander Theodore Shulgin and Ann Shulgin, *Tihkal: The Continuation* (1997).

[9] Available in multiple versions and translations at http://www.thedrugswheel.com

[10] *New Psychoactive Substances (NPS)"*, Energy Control, https://energycontrol.org/tiposustancia/nuevas-drogas/.

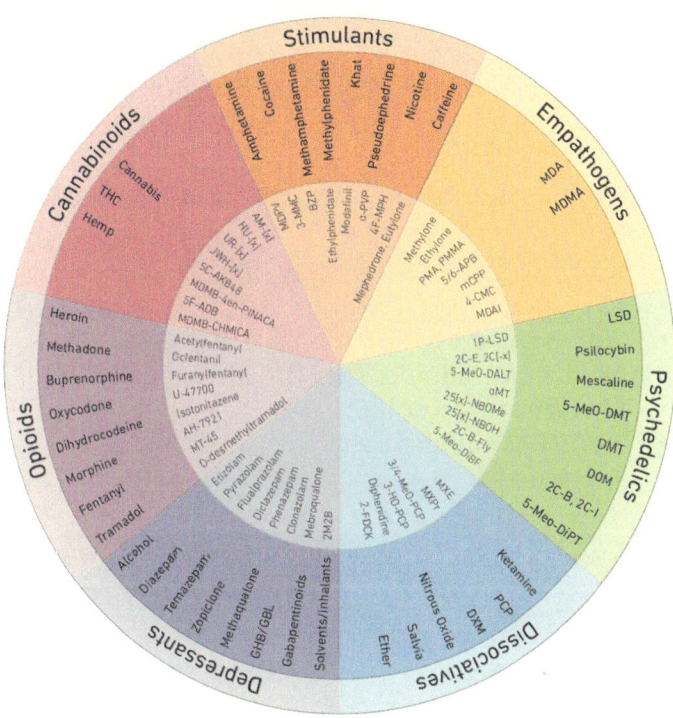

The Drugs Wheel, drug classification by effects.
(by Mark Adley, available at http://www.thedrugswheel.com).

Based on this basic classification of drugs according to their effects, let's define each of these 7 categories, as well as their main uses and risks:

STIMULANTS

Stimulants are mainly those substances that activate, energize, cause euphoria, increase concentration, raise alertness, etc. In most cases, they do this through their direct or indirect action on the neurotransmitters dopamine and norepinephrine, their neuroreceptors, or their systems. These substances tend to increase brain activation and hence their name "stimulants." Some examples of this category are:
- Caffeine (coffee, tea, energy drinks).
- Cocaine ("coke", "blow").
- Amphetamines ("speed", Adderall®).
- Methamphetamines ("meth", Desoxyn®).
- Nicotine (tobacco).
- MDPV ("cannibal drug").
- Alpha-PVP ("flakka").

Caffeine from coffee or tea is the most famous and consumed stimulant in the world.
(Zacharias Korsalka from Vienna, Austria, PDM-owner, via Wikimedia Commons).

Main Uses

Some stimulants such as methylphenidate or amphetamine are used in medicine for the treatment of attention-deficit/hyperactivity disorder (ADHD), the treatment of narcolepsy[11] or accompanying treatments that can cause drowsiness (caffeine, pseudoephedrine, etc.), and also to accelerate weight loss in specific cases (amphetamines and methamphetamines), such as bronchodilators (amphetamines) or local anesthetics (cocaine).

They are also used as nootropics, or cognitive enhancers, in academia and in the workplace. In fact, caffeine is the most used stimulant worldwide, with millions of doses consumed daily, followed by the next widely consumed stimulant, nicotine, in the form of tobacco.

They are also widely used alone or combined, at a recreational level, in leisure spaces such as nightclubs and festivals, as well as other illegalized stimulants such as cocaine or amphetamine.

Main Risks

All drugs have risks, and stimulants are no less. This does not mean that most of these risks are always inherent to the substance itself but rather that an important part derive from the use that is made of them, influenced by important variables related to the substance itself (like type, dose, frequency, purity, adulterations, route of administration, etc.), to the user (state of physical and mental health, psychological state, emotional state, intention, tolerance, combinations with other drugs, etc.) and the context of use (social context, legal status, risky activities, driving, etc.). Therefore, these risks will depend on many

---

[11] Disease that makes it difficult to regulate sleep-wake cycles, causing people to suffer from extreme sleepiness at any time of the day.

variables and, most of the time, can be reduced, although they can never be completely ruled out.

In the worst cases, the use of stimulants can lead to cardiovascular problems (such as heart attacks, strokes or other cerebrovascular accidents, arrhythmia, tachycardia, high blood pressure), dehydration and hyperthermia ("heat stroke"), hyponatremia[12], or transient psychological problems such as insomnia, anxiety, paranoia, and even stimulant psychosis[13].

Likewise, accidents can occur derived from the euphoria and recklessness produced by the substance (which makes driving a dangerous activity), and in certain people and conditions they can produce antisocial behavior such as aggressiveness.

Some stimulants can cause hangovers, neurotoxicity, or emotional comedowns, especially in high doses or when mixed with alcohol or other substances.

The long-term risks of stimulant use are highly dependent on the type of stimulant, the person using it, the frequency of use, and the doses taken. High frequency or high doses can lead to physical tolerance, psychological addiction, neuropsychiatric abnormalities, and cardiovascular diseases such as cardiomyopathy. The use of some types of stimulants can be highly addictive, both physically and psychologically, and faster routes of administration (such as injection, vaporization, or insufflation) are often more problematic than slower routes (oral administration). Neural adaptations to long-term effects can also be problematic, making it difficult to quit after chronic use.

---

[12] Condition where sodium levels are low due to excess water, lack of nutrition and drug-altered urinary excretion; very rare but dangerous.

[13] Stimulants at high doses can produce psychosis in predisposed people, and also an episode of transient psychosis called "stimulant psychosis" or "toxic psychosis", usually in poorly rested people.

Depressants

Substances that mainly relax, disinhibit, sedate, cause euphoria, etc. are considered depressants, generally due to its action on GABA neuroreceptors. They reduce neuronal and cerebral activation – hence their designation as "depressants." Paradoxically, depressant substances, at low doses, tend to produce a feeling of energy and euphoria, which is actually related to disinhibition. Some examples are:
- Alcohol (beer, wine, rum, gin, whiskey, vodka, etc.).
- Benzodiazepines (alprazolam, lorazepam, diazepam, Orfidal®, Valium®, Trankimazin®).
- Barbiturates.
- GHB (or its precursor, GBL) misnamed "liquid ecstasy" (and "G", "juice", Xyrem®).
- 2M2B.
- Mebroqualone.

Red wine glasses. Alcohol is the most widely known and consumed depressant in the world.
(Maria Eklind, CC BY-SA 2.0 <https://creativecommons.org/licenses/by-sa/2.0>, via Wikimedia Commons).

Main Uses

Depressant drugs are used in medicine as anxiolytics, muscle relaxants, sedatives, hypnotics, and anesthetics.

Outside the medical world, they are widely used in the recreational field for their disinhibiting and social properties, with alcohol being one of the three most consumed drugs in the world, behind coffee (caffeine) and tobacco (nicotine).

There have also been uses in the criminal field as a chemical submission[14] tool.

Main Risks

As we commented with respect to stimulants, the risks of depressant drugs will depend a lot on the variables of the substance itself (type, dose, frequency, purity, adulterations, route of administration, etc.), the consumer (state of physical and mental health, psychological state, emotional state, intention, tolerance, combinations with other drugs, etc.) and the context (social context, legal status, risk activities, driving, etc.) – risks that can be reduced but never completely eliminated.

In the worst cases, the consumption of depressants can lead to dizziness, vomiting, coma and even cardiorespiratory arrest.

Some depressants such as GHB/GBL or benzodiazepines (especially if they are not sold already in doses) have a lot of pharmacological potency, so accidental overdoses can occur. They can also facilitate accidents due to their effects on coordination and reflexes (driving or any motor activity can be dangerous). Depressant substances, such as alcohol, can also cause aggressiveness and recklessness in some people.

Some depressants can be toxic, especially in high doses, or if they are mixed with other substances. In the case of alcohol, it is

---

[14] Chemical submission is to drug a victim to facilitate a crime, such as robbery, sexual assault, kidnapping, etc.

common for it to produce a multifactorial phenomenon known as a "hangover" that is derived from a combination of lack of rest, dehydration, stomach irritation, toxic effects on the brain and liver, headache, neuroinflammation, nausea and neuroadaptive effects. The long-term risks of using depressant substances depend very much on the type, the person, the frequency of use and the dose. High frequency or high doses can lead to addiction, liver and brain damage (particularly alcohol), cardiovascular disease, cancer, and neurotoxicity.

Depressants can be physically and psychologically addictive. Furthermore, since some are widely available and accepted in many societies, such as alcohol or benzodiazepines, the social context may mask addiction or encourage increased consumption, especially in the case of alcohol.

If the consumption of depressants such as alcohol is maintained over time, the brain can develop adaptations that make it dangerous to stop abruptly. In the case of alcohol, a syndrome known as "delirium tremens" may develop, which could even lead to death. Because of this, slow and well-planned detoxification or the use of other depressant psychoactive drugs is often temporarily necessary. This chronic consumption also takes its toll on many areas of the brain, especially those related to memory, and can produce forms of dementia, such as the well-known Wernicke-Korsakoff syndrome. Not only does the brain suffer from chronic alcohol consumption, but this condition is also particularly damaging to the liver. In cases of chronic consumption, fatty liver, cirrhosis or liver failure may occur. Long-term alcohol consumption is also related to cardiovascular and metabolic diseases.

OPIOIDS

Opioids are considered those substances that produce analgesia, well-being, euphoria, etc. through their action on opioid receptors in the brain, emulating the effect of endorphins. Their name comes from its similarity to the substances present in opium, such as morphine. As with depressants, although their action is fundamentally inhibitory, at low doses they produce a subjective sensation of stimulation.

Some examples are:
- Morphine (opium, poppy).
- Heroine (horse).
- Codeine.
- Methadone.
- Buprenorphine.
- Tramadol.
- Fentanyl.
- Ocfentanyl.
- MT-45.

Bottle of morphine for hospital use, the best known natural opioid. *(Vaprotan, CC BY-SA 3.0 <https://creativecommons.org/licenses/by-sa/3.0>, via Wikimedia Commons).*

Main Uses

Some opioid drugs are used in medicine as analgesics, anesthetics, antitussives or antidiarrheals.

Drug policy has always had a complicated relationship with opioids, since they are very addictive substances but very necessary and difficult to substitute in the treatment of pain.

Main Risks

As we commented with respect to stimulants and depressants, the risks of opioid drugs will depend a lot on the variables of the substance itself (type, dose, frequency, purity, adulterations, route of administration, etc.), the user (state of physical and mental health, psychological and emotional state, intention, tolerance, combinations with other drugs, etc.) and the context (social context, legal status, risky activities, driving, etc.) – risks that can be reduced but never completely eliminated.

In the worst cases, opioid use can lead to dizziness, vomiting, coma, or even cardiorespiratory arrest.

Most opioids are pharmacologically very potent and have a low safety ratio, so accidental overdoses can easily occur if their purity, adulteration and dosage are not well known.

In the long term, opioids are highly addictive substances, and they generate tolerance very quickly, so their therapeutic use should be as short as possible.

It is worth mentioning that some common routes of administration of opioids, such as intravenous injection, can present risks themselves in certain contexts, such as the transmission of diseases like hepatitis or HIV if sterile equipment is not used.

CANNABINOIDS

Cannabinoids are considered those substances that produce calm, sensory distortions, creativity, laughter and other effects through their action on cannabinoid receptors in the brain. These substances act on cannabinoid neuroreceptors in the brain and other areas of the body. Its name comes from its presence in the cannabis sativa plant. Some examples include the active ingredients of cannabis, THC and CBD, of which THC is the most responsible for its psychoactive effects and CBD has a modulating action on these; but in the field

Cannabis sativa plant in bloom.
(Pavel Sevela, CC BY-SA 3.0 <https://creativecommons.org/licenses/by-sa/3.0>, via Wikimedia Commons).

of new psychoactive substances we can also find a string of new synthetic cannabinoids such as 5C-AKB48 and MDMB-4en-PINACA.

Main Uses

In recent decades, much research has been done on the therapeutic use of cannabis and cannabinoids for the treatment of different diseases, and there is a growing number of countries or regions that have already authorized their medical use for conditions such as chronic pain, Parkinson's, chemotherapy nausea, epilepsy, glaucoma, PTSD, etc. Its non-medical use is also widespread, being considered the most widely used illegalized drug in the world.

Main Risks

As with previous substances, the risks of cannabinoid drugs will depend a lot on the variables of the substance itself (type, dose, frequency, purity, adulterations, route of administration, etc.), the user (state of physical and mental health, psychological and emotional state, intention, tolerance, combinations with other drugs, etc.) and the context (social context, legal status, risky activities, driving, etc.) – risks that can be reduced but never completely eliminated.

At the risk level, it is convenient to establish a clear distinction between natural cannabinoids, present in the *Cannabis sativa* plant, and those of synthetic origin, sometimes called "spice."

In the worst cases, the use of natural cannabinoids could lead to anxiety, paranoia, psychotic episodes or other mental disorders.

Although on a physical level it is generally considered safe, high doses can produce a "whitey" or "green out", characterized by tachycardia, hypotension or dizziness, so they can pose a risk for people with heart problems. Nevertheless, it is not considered toxic at a physiological level and, despite its large consumer base, deaths associated with cannabis are hardly reported except in very specific situations. One of the most common adverse effects is the above mentioned "whitey", episodes of dizziness and transient discomfort normally associated with high doses. Still, as we have seen, they have psychological risks, being able to advance the manifestation of psychotic disorders in predisposed people.

A common risk in the consumption of cannabis is the overdose associated with consuming it orally in the form of confectionery or cannabis cooking, with absorption and potency being much greater by this route. In addition, since it takes several hours for the effects to be noticed when being ingested orally, there are cases of redosing due to impatience which end up producing an overdose that, although not fatal, can be a frankly unpleasant experience.

Regarding synthetic cannabinoids, they are new, unknown and extremely powerful substances, pharmacologically speaking, so it is very easy to accidentally overdose on them and expose yourself to risks much greater than those of natural cannabis consumption.

EMPATHOGENS-ENTACTOGENS

Empathogenic or entactogenic are substances that have the peculiarity of generating mostly empathy, love and connection with other people and with oneself, as well as positive emotions, well-being, sociability, emotionality, etc., mainly by releasing large amounts of serotonin from our neurons, but also other neurotransmitters such as dopamine, norepinephrine and oxytocin.

The word "empathogen" alludes to its ability to generate empathy, while "entactogen" is derived from the root *en* (Greek for "within"), *tactus* (Latin for "tactile") and *gen* (Greek for "produce"), that is, to produce contact with oneself, to connect with oneself.

These substances can also have stimulant and psychedelic properties at high doses but are not distinguished by them (this is why some empathogen-entactogen substances like MDMA are also considered to be semi-psychedelic or atypical psychedelics).

Ecstasy pills (MDMA), the most famous empathogenic-entactogenic substance.

The main substances in this category are:
- MDMA (ecstasy).
- MDA.
- 6-APB ("benzofury").
- MDMC (methylone).

Main Uses

Currently, empathogenic-entactogenic drugs do not have an officially authorized medical use, but MDMA is well advanced in clinical trials to be authorized in the treatment of posttraumatic stress disorder (PTSD) in the next few years. Since it is already in the process of being evaluated by some very important regulatory agencies (FDA, EMA), in some countries its compassionate use can be requested in certain cases when conventional treatments are not working.

The recreational use of empathogens such as MDMA ("ecstasy") is widespread in leisure spaces, such as music festivals, concerts or nightclubs.

Main Risks

As with all other previous substances, the risks of empathogenic-entactogenic drugs will depend a lot on the variables of the substance itself (type, dose, frequency, purity, adulterations, route of administration, etc.), the user (state of physical and mental health, psychological and emotional state, intention, tolerance, combinations with other drugs, etc.) and the context (social context, legal status, risky activities, driving, etc.) – risks that can be reduced but never completely eliminated.

In the worst cases, the consumption of empathogens-entactogens can lead to cardiovascular risks (such as heart attacks, strokes, arrhythmia, tachycardia, high blood pressure), hyperthermia (heat stroke), dehydration, hyponatremia, combination with other substances and accidents derived from the euphoria produced by the substance.

In the specific case of empathogens-entactogens, given their relationship with the serotonin system, it is especially important to control body temperature and hydration to avoid a heat stroke. Likewise, avoid overdoing it with water or non-isotonic drinks, since there is also a risk of hyponatremia.

If taking high doses, redosing, or combining it with other substances, an MDMA hangover can occur after a day or two. This hangover is characterized by being very emotional and can manifest itself as sadness, tiredness, emptiness, restlessness or melancholy that does not usually last more than a day but can last longer.

The long-term risks of MDMA use depend very much on the frequency and doses consumed. High frequency or high doses can facilitate the onset of psychological disorders such as depression, cardiovascular disease, and even addiction, because, although not to the same extent as other stimulants, long-term abuse of MDMA does present some risk of psychological and physical addiction.

The risk of having a psychotic reaction is extremely low and has not been shown to be a risk for healthy people, so it could be greatly minimized by avoiding the use of empathogens-entactogens in people with known psychosis, bipolarity, or psychotic disorders, or people with a family history of these mental issues. It can be difficult to know if someone is at risk of a psychotic reaction, especially if someone is still very young, which is one of the reasons why the use of substances with psychedelic-like effects is generally less risky in older and more mature people and in controlled clinical settings with appropriate professional supervision.

Despite popular belief, numerous population studies[15], with sample sizes in the hundreds of thousands of people, have shown that at the population level there is no correlation

---

[15] Teri S. Krebs and Pål-Ørjan Johansen, *Psychedelics and mental health: A population study*," *PLoS One* 8, 8 (2013-08-19): e63972.

between the use of MDMA, or psychedelics, and mental illness of any kind[16]. In fact, the correlation indicates that the use of MDMA or psychedelics is associated with better mental health, less stress[17], less depression[18] and fewer suicidal thoughts[19]. Although correlation does not imply causation, these studies show that the image of MDMA or psychedelics as substances that cause mental illness or that attract people with mental illness is distorted by the media and by prevention campaigns based on fear, especially because these correlations do not occur, even taking into account that as of today, only in the U.S., about 30 million people have tried psychedelics[20].

Dissociatives

They are substances that mainly dissociate or separate us from our bodies, anesthetize and incoordinate us, generally by blocking glutamate receptors, and can have psychedelic properties at high doses (this is why some dissociative

---

[16] Pål-Ørjan Johansen and Teri Suzanne Krebs, *Psychedelics not linked to mental health problems or suicidal behavior: A population study*," Journal of Psychopharmacology 29, 3 (March 2015): 270-79.
[17] Peter S. Hendricks et al., *Classic psychedelic use is associated with reduced psychological distress and suicidality in the United States adult population*", Journal of Psychopharmacology 29, 3 (March 2015): 280-88.
[18] Grant M. Jones and Matthew K. Nock, "*Lifetime use of MDMA/ecstasy and psilocybin is associated with reduced odds of major depressive episodes*," Journal of Psychopharmacology 36, 1 (January 2022): 57-65.
[19] Grant M. Jones and Matthew K. Nock, *MDMA/ecstasy use and psilocybin use are associated with lowered odds of psychological distress and suicidal thoughts in a sample of U.S. adults*," Journal of Psychopharmacology, 2022.
[20] Teri S. Krebs and Pål-Ørjan Johansen, "*Over 30 million psychedelic users in the United States*," F1000Research 2 (March 28, 2013): 98.

Bottles of ketamine for hospital use.

substances like ketamine are also considered to be semi-psychedelic or atypical psychedelics).

Some examples of this category include:
- Ketamine ("Special K", "Kit Kat", "K").
- PCP (phencyclidine).
- N2O (laughing gas).
- MXE (methoxetamine).
- 2-FDCK.

Main Uses

Some dissociative drugs are used in medicine as analgesics and anesthetics, for example, ketamine or laughing gas. Recently, a purification of ketamine, esketamine, has been patented by the pharmaceutical company Janssen (part of Johnson & Johnson) and approved for the treatment of major depression, becoming the first compound with psychedelic effects approved for the treatment of mental illness.

Its recreational use is also quite widespread, although originally associated with *rave* culture, in recent years its use has become popular in other contexts.

Main Risks

As with all previous substances, the risks of dissociative drugs will depend a lot on the variables of the substance itself (type, dose, frequency, purity, adulterations, route of administration, etc.), the user (state of physical and mental health, psychological state, emotional state, intention, tolerance, combinations with other drugs, etc.) and the context (social context, legal status, risky activities, driving, etc.) – risks that can be reduced but never completely eliminated.

In the worst cases, the use of dissociatives can lead to hypertension, dizziness, nausea, confusion, anxiety and, since dissociative substances produce a lot of motor incoordination and loss of sensations, they are dangerous if there is a risk of falling or driving, and at high doses they can produce an extreme dissociation experience known as "falling into a k-hole", which can be unpleasant. Very, very high doses of ketamine could cause death, but these doses are very rare.

Like classic psychedelics, such as LSD or psilocybin, ketamine and nitrous oxide have low toxicity even at high doses. Therefore, physical and physiological safety is generally not a concern unless the person has accidentally taken a very high dose that could affect breathing, or if they drive, fall, or engage in any other physically hazardous activity. Because ketamine slightly raises blood pressure and there is the possibility of intense experiences that can generate anxiety, people with a history of cardiovascular or psychiatric diseases should refrain from using it. Likewise, the continued use of nitrous oxide can lower the levels of vitamin B12 in the body and lead to neuronal problems, so it may pose a risk in people with low levels of this vitamin.

The main risk found in psychedelic experiences that can come from a high dose of ketamine is psychological, such as having a difficult experience ("bad trip"), a psychotic reaction that can occur in people with a predisposition or in very, very rare cases, "flashbacks" (hallucinogen persisting perception disorder or HPPD, although few cases are known). These risks increase at higher doses.

The probability of having a difficult experience or "bad trip" is low and could be greatly minimized with a good set and setting. Long-lasting psychological difficulties resulting from such an experience (such as negative trauma, long-lasting anxiety or fear) are very rare, but can occur especially if the substance is taken without prior experience, in highly uncontrolled environments, without adequate preparation of the user and their context (set and setting). Substances with psychedelic effects can amplify mental states, so using them with fear, worry, anxiety, or in uncomfortable or insecure contexts can make it easier to have bad experiences.

The risk of having a psychotic reaction is very low and has not been shown to be a risk for healthy people, so it could be greatly minimized by avoiding the use of ketamine in people with known psychosis, bipolar or psychotic disorders, or people with family history of these mental disorders. It can be difficult to know if someone is at risk of a psychotic reaction, especially if someone is still very young, which is one of the reasons why the use of substances with psychedelic effects is generally less risky in older and more mature people and in controlled clinical settings with appropriate professional supervision.

Although the long-term risks of ketamine use depend very much on the frequency and the doses used, there are some specific long-term risks, such as addiction, tolerance, bladder problems, and urinary tract infections (common side effects of long-term ketamine abuse due to the way it is metabolized and excreted from the body), neurotoxicity and withdrawal syndrome. But using them without taking into account underlying mental conditions such as psychosis, bipolarity or psychotic disorders could worsen the course of these disorders and contribute negatively to the long-term outcome.

The neurotoxicity of ketamine is still debated, but it appears that it could produce some indirect excitotoxicity at very high doses and frequencies of use. However, it appears that no long-term cognitive impairments have been found to result from this, and short-term cognitive impairments appear to recover upon discontinuation of ketamine.

PSYCHEDELICS

Psychedelic substances (also called hallucinogens or entheogens) are those substances that alter our perception and thinking, induce visions, amplify our senses, expand our consciousness, induce laughter, connection with nature and our inner self, etc., mainly by activating serotonin 5-HT2A neuroreceptors, although it is not always its main mechanism. Some of these substances may also have stimulant or dissociative properties.

The term "psychedelic" derives from the Latin roots *psyche* (mind) and *delos* (to manifest), therefore, the term refers to its ability to "manifest the mind" or the underlying mental processes, making them conscious.

Although the current official name is "psychedelic compound", " psychedelic drug" or "psychedelic substance", these substances have received different names throughout history, such as hallucinogens, entheogens[21], psychotomimetics, and there is currently a (longstanding) debate[22] about what the most appropriate terminology is, or whether to recover the term hallucinogenic. Since this work and

---

[21] CA Ruck et al., "Entheogens," *Journal of Psychedelic Drugs* 11, 1-2 (January 1979): 145-46.

[22] Jonathan Otto, *Pharmacotheon: Entheogenic Drugs, Their Plant Sources and History (1993)*

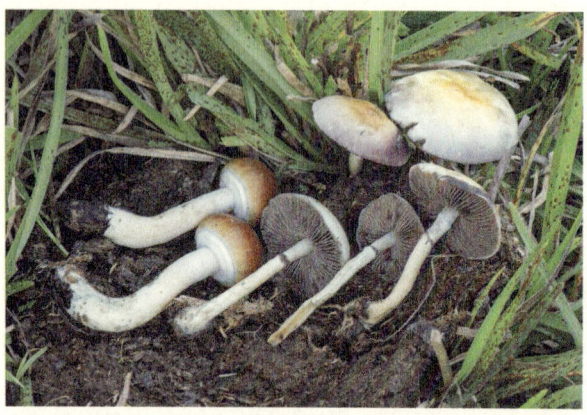

Psilocybe Cubensis mushrooms, known as "magic mushrooms", a classic psychedelic. *(Alan Rockefeller, CC BY-SA 4.0 <https://creativecommons.org/licenses/by-sa/4.0>, via Wikimedia Commons).*

collection are primarily informative in nature, we will stick primarily to current official terminology to avoid confusion, but these terms may be used interchangeably.

Some examples of substances in this category are:
- LSD ("acid", "blotter", "dots", "microdots").
- Psilocybin (hallucinogenic mushrooms, magic mushrooms).
- Mescaline (peyote, San Pedro cactus).
- DMT ("Dimitri", changa, ayahuasca).
- 5-MeO-DMT ("toad").
- 1P-LSD.
- 25i-NBOMe.

Main Uses

Currently, psychedelic substances are mostly considered high risk and have no authorized medical use, although this may change very soon and we will talk about this extensively in this book.

Main Risks

As with previous categories, the risks of psychedelic drugs will depend a lot on the variables of the substance itself (type, dose, frequency, purity, adulterations, route of administration, etc.), the user (state of physical and mental health, psychological and emotional state, intention, tolerance, combinations with other drugs, etc.) and the context (social context, legal status, risky activities, driving, etc.) – risks that can be reduced but never completely eliminated.

When talking about risks, we can distinguish between those from psychedelic substances with a stimulant profile (such as DOC, DOM, DOI, 25i-NBOMe), which therefore combine psychedelic and stimulant risks, with "pure" psychedelics or "classics" like LSD, psilocybin, DMT, which we will delve into in this book

Classic psychedelics like LSD or psilocybin are substances with very low toxicity, even at high doses, and in most cases no overdose deaths have yet been recorded in medical literature. Therefore, physical and physiological safety is generally not a concern beyond possible nausea or vomiting, unless the person is driving, falls, or engages in some other physically dangerous activity. In any case, and due to the possibility of intense experiences that can generate anxiety, people with a history of cardiovascular disease should refrain from using them.

The main risk found in psychedelic experiences is psychological, such as having a difficult experience or "bad trip", a psychotic reaction that can occur in people with a predisposition or in very, very rare cases, "flashbacks" (hallucinogen persisting perception disorder or HPPD, although few cases are known). These risks increase at high doses.

The probability of having a bad trip is low and could be greatly minimized with a set and setting, as we will see later. Long-lasting psychological difficulties resulting from such an experience (such as negative trauma, long-lasting anxiety or fear) are very rare, but can occur especially if the substance is taken without prior experience, in highly uncontrolled environments, without adequate preparation of the user and their context (set and setting). Substances with psychedelic effects can amplify mental states, so using them with fear, worry, anxiety, or in uncomfortable or insecure contexts can make it easier to have bad experiences.

The risk of having a psychotic reaction is very low and has not been shown to be a risk for healthy people, but rather for those with a propensity, so it could be greatly minimized by avoiding the use of psychedelics in people with known psychosis, bipolarity or psychotic disorders, or people with a family history of these mental issues. It can be difficult to know if someone is at risk of a psychotic reaction, especially if someone is still very young, which is one of the reasons why the use of substances with psychedelic effects is generally less risky in older and more mature people and in controlled clinical settings with appropriate professional supervision.

Although the long-term risks of psychedelic use depend largely on the frequency, doses and type of use, no specific long-term risks of psychedelic use are known, due to their low potential for toxicity, low addictive potential and high tolerance that prevents the creation of a habit (the desire to consume them usually decreases with use) and there is no withdrawal syndrome. Studies have found no detrimental effects in healthy people with long-term psychedelic use. But taking them despite underlying mental conditions such as psychosis, bipolar, or psychotic disorders is very risky and could worsen the course of these disorders and contribute negatively to long-term outcomes.

Long-term use of psychedelics tends to be very spaced in time, as the experiences are very intense and require time to integrate and reflect on. Tolerance also prevents frequent use, with potency reduced to half if consumed in the following days. It takes approximately 3 days of abstinence for tolerance to decrease by 50% and 7 days to return to baseline in the absence of further consumption. Despite popular belief, numerous population studies[23] with sample sizes in the hundreds of thousands of people, have shown that, at the population level, there is no correlation between the use of MDMA or psychedelics and mental illness of any kind[24]. In fact, the correlation indicates that the use of MDMA or psychedelics is associated with better mental health, less stress[25], less depression[26] and fewer suicidal thoughts[27]. Although correlation does not imply causation, these studies show that the image of MDMA or psychedelics as substances that cause mental illness or attract people with mental illness is distorted by the media and by prevention campaigns based on fear, especially because these correlations do not occur, even taking into account that as of today, only in the U.S., around 30 million people have tried psychedelics[28]. The risks of these substances, although real, have been greatly exaggerated and very rarely produce lasting negative effects[29].

Next, let's see a graphic summary of the wheel with the effects and some risks of each of the categories mentioned above:

---

[23] Krebs and Johansen, "Psychedelics and Mental Health: A Population Study."
[24] Johansen and Krebs, *Psychedelics Not Linked to Mental Health Problems or Suicidal Behavior: A Population Study.*
[25] Hendricks et al., *Classic psychedelic use is associated with reduced psychological distress and suicidality in the United States adult population.*
[26] Jones and Nock, *Lifetime use of MDMA/ecstasy and psilocybin is associated with reduced odds of major depressive episodes."*
[27] Jones and Nock, *MDMA/ecstasy use and psilocybin use are associated with lowered odds of psychological distress and suicidal thoughts in a sample of U.S. adults."*
[28] Krebs and Johansen, *Over 30 million psychedelic users in the United States."*
[29] Anne K. Schlag et al., *Adverse effects of psychedelics: From anecdotes and misinformation to systematic science," Journal of Psychopharmacology*, February 2, 2022

ESSENTIAL GUIDE TO THE PSYCHEDELIC RENAISSANCE

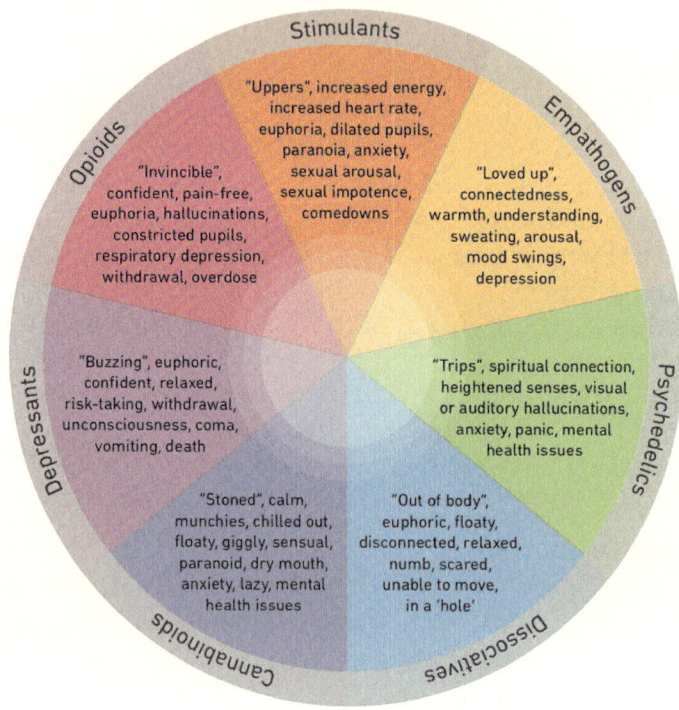

The drugs wheel with general effects and some risks.
(by Mark Adley, available at http://www.thedrugswheel.com).

HISTORY OF PSYCHEDELICS IN THE WEST

PRE-LSD

It is not the purpose of this book to delve into humanity's rich, millennia-long history with psychedelic substances. It is an exciting topic but too extensive for the format of this collection, and it has already been covered masterfully by other specialized works[1]. Therefore, I will focus especially on the Western scientific perspective and on what happened during the 20th century and in recent decades, which have come to be known as the "psychedelic renaissance."

---

[1] J. P. M. Brenan, Richard Evans Schultes, and Albert Hofmann, *Plants of the gods: Origins of hallucinogenic use*, Kew Bulletin, 1980. Ott, *Pharmacotheon: Entheogenic Drugs, Their Plant Sources and History*. Antonio Escohotado, *Historia general de las drogas: incluyendo el apéndice Fenomenología de las drogas* (Planeta Publishing Corporation, 1998).

Although psychedelic substances have been used for millennia[2] for various socio-cultural, political and religious reasons, Western societies abandoned its use centuries ago. Throughout history, these substances have been linked to important aspects of societies, whether medicinal, spiritual, religious, divinatory, ritualistic... In many cases they were the sacred sacrament of a religion or a god. Except for some explorers and intellectuals in recent centuries, few Westerners had had contact with or interest in psychedelic substances until the end of the 19th century and, especially, the middle of the 20th century, when science began to be interested in these mysterious substances...

Mescaline, the active ingredient in the peyote (*Lophophora williamsii*) and San Pedro (*Echinopsis pachanoi*) cacti, which had been used for thousands of years by Native Americans, was the first psychedelic substance to be isolated and to enter Western science. The German pharmacologist Arthur Heffter isolated the active ingredients of peyote in 1897, and tested its psychedelic effects on animals and on himself.

As early as 1919, the Austrian chemist Ernst Späth managed to synthesize mescaline. By then, some psychologists, such as the American Weir Mitchell, considered the father of neurology, and the Englishman Havelock Ellis, had already described their experiences with cacti. But it was the German American Heinrich Klüver who studied its effects in greater detail in the book *Mescal: And Mechanisms of Hallucinations*[3], published in 1928, proposing its use to explore the unconscious.

---

[2] Melanie J. Miller et al., "Chemical evidence for the use of multiple psychotropic plants in a 1,000-year-old ritual bundle from South America," *Proceedings of the National Academy of Sciences of the United States of America* 116, 23 (June 4, 2019): 11207-12.

[3] Heinrich Klüver, *Mescal: And Mechanisms of Hallucinations* (University of Chicago Press, 1928).

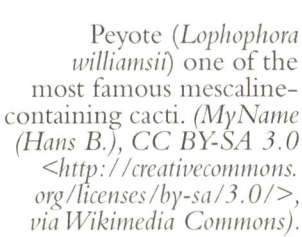

Arthur Heffter, who isolated the active principles of peyote in 1897, and whose psychedelic effects he also tested. *(Erwin Raupp, 1863–1931, Public domain, via Wikimedia Commons).*

Peyote (*Lophophora williamsii*) one of the most famous mescaline-containing cacti. *(MyName (Hans B.), CC BY-SA 3.0 <http://creativecommons.org/licenses/by-sa/3.0/>, via Wikimedia Commons).*

Post-LSD

The event that would mark the beginning of Western scientific interest in psychedelic substances happened on April 16, 1943, in Basel, Switzerland, where Dr. Albert Hofmann, researcher at Sandoz pharmaceutical laboratories, was working on synthetic derivatives of ergotamine (a compound present in the fungus *claviceps purpurea,* known as ergot) in search of an analeptic (a stimulant for the respiratory and circulatory systems) when he began to feel unwell, to the point of needing to go home, as he would write years later:

> *(...) I was forced to interrupt my work in the laboratory in the middle of the afternoon and return home, affected by a marked restlessness, combined with a slight dizziness. At home I lay down and sank into a not unpleasant intoxicated-like condition, characterized by an extremely stimulated imagination. In a dreamlike state, with my eyes closed (daylight was uncomfortably dazzling to me), I perceived an uninterrupted stream of fantastic images, extraordinary shapes with intense and kaleidoscopic play of colors. After about two hours, this condition dissipated*[4]*.*

The compound he was working on at the time was not entirely new, since it was a molecule that he himself had synthesized five years earlier: number 25 in a series of molecules derived from lysergic acid, lysergic acid diethylamide, annotated by its German acronym as LSD-25, but which had shown no interesting pharmacological properties in animal tests and had been discarded.

Intrigued by the origin of these strange effects that he had felt, and in case they could be due to some kind of accidental ingestion of that compound with which he was working, three days later, on April 19, he decided to do a little experiment on himself. He ingested a quarter of a milligram (or 250

---

[4] Albert Hoffman, *LSD, My Problem Child* (McGraw-Hill, 1980).

Albert Hofmann in his laboratory, holding a molecular model of his famous creation: LSD-25.
(Photo taken from www.salte.com).

millionths of a gram) of the compound, an amount that, at that time, was considered minuscule for any known compound and therefore of little risk, but that would prove to be a high dose in the case of this powerful new molecule.

Within half an hour, he began to feel strange again; his senses and his perception of things began to change. He felt like laughing and it was difficult for him to speak, so he asked his assistant to accompany him home. He rode his bicycle since it was his usual means of transport at the time, due to the restrictions on motor vehicles due to the Second World War. Along the way, his condition intensified with strong visual and time distortions, so when he got home, fearing that he had been poisoned and that he was in danger, he asked that they bring him milk as a non-specific antidote and that they call the doctor. After examining him, the doctor did not see that any of his vital signs were altered, and did not notice anything unusual in his condition, except for his two enormous pupils.

Seeing that his body was fine, that everything came from his mind, and that he would not die or be harmed, he began to feel calmer and more confident that he was not going insane. Years later he described:

> (...) *little by little I could begin to enjoy the unprecedented colors and plays of shapes that persisted behind my closed eyes. Kaleidoscopic, fantastic images surged in on me, alternating, variegated, opening and then closing themselves in circles and spirals, exploding in colored fountains, rearranging and hybridizing themselves in constant flux. It was particularly remarkable how every acoustic perception, such as the sound of a door handle or a passing automobile, became transformed into optical perceptions. Every sound generated a vividly changing image, with its own consistent form and color[5]. (...)*

The next day, after the experience, he felt tired but very well, renewed:

> *I woke up next morning feeling refreshed, with a clear head, though still somewhat tired physically. A sensation of well-being and renewed life flowed through me. Breakfast tasted delicious and gave me extraordinary pleasure. When I later walked out into the garden, in which the sun shone now after a spring rain, everything glistened and sparkled in a fresh light. The world was as if newly created. All my senses vibrated in a condition of highest sensitivity, which persisted for the entire day[6].*

And, indeed, in a way, a new world had been created, because that April 19, 1943, would go down in history as "Bicycle Day," the first LSD trip in history, and the first psychedelic trip of a Western scientist in history that would become famous, ushering in a new era in neuroscience, psychotherapy, and spurring a sociocultural and political revolution that would ultimately lead to its own ban, as we'll see later.

After Albert Hofmann's discovery, the pharmaceutical company Sandoz began to thoroughly investigate this new and intriguing substance, patenting it and marketing it under the name Delysid®, starting in 1947.

---

[5] Hoffmann.
[6] Hoffmann.

LSD blotter commemorating "Bicycle Day": April 19, 1943. Each square of cardboard usually contains an impregnated dose of LSD that is between 100 and 150 micrograms, half of what Albert Hofmann took that day. *(Photo taken from https://www.blotterstore.com).*

At a time when psychoanalytic paradigms prevailed in psychiatry, Sandoz began sending samples of LSD-25 to various universities, research centers, or individual therapists, offering to work with the substance, and asking them to send information about its possible applications. It soon began to be used to study schizophrenia because it was thought to be a psychotomimetic substance[7], allowing psychiatrists to experience, in the first person, a state that was considered similar to psychosis, and to investigate brain neurochemistry, which in those years was very poorly developed. The study of LSD sparked interest in other tryptamines, a large family of compounds derived from the amino acid L-tryptophan, which includes endogenous neurotransmitters present in the human brain (such as serotonin or melatonin), and some psychedelic compounds (such as psilocybin, psilocin and dimethyltryptamine or DMT) that, at the brain level, share their affinity for serotonin neuroreceptors. In fact, the discovery of LSD had a great impact on the discovery and characterization of serotonin, in 1948, and on the study of the serotonergic system and its imbalances, in addition

---

[7] Substance that emulates a psychosis.

to fueling a change in the prevailing psychoanalytic paradigm on psychological and emotional disturbances towards a more neurochemical one.

Over the years, in the field of clinical psychiatry, a new use for LSD appeared in Europe: its therapeutic use in the form of psycholytic psychotherapy. It consisted in administering successive low doses of LSD in psychoanalysis sessions, in order to facilitate patients' access to their experiences and progressively change their behavior patterns, but without the patient entering a deep psychedelic experience. In the development of psychotherapies with psychedelics in Europe, it is worth mentioning the contribution of the Czech psychoanalyst Stanislav Grof, who would later develop transpersonal psychology, which works on altered states of consciousness. Also, the work of British psychiatrist Ronald A. Sandison.

In the early 1950s, at the Saskatchewan Hospital in Canada, the psychiatrist Humphry Osmond and the biochemist and psychiatrist Abram Hoffer, formed a group dedicated to the biochemical investigation of schizophrenia. This was

LSD   **Serotonin**

Molecular structure of LSD compared to that of serotonin. (David E. Nichols, "*Dark classics in chemical neuroscience: Lysergic acid diethylamide (LSD)*", *ACS Chemical Neuroscience* 9, 10 (October 17, 2018): 2331-43).

a revolutionary idea at the time, compared to the prevailing conventional psychiatric practices, which gave it an exclusively psychological explanation. Humphry Osmond had already used mescaline as a psychotomimetic in the study of schizophrenia, hypothesizing that schizophrenia could be caused by an autointoxication with endogenous psychedelic products. In an attempt to improve his model of psychosis, he stockpiled every known psychedelic substance and continued self-experimentation until, finally, they decided to limit themselves to the use of LSD. They used LSD as a psychotomimetic on healthy individuals and thus test treatments with them, based on the premise that what worked with them would also work with schizophrenia patients.

In 1954, in the same Saskatchewan Hospital, LSD also began to be used to treat thousands of alcoholic patients, under the premise that it could help them in the beginning of their withdrawal process, by causing them experiences that could be similar to *delirium tremens*[8] to make them "hit rock bottom," to cause a dissuasive effect in a controlled way. This would help in their recovery process within the Alcoholics Anonymous program, avoiding the physical and social risks of reaching that same state with alcohol. But the results, far from producing this unpleasant effect, were that patients were enjoying the experience and even finding it revealing. The impact of the psychedelic experience was making it easier for alcoholics to identify their deep motivations for drinking, be able to work on them and accept themselves as they were. Unbeknownst to them, Abram Hoffer and Humphry Osmond had just founded psychedelic-assisted psychotherapy, a new psychedelic-using psychotherapeutic approach that, unlike the prevailing psycholytic therapy in Europe, used large doses of LSD, in one or a few sessions which invited introspection. The patient did not interact with the therapist unless necessary, looking

---

[8] Alcohol withdrawal syndrome, characterized by delusions, and which can be fatal.

Saskatchewan Hospital (Courtesy University of Saskatchewan, *University Archives & Special Collections, Pamphlet Collection, LXX-1643*, via https://www.thecanadianencyclopedia.ca/en/article/psychedelic-research-in-1950s-saskatchewan).

to reach "peak experiences" or "mystical experiences." At this point they had the collaboration of Alfred Hubbard, a self-proclaimed expert on psychedelics, who helped Osmond's team perfect their technique of working with psychedelic psychotherapy.

Within the 3000 patients who followed the treatment at the Saskatchewan Hospital, the rate of recovery obtained with severe alcoholics who achieved abstinence after one year of treatment reached 50 %[9] compared to an effectiveness of 20 % obtained in Alcoholics Anonymous in those years. Because of this, the co-founder of Alcoholics Anonymous, Bill Wilson, came to consider that the psychedelic experience could be a very valuable part in the process. Betty Eisner, a psychotherapist who worked with Bill Wilson, continued to perfect the

---

[9] J. Ross MacLean et al., *"LSD-25 and mescaline as therapeutic adjuvants," The Use of LSD in Psychotherapy and Alcoholism*. Indianapolis: Bobbs-Merrill, 1967.

model of the new psychedelic-assisted psychotherapy, together with her colleague Sidney Cohen, by introducing the simultaneous work of two therapists (female and male) during the sessions where psychedelics were administered. Something that almost all psychedelics have in common is the passion and interest that they have aroused in many people, to the point of creating "apostles" so fascinated with their therapeutic, spiritual, scientific potential, to name a few, that they devoted themselves to the dissemination of their findings in different fields: scientific, political, therapeutic and even social. Alfred Hubbard, also known as "*Captain Hubbard*", was one of the first great disseminators of LSD among the upper classes, politicians, government officials, etc., taking advantage of his enormous network of contacts. But then many more people with very similar goals would appear.

In 1952, Ernst Jünger published his book *Visit to Godenholm*[10], in which he narrates his experiences with LSD, consumed with Albert Hoffmann a year before, but it did not receive much attention at the time. Quite the opposite of the famous English writer Aldous Huxley, to whom Humphry Osmond had supplied mescaline a year before, and who published *The Doors of Perception*[11] in 1954, a work that would begin to popularize psychedelics for the non-scientific public, a phenomenon of increasing popularization that would mark the following decades. The relationship between Huxley and Osmond would also bring about the term "*psychedelic*" in 1956. It was invented by Osmond by fusing the Greek words *psyche* (mind) and *deloun* (reveal, manifest); he later proposed it to Huxley in his letters. Despite the fact that the term "hallucinogenic" has always been widely used, the hallucinatory property as we currently understand it would only refer to one of the

---

[10] Ernst Jünger, *Besuch Auf Godenholm*, 1952.
[11] Aldous Huxley, *The Doors of Perception & Heaven and Hell*, ed. Harper & Brothers (Harper & Brothers, 1954 & 1956).

Aldous Huxley, author of *The Doors of Perception*, had a fascination with psychedelics.

many possible characteristics of experiences with this type of substance, although there is still terminological debate.

Aldous Huxley, who was impressed with the potential of psychedelics and devoted much writing and public appearances to making them known, wrote:

> I suspect that these drugs [psychedelic drugs] are destined to play a role in human affairs at least as important as alcohol has hitherto, and incomparably more beneficial. [...] It enables one to know by experience that "God is love" feeling, that, in spite of death and suffering - everything is, in some way and in the final instance, all right[12].

When he died of cancer in 1963, despite having been off psychedelics for several years, he asked to be given LSD on his deathbed, something that would soon begin to be tested on terminally ill patients, to help them lose their fear of death, accept their condition, reconcile with life and enjoy their last months of existence.

---

[12] Huxley. Quoted by Antonio Escohotado, *Historia Elemental de Las Drogas* (Anagrama, 2006).

In fact, the following year, a study by Erik Kast of the University of Chicago investigated the supposed analgesic power of LSD compared to common painkillers such as dihydromorphine and meperidine. In a group of fifty very sick patients with various pains mostly related to cancer, he obtained an unexpected result by revealing that, in this type of patients, LSD produced a greater effect than those analgesics[13]. This result was highly surprising and would be almost implausible were it not for the researchers' observation that some of this analgesic power was not strictly pharmacological or physical, but rather seemed to come from an improvement in the patients' mood and from the reappraisal that some of them made of their terminal situation and the acceptance of their probable death.

This same author continued to carry out studies related to LSD and pain, but increasingly focusing on other psychological parameters of his patients, such as their mood, their attitude towards their terminal state, their sleep patterns, their perception of pain...and noting that, with a single administration of LSD, positive changes were produced in these parameters that lasted more than three weeks. In successive studies, he continued to change his approach to study the influence that these experiences had on his patients in the religious and philosophical realm. To do this, he subjected terminally ill patients to the administration of a moderate dose of LSD, perceiving the changes mentioned in his previous studies. But what was peculiar in this case was that he also observed improvements in patient communication, along with feelings of unity and calm that lasted up to 12 days. With these studies, a new approach had just been born[14] that would have much

---

[13] E. C. Kast and V. J. Collins, "Study of lysergic acid diethylamide as an analgesic agent," *Anesthesia and Analgesia* 43 (May 1964): 285-91.

[14] E. Kast, "LSD and the dying patient," *The Chicago Medical School Quarterly* 26, 2 (Summer 1966): 80-87.

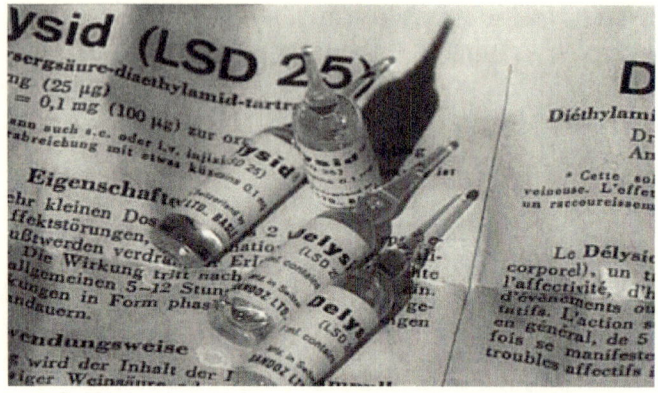

Vials of Delysid®, marketed by the pharmaceutical company Sandoz, which contained a dilution of LSD-25.
(Via https://www.neoteo.com/el-primer-estudio-sobre-el-lsd-en-40-anos-le-vuelve-encontrar-potencial-terapeutico/).

future development: psychedelic-assisted psychotherapy for post-diagnostic terminal depression and its associated anxiety.

Based on these studies, and on the anecdotal observations of alcoholics who claimed to live an experience akin to death and resurrection under the effects of LSD, the psychiatrist Sidney Cohen expressed in an article in 1965 his intention to initiate a program of study of the palliative use of LSD as antidepressant therapy for terminal cancer patients, to allow them to lose their fear of the experience of death and improve the last months of their life. Fortunately, other groups were also able to study and later replicate this approach, to the point that treating death depression with psychedelic psychotherapy ended up being reproduced with good results in contexts in which death was not the evident cause of depression, and it kept evolving until becoming a useful therapy in depression not associated with death.

Cohen would end up becoming a great defender of the therapeutic potential of psychedelics, but also one of the main disseminators of the dangers of use outside the clinic, publishing articles on the risks of misused psychedelics.

But scientists, doctors and intellectuals were not the only parties interested in harnessing the power of psychedelics. Between 1953 and 1973, the CIA carried out the secret project MK-Ultra (acronym for *mind control ultra*) performing illegal human experimentation, which sought to find substances and techniques that would facilitate interrogations, brainwashing, mind control, torture, and to explore their potential military use[15]. In the context of this secret project, multiple inhuman experiments were carried out with psychedelic, depressant and delirious substances[16], among other techniques, on volunteers or even civilians without their knowledge or consent. In some cases, these experiments ended in tragedy.

In 1955, the American banker and ethnobotanist Robert Gordon Wasson and his wife, the pediatrician and researcher Valentina Wasson, inspired by an article by the also ethnobotanist Richard Evans Schultes, traveled to Mexico to participate in a Mazatec ritual with psilocybe mushrooms invited by curandera María Sabina and, upon his return, Gordon published an article in the popular magazine *Life* titled "In search of the magic mushroom[17]", in 1957. They also accompanied the French mycologist Roger Heim to take samples, which he would later cultivate in France and send to Albert Hofmann for study, with the suspicion that it might contain a substance similar to LSD. After carrying out another first-person experiment with mushrooms, realizing their similarity to LSD, Albert Hofmann isolated, synthesized and described their active ingredients: psilocybin and psilocin, psychedelic tryptamines very similar to LSD at the structural and pharmacological level,

---

[15] Martin A. Lee and Bruce Shlain, *Acid Dreams: The Complete Social History of LSD: The CIA, the Sixties, and Beyond* (Grove/Atlantic, Inc., 2007).

[16] Category of substances that, unlike psychedelics, induce delirium. They normally have an anticholinergic effect on the brain.

[17] Robert Gordon Wasson, "Seeking the magic mushroom," *LIFE* (Time Inc, May 13, 1957).

María Sabina prepares psilocybe mushrooms while Robert G. Wasson takes notes. (Robert Gordon Wasson, "Seeking the magic mushroom", *LIFE* (Time Inc., May 13, 1957).

although with different pharmacokinetics, less pharmacological potency and duration of effects. Sandoz began marketing psilocybin under the trade name Indocybin® with similar indications as LSD. At this point in history, Albert Hofmann had already become a scientist whose career would be marked by the various psychedelic tryptamines that he himself discovered and described for Western science, convinced of their scientific and therapeutic usefulness, but which would suffer severe legislative setbacks yet to come.

In the late 1950s, LSD was already very popular in psychiatry. Some psychoanalysts at the time considered that LSD allowed them to reach depths inaccessible to traditional therapeutic methods, and much more quickly, saving years of therapy. Sometimes therapists even used LSD with their patients to facilitate empathic bonds. In 1959, psychiatrist Duncan Blewett, along with Al Hubbart and Humphry Osmond, published the *Handbook for the Therapeutic Use of LSD*[18], consi-

---

[18] N. Chwelos, D. B. Blewett, Handbook for the Therapeutic Use of Lysergic Acid Diehylamide 25 - Individual and Group Procedures, 1959.

dered one of the best guides to the clinical use of this substance. Blewett himself was so convinced that his approach was working above all other therapy, that he considered LSD psychotherapy to produce better results in a single afternoon than several years of conventional therapy.

Some personalities of the time had the opportunity to access these new psychedelic psychotherapy treatments with very positive results, such as the wife of then U.S. Senator Robert Kennedy (who would later defend the medical potential of LSD before its imminent prohibition) or the famous actor Cary Grant, who declared that he felt like a man "reborn" after several sessions of LSD. These experiences were widely aired by the media and gave a certain glamor to these new experiences. Unfortunately, however, results were not always so positive and there were those who, outside of normally controlled clinical use, sometimes had negative experiences. Although these cases fortunately rarely had lasting results, they were juicy enough for the most puritanical tabloid press.

By the early 1960s, LSD's popularity had moved out of scientific and therapeutic circles and onto the streets, where it was being used without medical supervision for recreational, spiritual, and self-exploration purposes. They were closely associated with youth counterculture movements, such as the *hippy* movement, with input from Beat Generation artists and writers such as William Burroughs, Allen Ginsberg and many others who were beginning to experiment with LSD. In California, a group of young people calling themselves *The Merry Pranksters,* formed by some famous names from the world of the arts, such as the writer Ken Kesey, who had been a volunteer for the MK-Ultra project, began to tour the country giving LSD to people as a rite of passage known as *acid-test* and greatly popularizing its use at the street level. It was precisely at this time that the first problems for LSD began, with the popularization of its use outside of controlled research settings.

The Merry Pranksters bus on tour in the U.S. with their *acid-test*. (Scott Brenner, "The Merry Pranksters," The American Century, https://omeka.wlu.edu/americancentury/items/show/185).

Echoes of this countercultural movement reached Harvard in 1962, where Professor Timothy Leary was very interested in the use of psychedelics since he had had experiences with psilocybin mushrooms – even claiming that he had learned more about psychology in 5 hours with them than in his 15 years of research. He began to conduct first-person experiments, organize studies together with his colleagues Ralph Metzner and Richard Alpert (later known as Ram Dass), and to include them in his classes with his students in what is known as the *Psilocybin Project,* until the university decided to expel them in 1963 after the famous "Good Friday" experiment[19], in which several theology students (among them the later famous Huston Smith), received psilocybin to attend mass and study

---

[19] Walter Norman Pahnke, "Drugs and mysticism: An analysis of the relationship between psychedelic drugs and the mystical consciousness: A thesis" (Harvard University, 1963).

whether it produced a mystical experience in them, which it did, in all of them, as opposed to those who only received a placebo.

After his expulsion from Harvard, Leary moved to a country house in Millbrooke, from where he founded a psychedelic commune, in which many young people came together and which served as the first great experiment in the social consumption of psychedelics for "psychological and spiritual development." This place served as a loudspeaker for the model that they intended to export to the entire American society, advocating that youth abandon their studies and join the movement, an invitation that years later would spread using the slogan *"Turn on, tune in, drop out."* One of the regulars at Millbrooke was Mary Pinchot (lover of President John F. Kennedy) who, together with Leary, planned to initiate different political personalities in the use of psychedelics and thus reduce the military tensions of the cold war. It has always been speculated that President John F. Kennedy himself may have experienced an LSD or psilocybin trip facilitated by Pinchot.

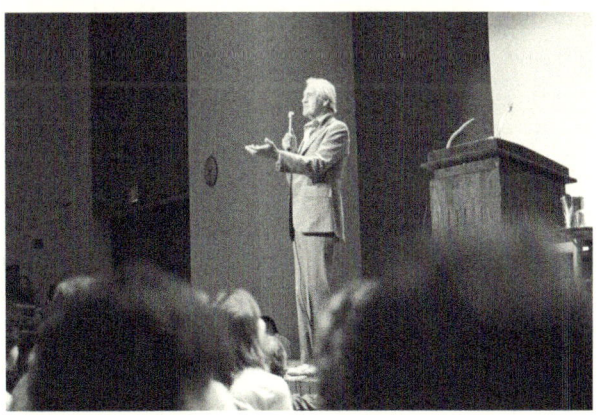

Timothy Leary, speaking at Southern Illinois University at Carbondale, Student Center (Brian Crawford, CC BY-SA 2.0, via flickr.com).

From Millbrooke, Albert Hofmann and Sandoz received a request for a large quantity of LSD (200g) and psilocybin (500g) which they rejected, stating these substances were still in the research phase and that they disapproved of the uncontrolled use of psychedelic tryptamines taking place at the commune. Albert Hofmann refused to take part in that movement and accused them of discrediting all the scientific work that was being done at that time, putting it at risk. At this point, tensions gradually began to grow between the controlled investigative use and uncontrolled social use of psychedelics, which would continue until their complete prohibition years later.

Most of the scientific community at the time censored what was happening at Millbrook, and saw years of research with psychedelics jeopardized if their popularization outside controlled environments could not be stopped. But Sandoz's restriction of supplies did not achieve its goal. Instead of reducing the uncontrolled use of its molecules, when Millbrook's supply ran out, anthropologist Nick Sand, who was a member of the commune and had a background in chemistry, began to manufacture millions of doses. This enabled them to become self-sufficient and supply the black market, which they continued to do years later when they moved to California – even making them the main LSD supplier of the American market for years.

Another important development of those years was the study of psychedelic substances as enhancers of creativity, associated with the field of business innovation, fundamentally applied to science and technology. A series of experiments by the research team of James Fadiman and Myron J. Stolaroff, among others, showed how low or medium doses of these substances could unlock breakthroughs or make it easier to solve technical problems[20]. In this area, the use of psychedelics as enhancers of creativity began to have many defenders within

---

[20] W.W. Harman et al., "Psychedelic agents in creative problem-solving: A pilot study", *Psychological Reports* 19, no. 1 (August 1966): 211-27.

the world of science, technology and art, a trend that has continued to this day, and that along the way has had the support of personalities such as Steve Jobs (Founder and Chairman of Apple), Francis Crick (Nobel Prize for his discovery of the DNA double helix), neuroscientist John C. Lilly, Kary Mullis (Nobel Prize for the discovery of PCR), Richard Feynman (Nobel Prize in Physics), Oliver Sacks, Jean Paul Sartre, Michel Foucault, and countless artists and musicians (The Beatles, Pink Floyd, The Doors, The Grateful Dead, Brian Wilson, Ray Charles, Eric Clapton, The Beach Boys, Jimi Hendrix, etc.).

Another event that would eventually prove to be of great importance, is the synthesis of ketamine in 1962 by the chemist Calvin Lee Stevens of Wayne State University who was working as a consultant for the pharmaceutical company Parke-Davis (now part of Pfizer). After passing clinical trials in prisoners, it was shown to be a much safer anesthetic with more controllable effects and a shorter duration than phencyclidine (PCP), producing "disconnection" effects that some

Parke-Davis Pharmaceuticals, currently part of Pfizer. *(U.S. Farm Security Administration-Office of War Information, Public domain, via Wikimedia Commons).*

researchers said resembled a "sleep" state, although they were later defined as "dissociative." This substance would finally be approved as an anesthetic by the Food and Drug Administration (FDA) in 1970 and, since then, its use in medicine has been very extensive, given its efficacy and safety. Although various researchers also began to be interested in these "dissociative" states induced by the substance and their work would ultimately be of great therapeutic and recreational interest.

In the early 1960s, a political and managerial change at the Saskatchewan Hospital in Canada, together with Abram Hoffer's confrontation with conventional psychiatry (which feared the excessive popularization of the still novel psychedelic psychotherapy) and the appearance of information in the media linking LSD to chromosome damage, defects in fetuses, cancer, accidents and cases of psychosis and suicides, complicated the operation of the Canadian investigation. Years later it was demonstrated that much of this news was untrue, and that the cases of psychosis were mostly the product of failures in the administration of LSD, using unsuitable subjects (who should have been discarded), or without adequate preparation. In addition, clinical suicide rates were proven to be even lower than those of conventional therapies. Still, the damage to political and public opinion had already been done.

Some meta-analyses and questionnaires have been conducted to study the safety and risks of psychotherapy with psychedelics, especially LSD and psilocybin. In the United States it was Dr. Sidney Cohen, psychiatrist and professor at the University of California in Los Angeles, UCLA, who published in this regard in 1960; and in England it was the psychiatrist of the Royal Society, Dr. Nicolas Malleson. The results of the studies (with 25,000 observations, in the case of Cohen, and 49,500 in the Malleson study) showed a very low hazard level of these substances in controlled psychotherapeutic settings, despite the fact that the psychedelic technique was not yet optimized, which did not correspond with the discourse of danger that was increasingly being offered by governments and the media.

In 1963, at Spring Grove Hospital, the U.S. National Institute of Mental Health (NIMH) financed a study of LSD-assisted psychotherapy in alcoholics, which confirmed the good results that this type of therapy offered, achieving great visibility with the broadcast of a report on the CBS television network. This study also allowed for an improvement in the technique, by giving value to factors that had previously been little attended to, such as the patient's physical environment and their mental state at the time of taking the psychedelic, what came to be known as *set and setting*, for which an adequate prior screening was vital to guarantee that the patients who accessed the treatment were in a position to benefit from it as much as possible, minimizing the risks.

Despite all these developments, in 1963 in Canada, a series of very notorious negative events related to the recreational use of LSD in young people prompted the country's new government to impose strict control measures on the substance, which would seriously hinder research and lead many of its researchers

Sanford Unger, a researcher at Spring Grove, with a patient in an LSD psychotherapy session.
("LSD: The Spring Grove Experiment," CBS Reports, produced by John Sharnik and Harry Morgan, aired May 17, 1966 (New York: CBS News Archives, 2016), DVD).

to abandon their work (as was the case with the Saskatchewan Hospital group) and would contribute to the growth of a black market for the substance, which, in turn, was accompanied by a greater number of public health problems in the country.

In the mid-1960s, after the publication of the manual *The Psychedelic Experience: A Manual Based on the Tibetan Book of the Dead*[21] and the continuous growth of the the hippie culture and the pacifist movement against the Vietnam War, San Francisco began to bring together a large number of young people who came from all over the country and whose poorly controlled use of psychedelic substances began to increase the incidence of problems related to them. The consumption of psychedelics was beginning to be considered a problem of public order, not only because of its implications for daily functioning in cities, but also because of the changes in political, ethical and cultural values to which it was linked. Particularly relevant was the rebellious nature of the pacifist and civil rights movements, strengthened by the experiences of unity and empathy that were associated with the psychedelic experience in a propitious context such as that of the Vietnam War, to which thousands of young people were sent against their will – all this mixed with a potentially destabilizing countercultural revolution and a questioning of the moral legitimacy of the authorities. It would be very risky to say that psychedelics were the cause of these social changes, but it is undeniable that they were associated with them, if only because of their repeated use by their promoters and members. In this context, public administrations and the press began to project a very distorted image of psychedelics, associating them with everything that was wrong: suicides, murders, malformations, accidents, sects... and disseminating large dissuasive advertising campaigns about its consumption, unleashing a panic that joined the already existing one in the most puritanical sectors of the U.S. USA

---

[21] Timothy Leary, Ralph Metzner, and Ram Dass, *The Psychedelic Experience: A Manual Based on the Tibetan Book of the Dead* (University Books, 1964).

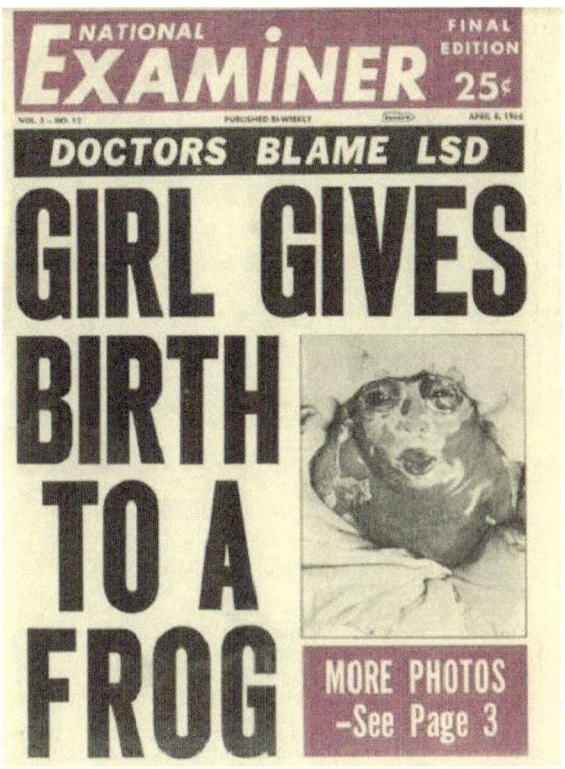

"Woman Gives Birth to Frog, Doctors Blame LSD". The media spread many sensational fake news against psychedelics.

In 1966, at a congressional subcommittee evaluating the restriction of psychedelics chaired by Senator Robert Kennedy, who was opposed to its complete prohibition, he declared:

> Why if [clinical LSD projects] were worthwhile six months ago, why aren't they worthwhile now? I think we have given too much emphasis and so much attention to the fact that [LSD] it can be dangerous and that it can hurt an individual who uses it that perhaps to some extent we have lost sight of the fact that it can be very, very helpful in our society if used properly.

Thousands of young people gathered in San Francisco in the summer of 1967, "The Summer of Love." *(Fantasy Fair, Mill Valley, 1967. To be featured in On the Road to the Summer of Love, on view at the California Historical Society. Photo by Elaine Mayes).*

In October 1966, the state of California decided to ban LSD for all uses. In the eyes of the administration, condemning the possession and use of psychedelics was not only a way of showing the electorate their commitment to preserving health, morals and public order, but it was also a way of being able to take legal action against members of a social movement that was becoming extremely uncomfortable for the government at the time. This ban led to demonstrations and riots in the U.S, like the famous protest at the Golden Gate Park in San Francisco, where 20,000 people gathered to consume psychedelics. Nor did this legislation prevent the phenomenon from continuing to grow in that city, especially in the Haight-Ashbury neighborhood, giving rise to what was known as the "Summer of Love" in 1967, one of the great moments of the *hippy* movement, but further evidence of the lack of control that was being practiced in the use of these substances outside clinics and laboratories.

The expiration of the Sandoz Delysid® patent was seen as an appropriate occasion to abandon the manufacture and sale of LSD, given the perception of great social turmoil offered by the press in the U.S. and Canada, blaming it on the use of the substance, and how badly this reflected on Sandoz; although its clinical use continued to be very promising and its controlled use did not seem to be causing any relevant problems, on the street, the perception was very different. Unfortunately, some researchers with access to the substance did not want to limit it to strictly clinical use, which justified much broader restrictions than would have been expected and led to its definitive ban for all uses.

In 1968, coinciding with student revolts in Europe and the U.S., LSD was definitively banned throughout the whole U.S. territory, which was a blow to the research that was in progress and forced promising ongoing studies, as well as its therapeutic use, to stop. But the main objective of curbing the use of LSD in society was not achieved, since a powerful black market had developed that would continue to supply the public from then until today. As proof of the lack of control that had been reached in the recreational use of psychedelics and the social impact of the counterculture of the time, Richard Nixon, president of U.S., immersed in a smear campaign of all uses of LSD and psychedelics (including scientific), years later apparently declared Timothy Leary "the most dangerous man in America."

This total prohibition movement did not mean the disappearance of LSD or psilocybin from the streets, since there was already a vast production and distribution network that was not only well supplied and very profitable (one gram of LSD gives about 10,000 doses, and mushrooms with psilocybin are easy and cheap to grow at home), but in many cases, this network claimed to have more political and even philanthropic purposes than economic (as in the case of the Brotherhood of Eternal Love), given that psychedelics had become the fuel of the counterculture and the *hippie* movement. The frequent confiscation of millions of doses did not reduce access to the

Signing of the United Nations Convention
on Psychotropic Substances of 1971.

substance; however, this movement did mean the end of all scientific and clinical research, which was blocked and had to be abandoned.

In 1971, the U.S. president, Richard Nixon, stated that drugs were "public enemy number one" and declared a *"war on drugs,"* a global campaign aimed at eradicating drugs through the use of all available legislative, police and military instruments. That same year, with the strong influence of the U.S., the United Nations Convention on Psychotropic Substances was signed in Vienna[22]. It imposed 4 lists or schedules for psychoactive substances, corresponding to 4 different levels of international control, where these substances were no longer only controlled because of their risk of addiction (as was the case of the 1961 convention on narcotic substances[23]) but because of their mind-altering

---

[22] The term psychotropic refers to substances that modify the mind, such as LSD, psilocybin and MDMA. The 1971 UN Convention on Psychotropic Substances focused on controlling them internationally based on their potential for abuse or risk.

[23] The term narcotic refers to substances that stimulate or depress the CNS, such as morphine or cocaine. The 1961 UN Single Convention

ability, alleged potential for abuse and risk to public health. These restrictions included their authorized medical uses, regardless of their addictiveness (most classic psychedelics are not addictive). Psychedelics (LSD, psilocybin, mescaline and DMT) were placed on the most controlled list, Schedule I, reserved for substances "with great potential risk to public health and no recognized medical use."

MDMA

3,4-methylenedioxymethamphetamine (MDMA, also known today as ecstasy) was synthesized for the first time in 1912 by the German chemist Anton Köllisch for the pharmaceutical company Merck (and patented by them as well) as an intermediate compound for the synthesis of a hemostatic agent[24]. It wasn't until the 1950s that it began to spark some interest, and the U.S. military performed some studies with it, among others, in the context of its MK-Ultra project. In 1965, Alexander "Sasha" Shulguin, a biochemist working for Dow Chemical, began working with this compound. In the 1970s, after the prohibition of MDA (a drug similar in molecular structure and effects, which had become popular), cases of recreational use of MDMA began to appear in the Chicago area.

In 1976, after talking to two of his students that had tried MDMA, Alexander Shulgin decided to try it and was very impressed with its effects on the emotional plane, publishing the first scientific article on its effects on humans, together with biochemist David E. Nichols, describing them as "an easily

---

on Narcotic Drugs focused on controlling drugs internationally based on their risk of addiction.

[24] A hemostatic agent is a substance that facilitates blood coagulation and thus stops bleeding.

Alexander "Sasha" Shulgin, rediscoverer and "godfather" of MDMA, and discoverer of hundreds of new psychedelic molecules. *(Photo via erowid.org).*

controllable altered state of consciousness with emotional and sensual overtones," comparable to "marijuana, psilocybin devoid of its hallucinatory component, or low levels of MDA"[25].

Sensing that its effects could be of enormous help for psychotherapy, he showed it to psychotherapist Leo Zeff, who was impressed by its potential and introduced it to the circles of psychotherapists and psychiatrists, teaching thousands of professionals to work with the substance. He nicknamed it "Adam", alluding to its ability to put people in states of "primordial innocence." MDMA was used in combination with psychotherapy, improving the capacity for introspection, work on the traumatic past, therapist-patient connection, and was able to accelerate the treatment of diseases such as post-traumatic stress disorder, depression, addictions, and even couple conflicts, thanks to its ability to induce empathy, positive emotions, improve

---

[25] T. Alexander and David E. Nichols, "Characterization of three new psychotomimetics," *The Psychopharmacology of Hallucinogens* (Elsevier, 1978), 74-83.

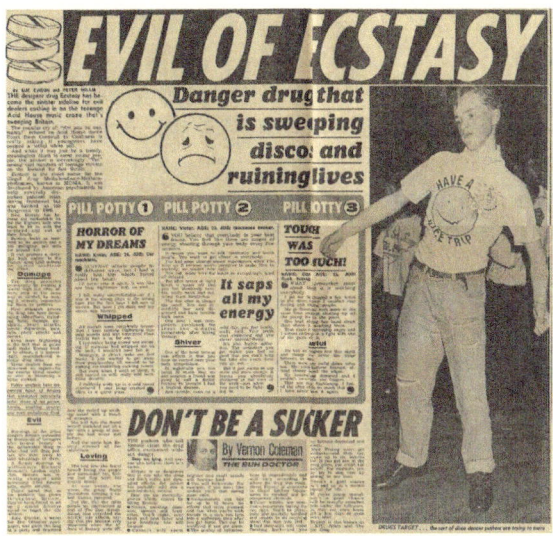

"The evil of ecstasy. The dangerous drug that is sweeping nightclubs and ruining lives. A nightmare. Don't be a fool." As with LSD and other psychedelics, MDMA also had its own campaign of sensationalism.

communication and facilitate forgiveness, because, among other things, MDMA "does not open the doors of perception [like classic psychedelics] as much as of emotionality"[26].

Although MDMA was known as "empathy" or "Adam", the press preferred to popularize the term "ecstasy" (XTC or X) coined in relation to the effects of its recreational use. Its recreational heyday came in the mid-1980s, with the *new age* movement and the *rave* scene; and, just as it had happened with psychedelics, based on negative reports and some deaths from heat stroke or overdose, the media began to publish highly exaggerated, sensational and even fake news about the substance and what happened in those

---

[26] Escohotado, *Historia Elemental de Las Drogas*.

"raves" among the young people who consumed it, initiating a moral panic that would quickly spread.

In 1985, the U.S. Drug Enforcement Administration (DEA) urgently banned MDMA for all uses, despite the fact that many therapists and psychiatrists testified against this ban citing the "almost incredible capacity of MDMA to facilitate subjective communication and access to repressed feelings", arguments that were not taken into account when the substance was also prohibited for clinical use and research.

Soon after, the expert committee of the World Health Organization (WHO) concluded that:

> *There are no data available on propensity for clinical abuse, nor on social or public health issues, nor epidemiological ones, linked to the use or abuse of this substance. There is no well-defined therapeutic use, but many professionals state that it has great value as a psychotherapeutic agent [...] There was, however, sufficient interest expressed to recommend that investigations be encouraged to follow up these preliminary findings. To that end, the Expert Committee urged countries to use the provisions of Article 7 of the Convention on Psychotropic Substances to facilitate research on this interesting substance.*

Despite all this, it was included in Schedule I of the Convention on Psychotropic Substances of the UN as a substance "with a great potential risk to public health and no recognized medical use," dashing any hope of further use by the medical and research communities.

In 1986, the year after the prohibition of MDMA, which was the last great promise in the field of psychedelics with clinical potential, Rick Doblin founded the Multidisciplinary Association for the Study of Psychedelics (MAPS), a non-profit scientific-activist organization, to continue promoting rigorous scientific research into the therapeutic use of psychedelics and appeal to the necessary legal channels to return these substances to clinics, laboratories and a future society that knows how to use them with responsibility and discretion.

After the Ban

Despite the fact that, by the mid-1960s, the clinical use of psychedelics had already led to the publication of dozens of books and the organization of several international conferences, in addition to the publication of more than 1,000 peer-reviewed scientific articles in which these substances had been administered to more than 40,000 participants[27], research in psychotherapy with LSD and psilocybin failed to take root. Initially, it was due to the fact that the science used in the 1950s, mainly at the Saskatchewan Hospital, did not meet all the scientific standards that would be required years later, nor was it as methodical or controlled as it should have been to give the irrefutable results that would leave a greater mark on the world of psychiatry[28]. The effects of these substances were also more difficult to predict in those early years, something that was uncomfortable to manage in the clinic.

However, starting in the 1960s, when its application, safety and predictability seemed to improve, its great failure was not having been able to detach itself from the sociopolitical context and thus prevent the popularization of the use of LSD on the streets, with former researchers promoting its massive use, and their inevitable association with the counterculture, student protests, peace movements and movements against Vietnam, which ended up polarizing the position of governments that would end up banning them; and with them, any legitimate use of these (until then) promising substances for research purposes.

---

[27] L. Grinspoon and J. B. Bakalar, "The psychedelic drug therapies," *Current Psychiatric Therapies* 20 (1981): 275-83.
[28] Erika Dyck, "Flashback: Psychiatric experimentation with LSD in historical perspective", *Canadian Journal of Psychiatry. Revue Canadienne de Psychiatrie* 50, no. 7 (June 2005): 381-88.

Logo of the Multidisciplinary Association for the Study of Psychedelics, founded by Rick Doblin in 1986 after the prohibition of MDMA.

With the exception of ketamine, the history of the classic psychedelics (psilocybin, LSD, mescaline) and that of MDMA had followed a similar script: substances with promising scientific and medical use, but which were banned when they became popular outside of clinics and laboratories, becoming a scapegoat to control certain youth or political movements. Unfortunately, the ban was only effective in crippling scientific research and the clinical use of these substances because, as is the case with almost all drugs, the ban did not have the expected effect on their recreational or non-laboratory use. Quite the opposite, their popularity in these contexts continued to grow, counting the doses consumed around the world, and confiscated, each year in the millions. All this resulted in an even less informed use due to taboo, an increase in the adulteration of the substance, and therefore, an increase in physical and mental health risks.

Despite the ban, unofficial research into psychedelics and underground treatments continued in the following decades, with psychedelic-assisted psychotherapies sometimes using other non-illegalized psychedelic compounds or other non-pharmacological techniques to access altered states of consciousness, such as holotropic breathing. Given the illegal nature of many of these investigations and treatments, there were few publications about them, but some people dared to do so, such as George Greer, Myron Stolaroff, Athanasios Kafkalides or the Shulgins.

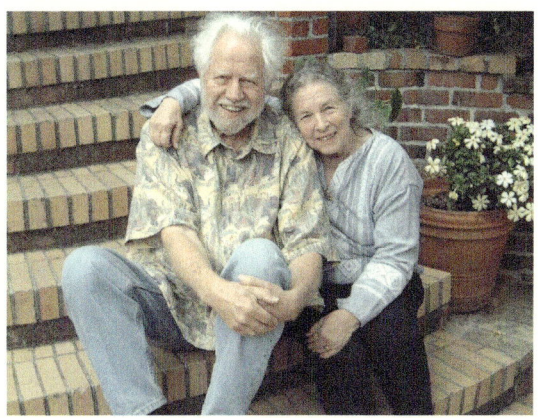

Alexander "Sasha" Shulgin and his wife, Ann Shulgin, at their home in California.
(Shulgin with his wife Ann at their home in Lafayette, California, USA in 2002. Photography: Anthony Pidgeon/Redferns).

Biochemist Alexander "Sasha" Shulgin and his wife Ann Shulgin, who had extensively researched the chemistry and effects of different psychedelics on the body, especially MDMA, feeling that these pharmacological tools had been unfairly banned for reasons unrelated to science, decided to share their knowledge to encourage research and self-exploration by publishing in 1991 the book *PiHKAL: A chemical love story*[29], acronym for "Phenethylamines I Have Known and Loved", and in the book they tell their own story with 179 substances from this chemical family (which includes psychedelics such as mescaline, and empathogens-entactogens with psychedelic properties such as MDMA), most of them discovered by Shulgin, as well as the recipes to synthesize them, dosages, laboratory notes, etc.

---

[29] Shulgin and Shulgin, *Pihkal: A Chemical Love Story*.

The DEA (Drug Enforcement Administration), was angry with the chemist and decided to raid and close his laboratory in 1994, revoking his license to investigate and produce illegalized drugs.

In response to this, the couple was reinforced in their conviction to prevent these substances from falling into scientific oblivion, and in 1997 they published the book *TiHKAL: The continuation*[30], acronym for "Tryptamines I Have Known and Loved", which followed a very similar structure to the previous one, but this time focused on their experiences with 55 molecules of the chemical family of tryptamines (to which most classic psychedelics belong, such as psilocybin, psilocin, LSD, DMT, etc.).

---

[30] Shulgin and Shulgin, *Tihkal: The Continuation*.

The Psychedelic Renaissance

As we saw in the previous chapter, although natural psychedelics from plants, fungi, and animals had been used in some cultures for millennia, it was Albert Hofmann's discovery of LSD back in 1943 that really started and spurred the interest and research of these substances in the West, greatly advancing the study of the brain, as well as helping to lay the foundations for the relationship between neurochemistry and behavior, and allowing the development of very promising new models of experimental treatments in mental health using these substances, such as psychedelic-assisted psychotherapies. With these new treatment models, it was possible, for example, for people suffering from terminal cancer to recover their smile in their last months of life, or for people suffering from alcoholism to stop drinking[1]. But this whole movement became deadlocked due to various factors: its use (outside the clinic

---

[1] Teri S. Krebs and Pål-Ørjan Johansen, "Lysergic acid diethylamide (LSD) for alcoholism: Meta-analysis of randomized controlled trials", *Journal of Psychopharmacology* 26, no. 7 (July 2012): 994-1002.

or the laboratory) by countercultural and anti-Vietnam war movements (which made the U.S. government and various conservative sectors very uncomfortable); some highly oversensationalized cases by the press, the ignorance surrounding its neurological functioning and long-term consequences, plus the various campaigns in the media[2]. All these led the U.S. government at the time to ban them at the federal level in 1968 and, soon after, internationally. Thus began the famous "war on drugs", ending a prolific era of very promising clinical research. Years later, history would repeat itself with MDMA (ecstasy) using a very similar script, destroying a substance with enormous clinical potential after its prohibition in 1985, despite the opposition of a good part of the scientific community and its rediscovery and "sponsorship" by Alexander "Sasha" Shulgin & Ann Shulguin.

This could have been the end of the story. Psychedelics would be just another family of illegalized drugs with supposedly "great potential risk to public health and no recognized medical use" as the UN says – a marginal family of substances doomed to oblivion and within the reach of only a few avid psychonauts. It would have stayed this way if it had not been for the determination and tenacity of some people and organizations that, despite the legal difficulties imposed, maintained the conviction that psychedelics had enormous potential and could have an important place in our society if they were used and controlled properly.

Lately there is a lot of talk about psychedelics everywhere: studies of magic mushrooms to treat all kinds of problems, such as depression and addictions; *celebrities* doing ayahuasca retreats; LSD microdosing to improve productivity in Silicon Valley startups; MDMA (ecstasy) being one step away from becoming legalized to cure traumas; ketamine administered in

---

[2] Stephen Siff, *Acid Hype: American News Media and the Psychedelic Experience* (University of Illinois Press, 2015).

overpriced mental health clinics; debates in the U.S. Congress, where there is talk of lowering the legal control of psychedelics; prestigious universities creating psychedelic research centers; reputable scientific journals naming psychedelic therapies among the year's greatest scientific breakthroughs; "psychedelic" companies trading on Wall Street and receiving billions of dollars in investments; U.S. cities and states decriminalizing or even legalizing the possession and use of psychedelics; books on the subject becoming *best sellers*; podcasts with millions of listeners where celebrity guests share their psychedelic journeys; series on Netflix on the subject and many articles in all kinds of media. Without going any further, recently the very *New York Times* ran the following headline on its cover: "The Psychedelic Revolution Is Coming. Psychiatry May Never Be the Same[3]."

What's going on? Aren't they supposed to be dangerous drugs with no medical use? Why is this happening now?

THE RESEARCH

Although the official story of "dangerous drugs with no medical use" spread by governments and the press, together with legal restrictions, worked well as a deterrent at a scientific level for decades, relegating these substances almost to oblivion (in contrast with their recreational use, which continued to be very popular), since the end of the 20th century and especially in the beginning of the 21st century, some researchers, thanks to their conviction, and despite the great bureaucratic challenges, resumed official lines of research related to psychedelics.

---

[3] Andrew Jacobs, "The Psychedelic Revolution Is Coming. Psychiatry May Never Be the Same", *New York Times*, May 9, 2021, https://www.nytimes.com/2021/05/09/health/psychedelics-mdma-psilocybin-molly-mental-health.html.

Some were veterans of the research conducted in the 1950s, 1960s, and 1970s and others had held parallel lines to psychedelics, but newcomers joined the field as well.

This time, their seeds fell on fertile ground because at the beginning of this millennium numerous factors that had precipitated the prohibition of psychedelic substances in the late 1960s were changing, and many others appeared facilitating the conditions for lines of research with psychedelics to be resumed with due caution:

- In the sociopolitical context, there had been a stabilization with respect to the years in which its prohibition originated: appeasement of the student revolts and the pacifist movement; end of the political tension of the cold war; end of the anti-nuclear movement and no more wars that required forced recruitment... in short, the sociocultural context that had used psychedelics as an identity element of rebellion against the government was already extinct, as was the generation of politicians who had confronted them.
- In the epidemiological context, where mental illnesses such as depression, anxiety, post-traumatic stress, addictions or neurodegenerative disorders are a growing major problem, especially in Western societies (and even more so after the COVID-19 pandemic), it is becoming increasingly urgent to innovate and accelerate the progress of neuroscience, to understand the pathological mechanisms of these diseases, as well as to search for new and better treatments.
- Together with the above, there is an urgent need for new advances in treatments and psychopharmacology, which has been quite stagnant for decades, and has not made great progress since the discovery of antidepressants that inhibit the reuptake of different types of neurotransmitters (SSRIs, ISRNs, etc.) and benzodiazepines.

- In the research context, the development of neuroscience and neurochemistry, together with the development of neuroimaging techniques (such as positron emission tomography, PET, and magnetic resonance imaging, MRI), has facilitated the work, allowing a better theoretical understanding and practical observation of the mechanisms of action of psychedelic substances, and with it, improvements in the predictability and control of their risks, opening the way to apply their therapeutic and research potential, as well as the communication of said findings.
- The improvement of scientific standards, research designs and analytic tools, which make the results more solid and undeniable, in addition to establishing correlations and causalities more easily.
- Many of the researchers involved in the research of the 1950s and 1960s (although some were already at the end of their careers) were still close to the field and maintained their interest and conviction that these substances had a great role to play in modern science, having been able to lead or support the resurgence.
- In addition, a new generation of unprejudiced researchers is emerging, wanting to innovate and advance the field of neuroscience and therapy, challenging the taboos on substances that did not prove to be as dangerous or as useless as they were labeled, but extremely important.
- The financial support of scientific institutions such as the Multidisciplinary Association for Psychedelic Studies (MAPS), the Heffter Research Institute, the Beckley Foundation, the International Center for Ethnobotanical Education, Research, and Service (ICEERS), etc., together with a greater openness and acceptance by the ethics committees of several prestigious research organizations and centers, such as Johns

Hopkins University, New York University (NYU), Harbor-UCLA Medical Center, University of New Mexico, Imperial College London, Psychiatric University Hospital of Zurich, Hospital Sau Pau of Barcelona, etc.

- The appearance of the internet and new communication technologies allowed information on this type of substance and its effects to circulate with greater freedom, speed and scope, without necessarily being subject to the moral scrutiny of the mass media, thus also favoring its demystification and scientific re-evaluation, as well as the dissemination of these past and present lines of research.

- Closely linked to the above, the Internet also facilitated the creation of networks of people interested in the subject, as well as the accumulation of anecdotal evidence with the creation of communities dedicated to psychonautics and the discussion of information on all kinds of psychoactive substances, such as Erowid, Reddit, Drugs-Forum, Bluelight, Cannabiscafe and others, formed by psychonauts interested in greater knowledge and self-experimentation, and whose publications are currently being analyzed by various scientific publications[4] that seek to take advantage of the experiences of these users to improve the predictability and safety of their use in clinical research. Likewise, the development of risk and damage reduction programs in recreational spaces has also made it possible to provide and validate information on how to safely manage bad experiences that may occur in

---

[4] Theresa M. Carbonaro et al., "Survey study of challenging experiences after ingesting psilocybin mushrooms: Acute and enduring positive and negative consequences", *Journal of Psychopharmacology* 30, no. 12 (December 2016): 1268-78.

clinical environments, such as, for example, the importance of *set and setting* or how to manage bad trips in the clinic. Also, the accumulation of more anecdotal evidence given its *underground* use.

- The review of the research carried out in the 50s and 60s using current standards, preparing systematic reviews and meta-analyses that have made it possible to reassess the safety and efficacy of treatments based on the work carried out at the time, since some of them accumulated many scientific publications.
- The recent acceptance of the possible medical uses of cannabis, which, in most legislation, was at the same level of prohibition as psychedelics, as in the case of the U.S., where they were labeled as Schedule I substances, officially defined as "of great risk to public health and with no therapeutic value." This acceptance also paved the way for the scientific and social acceptance of the investigation of other illegal substances, by casting doubt on the old classifications of drugs.
- Modern population studies[5] with sample sizes in the hundreds of thousands of people, showing that there is no correlation between the use of MDMA or psychedelics and mental illness of any kind[6]. In fact, the correlation indicates that the use of MDMA or psychedelics is associated with better mental health, less stress[7], less depression[8]

---

[5] Krebs and Johansen, "Psychedelics and mental health: A population study."
[6] Johansen and Krebs, "Psychedelics not linked to mental health problems or suicidal behavior: A population study."
[7] Hendricks et al., "Classic psychedelic use is associated with reduced psychological distress and suicidality in the United States adult population."
[8] Jones and Nock, "Lifetime use of MDMA/ecstasy and psilocybin is associated with reduced odds of major depressive episodes."

and fewer suicidal thoughts[9]. Although "correlation does not imply causation", these studies show the extent to which the image of MDMA and psychedelics as substances that cause mental illness or attract people with mental illness is distorted by the media and prevention campaigns based on fear. The risks of these substances, while real, have been greatly overestimated, and they very rarely produce lasting negative effects[10]. They don't even seem to be associated with arrests[11] or other indicators of antisocial or criminal activities that were blamed on them in the 60s and 70s.

Thanks to all these factors, and many others that have emerged along the way, starting in the 1990s, a few research groups began to carry out some studies with psychedelics. For example, in the U.S., some studies were published with MDMA (by Charles Grob's group) and DMT (by Rick Strassman), and in Europe with ayahuasca (by Jordi Riba and Manel Barbanoj), MDMA (by Magi Farré, Rafael de la Torre and Jordi Camí), and various other psychedelic substances such as psilocybin, MDMA, Ketamine, LSD (by Franz Vollenweider and Gouzoulis-Mayfrank). All this despite the fact that the rest of the scientific community was still, for the most part, highly influenced by the biased view of psychedelics that had spread (and continued to spread) from prohibitionist positions, and dissuaded by the ethical, legal and economic challenges to conduct research with highly controlled substances such as psychedelics.

---

[9] Jones and Nock, "MDMA/ecstasy use and psilocybin use are associated with lowered odds of psychological distress and suicidal thoughts in a sample of U.S. adults."

[10] Schlag et al., "Adverse effects of psychedelics: From anecdotes and misinformation to systematic science."

[11] Grant M. Jones and Matthew K. Nock, "Psilocybin use is associated with lowered odds of crime arrests in U.S. adults: A replication and extension", *Journal of Psychopharmacology* 36, no. 1 (January 2022): 66-73.

Unfortunately, until very recently, and even today, this research has found all kinds of obstacles and difficulties to develop, in most cases for reasons unrelated to science, as it has been the case from the 1970s. For example, in Spain, a promising study[12] on the safety and efficacy of MDMA-assisted psychotherapy in women suffering from post-traumatic stress after rape, led by José Carlos Bouso (current scientific director of ICEERS), which had begun in 2000 and was the first of therapeutic MDMA worldwide, was abruptly suspended before completion due to political pressure in 2002, despite its promising preliminary results.

Ketamine was the only substance with psychedelic properties with widely recognized medical use that had never been banned, and therefore research with it was more affordable, which allowed its antidepressant properties to be demonstrated in the year 2000[13], and meant the opening of a new research front that would advance very quickly.

But the global scientific interest in clinical research with psychedelics began to spread faster from 2006, when Roland Griffiths, a leading researcher in the field of psychopharmacology and addictions at the prestigious Johns Hopkins University in the U.S., together with a veteran of psychedelic research, William "Bill" Richards, and others, published a study[14] in which they simply administered psilocybin (the main stable active ingredient in "magic mushrooms") or placebo

---

[12] José Carlos Bouso et al., "MDMA-assisted psychotherapy using low doses in a small sample of women with chronic posttraumatic stress disorder," *Journal of Psychoactive Drugs* 40, no. 3 (September 2008): 225-36.

[13] Robert M. Berman et al., "Antidepressant effects of ketamine in depressed patients," *Biological Psychiatry*, 2000.

[14] R. R. Griffiths et al., "Psilocybin can occasion mystical-type experiences having substantial and sustained personal meaning and spiritual significance," *Psychopharmacology* 187, no. 3 (August 2006): 268-83; discussion 284-92.

to a group of people in a controlled environment and under direct professional supervision in order to evaluate, after the experience, what they had felt and if it had produced lasting changes in their mood. Two-thirds of the people who participated in the study rated the psilocybin psychedelic experience among the 5 most important and meaningful experiences of their entire lives, on the same level as the birth of a first baby or the death of a close family member. A third even ranked it as the most important and meaningful experience of their lives. In addition, those who participated in the study, and their relatives, friends, partners, etc., testified that positive and lasting changes in different aspects of the subject's personal and emotional well-being had occurred and lasted for months.

This study and the surprising results obtained, with such an apparently simple intervention, were widely publicized and had a great impact on the scientific community (among other things, because of the signatories and the institution performing the study), and little by little continued to add new publications from various centers of great scientific prestige (Johns Hopkins University, Imperial College London, NYU, UCLA, etc.), along with the work of existing teams (University of Zurich, Hospital San Pau) and the aforementioned veteran scientific-activist organizations, such as MAPS (1986), Heffter Research Institute (1993), Beckley Foundation (1998), or ICEERS (2008), which had been supporting and requesting more research on the therapeutic use of psychedelics for years. Since then, they have been greatly promoting the field of psychedelic study and specifically the development of psychedelic-assisted psychotherapy at a time when we are facing a true epidemic in the field of mental health, where disorders so difficult to treat like depression, anxiety or addictions have become the leading cause of disability worldwide (and now, with the advent of the COVID-19 pandemic, these numbers will continue to grow even faster, as various studies have already shown), while current conventional treatments

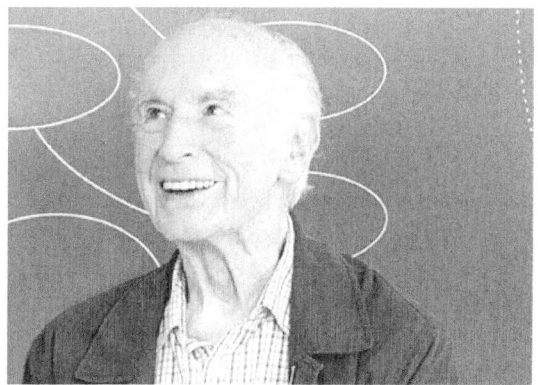

Albert Hofmann, on his 100th birthday
(Stepan, CC BY-SA 2.0 DE
<https://creativecommons.org/licenses/by-sa/2.0/de/deed.en>, via Wikimedia Commons).

do not achieve sufficient efficacy and efficiency rates to curb this increase in mental health problems and in many cases lead to safety problems and side effects.

In April 2008, at the age of 102, Albert Hofmann, the main person responsible for the discovery of psychedelics for Western culture, died in Basel, Switzerland. He had always lamented that his "problematic son" had been misinterpreted in the context of the countercultural movement, and that it had not been understood as a powerful therapeutic and spiritual tool, even declaring on his 100th birthday:

> *It gave me an inner joy, an open mindedness, a gratefulness, open eyes and an internal sensitivity for the miracles of creation... I think that in human evolution it has never been as necessary to have this substance LSD. It is just a tool to turn us into what we are supposed to be*[15].

But his death did not come without the satisfaction of seeing this psychedelic renaissance return "his" LSD to clinical

---

[15] Speech on his 100th birthday

research, since a year earlier, in 2007, Switzerland had authorized studies of LSD-assisted psychotherapy in terminally ill patients. These were the first studies of the therapeutic effects of LSD, conducted in humans, in 35 years.

Psychedelic-assisted psychotherapy is a treatment model in which a psychedelic is administered, in a controlled therapeutic setting, under the direct supervision of professionals, and as part of a broader psychotherapy treatment. Given that psychedelics are very safe substances at a physiological level, but have psychological risks, especially in certain people, they are only administered to patients who have already tried other treatments without success, who have undergone a psychological screening process to rule out latent illnesses (such as psychotic disorders or bipolarity), and who undergo psychological preparation sessions prior to the psychedelic experience, always maintaining safety protocols[16].

After the experience, in which the person has remained with their eyes closed, headphones on with selected music, and in the company and supervision of a team of professionals, an integration process is carried out that is crucial to work with all the material that emerged during the psychedelic experience.

What is important about this treatment model is that, unlike current treatments with antidepressants or anxiolytics, where the drug is taken daily, "masking" the symptoms, in psychedelic-assisted psychotherapy, the substance is only administered in one or two sessions throughout a psychotherapeutic treatment, the aim being to induce a transformative experience in those sessions, the therapeutic results of which last once the therapy is finished. That is to say, the psychedelic would only act as a "momentary catalyst", facilitating that transformative and

---

[16] M. W. Johnson, W. A. Richards, and R. R. Griffiths, "Human hallucinogen research: Guidelines for safety," *Journal of Psychopharmacology* 22, no. 6 (August 2008): 603-20.

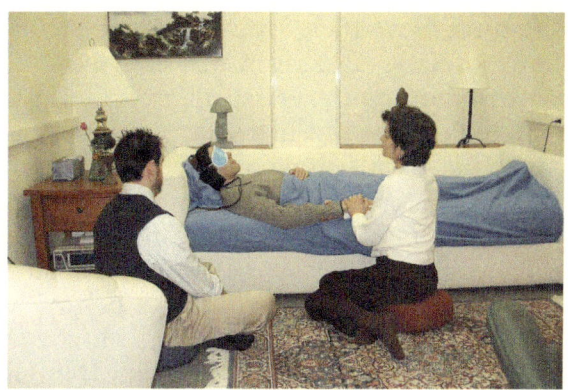

Psilocybin-assisted psychotherapy session at Johns Hopkins University. There are usually two therapists (female and male) to provide support throughout the session. *(Photo by Matthew W. Johnson CC BY-SA 3.0, via https://researchoutreach.org/).*

lasting experience, favoring access to the root of the problem and allowing therapist and patient to work on it.

And, indeed, most of this research is concluding that psychedelics, administered in a context of psychotherapy under direct professional supervision and in a controlled environment, are capable of catalyzing such transformative experiences, associated with long-lasting therapeutic results (that could last for years), quickly, safely (if done in well prepared patients) and effectively, in many cases facilitating the partial or complete remission of some mental disorders such as depression, anxiety, post-traumatic stress and addictions in patients who have not managed to improve with conventional therapies.

These types of disorders, today, usually require very extensive, expensive therapeutic processes and long-term pharmacological treatments with unwanted side effects. Following these control and supervision guidelines, the safety, effectiveness and durability rates that are being achieved in research are above the best current treatments, with fewer side effects and in much less time. Nevertheless, more research is still required to consolidate these results, given that at the moment most studies are carried out with very small groups of patients and given the intensity of the psychedelic experience, it is difficult to compare its effect with placebos.

To discuss and make all this research visible, a growing number of conferences, conventions and annual scientific congresses are organized to serve as a space for meeting and disseminating the latest advances in this field, such as Psychedelic Science, Breaking Convention, ICPR, Horizons, World Ayahuasca Conference, Beyond Psychedelics, INSIGHT, etc.

As proof of the rapid change in attitude that regulatory agencies, such as the EMA or the FDA, have had regarding psychedelic drugs, thanks to this scientific development, aided by better access to information and the experience of previous regulatory processes (such as medical cannabis), the stigmas surrounding research with psychedelics are disappearing, making the original impediments – legal, economic, technical and social – turn into advantages. As an example, the fact that the FDA (Food and Drug Administration) is approving the

INSIGHT 2021 Conference, in Berlin. *(Photo is property of the author).*

breakthrough therapy designation for many of these trials, based on their safety and efficacy, accelerating their development and medical authorization. Now this whole field is being greatly boosted with milestones that would be unimaginable just 5 years ago:
- MDMA, hand in hand with the NGO MAPS, is already concluding Phase III[17] clinical trials for the treatment of post-traumatic stress syndrome, which could lead to its authorization for controlled medical use in 2023.
- Psilocybin, from the Compass Pathways pharmaceutical company, is already in Phase II-III clinical trials for the treatment of major depression and could be authorized for controlled medical use around 2025.
- Esketamine (enantiomer of ketamine), from Janssen Pharmaceuticals, has already been authorized in 2019 for the treatment of depression, and is marketed for medical use under the name of Spravato® in the form of a nasal spray, both in the U.S. USA (FDA), in Europe (EMA) and many other countries. Likewise, racemic ketamine has long been used in mental health treatments at doctors' discretion.
- The study of psilocybin for the treatment of smoking has just received a major grant from the National Institute on Drug Abuse (NIDA) in the U.S. to continue evaluating its efficacy and safety in this type of disorder.
- And there are many other various psychedelic substances (ibogaine, DMT, ayahuasca, LSD, 5-MeO-DMT, psilocybin, MDMA) currently being investigated or considered for many other therapeutic conditions (addictions, social anxiety, anorexia, tinnitus, phobias,

---

[17] Clinical trials prior to the approval of a new drug are divided into phases I, II and III.

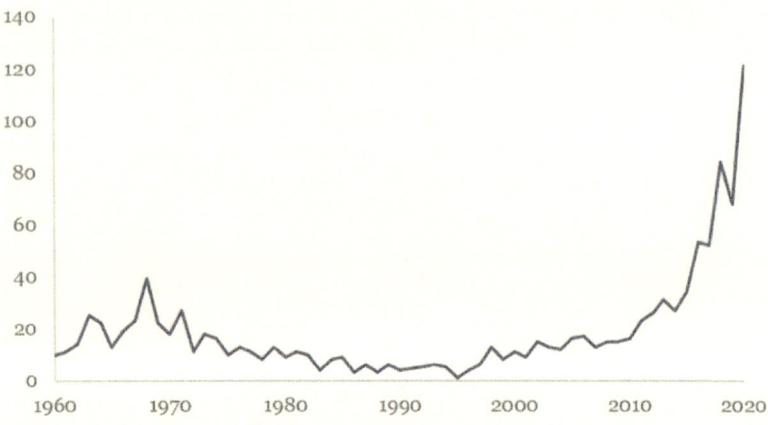

Number of scientific publications in PubMED, clearly showing that the "psychedelic renaissance" has already surpassed the research of the 60's and 70s. *(The Psychedelic Renaissance in 2020 by Josh Hardman from Psilocybin Alpha, via psilocybinalpha.com).*

anxiety, obsessive-compulsive disorder, dementia, Alzheimer's, stuttering, palliative care, chronic pain, etc.) and that are in different states and phases of development and authorization, so it seems that this revolution in the research and medical use of psychedelics has only just begun.

To give an idea of the magnitude of this scientific phenomenon, almost half of all scientific research published with psychedelics has come in the last decade (from 2010 to 2020), with those carried out in the United Kingdom, U.S., Switzerland, Spain and Brazil having the greatest impact[18].

---

[18] Aviad Hadar et al., "The psychedelic renaissance in clinical research: A bibliometric analysis of three decades of human studies with classical psychedelics", *Journal of Psychoactive Drugs*, January 9, 2022, 1-10.

The popular magazine *Science* included trials in MDMA-assisted psychotherapy for the treatment of post-traumatic stress in its list of the 10 greatest advances in science in 2021[19], while many universities and research institutions have already gone beyond their psychedelic research programs and have founded specialized centers. Some examples are the Center for Psychedelic Research at Imperial College London, the Center for the Science of Psychedelics at UC Berkeley, the Center for Psychedelic & Consciousness Research at Johns Hopkins University, the Center for Psychedelic Research & Therapy at the Dell Medical School of the University of Texas at Austin, the Center for Psychedelic Psychotherapy and Trauma Research of the Icahn School of Medicine at Mount Sinai, or the Psychae Institute in Melbourne.

In short, we are currently in a golden era for research with psychedelics, a moment which the first article on the subject published in a *mainstream* medium of relevance in 2010 called "The Psychedelic Renaissance[20]," baptizing this revolution in research and giving rise to what we are seeing today in the field of research, but also to what is being experienced in other fields. As was the case in the 1960s and 1970s, this originally investigative movement is already socially and culturally permeating very diverse fields and promoting new business, technological, cultural, informative and legal initiatives, which implies greater interest but, at the same time, could become a threat if the socio-cultural phenomena of the past were to occur again.

---

[19] Kelly Servick, "2021 Breakthrough of the year - A psychedelic PTSD remedy", *Science*, December 2021, https://www.science.org/content/article/breakthrough-2021.

[20] Steven Kotler, "The new psychedelic renaissance," *Playboy. April* 2010 (2010): 51-52.

Robin Carhart-Harris and Michael Pollan in conversation in the fMRI lab, Imperial Center for Psychedelic Research. *(Thomas Angus, Imperial College London, CC BY-SA 4.0 <https://creativecommons.org/licenses/by-sa/4.0>, via Wikimedia Commons).*

Social, Cultural & Legal

Since approximately 2015, references to psychedelics in the press, books, magazines and documentaries have multiplied. Prestigious popularizers, such as Michael Pollan, began to publish[21] on the subject in all kinds of mass media, and people unfamiliar with the field of psychedelics or other illegal substances became interested.

For years, the traditional, ceremonial and therapeutic use of psychedelics with strong cultural roots outside the West, such as ayahuasca, peyote, iboga and many others, had already been spreading throughout the world, allowing those interested to come into contact with these substances and their traditional medicinal uses, and disseminating its associated values and cultural elements; but it has been in recent years that they have become more visible and have had a greater socio-cultural impact outside the field of research, as a self-development tool.

---

[21] Michael Pollan, "The Trip Treatment", *The New Yorker*, February 1, 2015, https://www.newyorker.com/magazine/2015/02/09/trip-treatment.

The growing interest of society in the field of psychedelics is stimulating the appearance of more and more outreach initiatives in this field: new media like *Psychedelic Times,* magazines like *Double Blind Mag,* resources following the psychedelic revival such as *Psilocybin Alpha,* documentaries on Netflix like *Have a Good Trip, DOSED* or *Nine Perfect Strangers,* best-sellers like *How to Change your Mind*[22], podcast like *The Joe Rogan Experience* or *Psychedelics Today*[23]*,* apps like Mindleap Health or Maya and thousands of news articles published on the subject in the *mainstream* media, like *The New York Times,* CNN, the BBC, *The Washington Post,* etc. Likewise, more and more organizations and universities are creating courses, centers and specific groups for training and working with psychedelics.

Also, "psychedelic societies[24]" are flourishing in most cities in the world[25], allowing anyone with an interest in these substances to join, learn and contribute to this renaissance. All of this, together with the decentralized dissemination of information that the Internet and its forums allow, has given the general population access to much first-hand information on these substances. Thanks to resources such as PsychonautWiki, TripSit, Erowid, Bluelight, Drugs-Forum or Energy Control, anyone outside the academic field can access scientific information on substances and risk reduction techniques, which would have been very difficult to find years ago.

---

[22] Michael Pollen, *How to Change Your Mind: What the New Science of Psychedelics Teaches Us about Consciousness, Dying, Addiction, Depression, and Transcendence,* 2019.

[23] The addresses of many of these resources are available in the resource section of this book.

[24] Association model that has sprouted in various cities around the world to bring together people with an interest in learning, disseminating, doing activism and social relations, around a common interest.

[25] A directory is available in the resource section of this book.

Increase in Google searches for "psychedelics" between early 2016 and late 2020. *(The Psychedelic Renaissance in 2020 by Josh Hardman from Psilocybin Alpha, via psilocybinalpha.com).*

Similar to what already happened with cannabis 25 years ago, we are now also witnessing a number of popular legal initiatives that are facilitating the therapeutic use and decriminalizing the possession and use of psychedelics in various U.S. cities and states USA (such as Oregon, Colorado, Massachusetts, and California). In certain aspects, psychedelics seem to be following a similar evolution to that of therapeutic cannabis in its day, although given its characteristics, quite different access models and therapeutic objectives are being pursued. In the case of psychedelics, their decriminalization is running in parallel with their pharmaceutical and industrial development, and the possibility of their "non-medical" or even "recreational" use is not always viewed favorably by the scientific community, since these are extremely powerful substances with potentially high risks if used without proper control, and their use could itself become a risk-factor that could lead to repeating the events of the 1960s.

For example, in late 2020, Oregon voted and passed two legislative initiatives (109 and 110) aimed at decriminalizing illegal drugs and legalizing the therapeutic administration of psilocybin, becoming the first state in the U.S., and the world, to expressly legalize the therapeutic administration of a psychedelic through a state program. Also, after authorizing the use of psilocybin in terminal patients, Canada recently authorized the administration of psilocybin by doctors to patients with any condition, although it is still putting many obstacles to implement this new legislation, and an increasing number of dispensaries are now offering psilocybin mushrooms.

The Internet and various media outlets are also creating and giving visibility to some personalities of this movement. Without going any further, a year ago a list of the current 100 most influential living people of the psychedelic renaissance was published, mainly focused in the U.S., but including some international names as well, yet not including most of those who were active at the beginning of the investigation (some people already mentioned earlier in this chapter). Some of the people this list considers most influential today are: activist-scientists who started the movement and continue to have a huge impact like Rick Doblin (founder of MAPS), David Nichols (scientist and founder of the Heffter Research Institute), Amanda Feilding (founder of the Beckley Foundation), Stanislav Grof (developer of the transpersonal psychology), James Fadiman (Institute of Transpersonal Psychology & Sofia University) or the mycologist Paul Stamets (Fungi Perfecti); great communication figures and supporters of relevance such as Tim Ferriss (*The Tim Ferriss Show*), Joe Rogan (*The Joe Rogan Experience*, UFC), Sam Harris (*Making Sense* Podcast), Jordan B Peterson; writers and journalists like Michael Pollan, Hamilton Morris (Vice); artists like Alex Grey; famous athletes like Mike Tyson and Lamar Odom; philanthropists, investors, businessmen, billionaires and even politicians like former presidential candidate Andrew Yang. USA Andrew Yang. It also mentions some personalities from the world of clinical psychedelic science such as Robin Carhart-Harris (Imperial College London), Rick

Strassman (University of New Mexico), David Nutt (Imperial College London), Rosalind Watts (Imperial College London), Matthew Johnson (Johns Hopkins University), Roland Griffiths (Johns Hopkins University), Ben Sessa (Awakn), etc., leaving in the inkwell a large number of very important people at the scientific level, who are less visible nowadays.

Also, various *celebrities* of film, music, television, sports, etc., not mentioned in the previous list, have "come out of the psychedelic closet" recounting their therapeutic psychedelic experiences, as is the case of Sting, Seth Rogen, Miley Cyrus, Will Smith, Paul McCartney, Paul Simon, Megan Fox, Gwyneth Paltrow, Ben Lee, Daniel Carcillo, Kristen Bell...

Before the pandemic, the popularity of psychedelic-themed festivals such as Burning Man, BOOM, Psy-Fi or O.Z.O.R.A Festival was at an all-time high, as was the demand for risk reduction and care services for difficult psychedelic trips (known as *trip-sitting*) carried out by organizations that emerged within these festivals, such as Kosmicare in Portugal or the Zendo Project in the U.S., and new services such as remote assistance in difficult trips from the Fireside Project or TripSit, together with other essential risk reduction tools, such as information and drug analysis, provided by organizations such as Energy Control, Unity, Throw Head, Dance Safe, Safe'n Sound, etc.

This renaissance has its own "International Celebration Day", a cause for all kinds of meetings and celebrations. April 19, known worldwide as *"Bicycle Day,"* commemorates Albert Hofmann's bicycle ride in Basel, Switzerland, on April 19, 1943, from his laboratory to his home, where he began to feel "strange" after having ingested, for the first time in history, a dose of LSD.

Some surveys such as the Global Drug Survey have already shown in 2020 an increase in the number of people who say they are using psychedelics recreationally or to treat different mental health disorders at home, which logically generates discomfort in some circles that fear that consumption of these substances without adequate knowledge and control can cause problems.

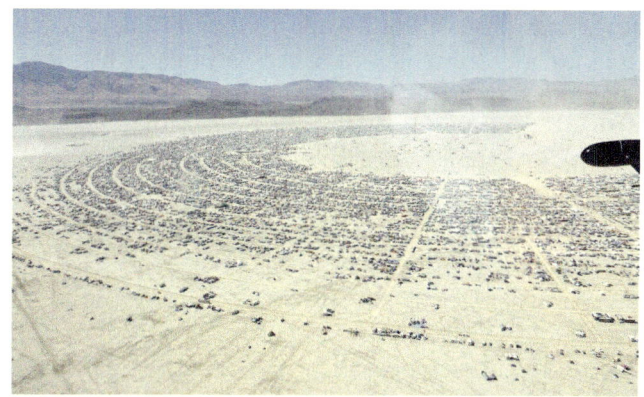

Aerial view of the Burning Man festival, in Black Rock, Nevada. USA (Photo by Steve Jurvetson, CC BY 2.0, via flickr.com).

At the moment, it is difficult to know the specific social impact of the popularization of psychonautical culture and "*DIY*" psychedelic-assisted psychotherapy. We know that it is a subject that is already being discussed with greater interest in forums and raising more questions, as there is greater and greater ease for disseminating and accessing information on the domestic cultivation of mushrooms or simple DMT extraction techniques, with the possibility to easily find companies that facilitate home production for self-consumption. Furthermore, in recent years, this revolution also coincided with an increase in the availability and purity of psychedelics, such as LSD, MDMA and DMT, on the unregulated market, as well as the appearance of new synthetic psychedelic substances that are not controlled and are very affordable, such as 1P-LSD and 4-AcO-DMT[26], which may be further indicators of increased demand or use.

But what does seem clear is that this rapid popularization in the West, where, unlike other cultures, there is still no good

---

[26] "European Drug Report 2021:Trends and Developments", https://www.emcdda.europa.eu/publications/edr/trends-developments/2021_en.

social understanding of the handling of psychedelic substances, their use outside controlled clinical settings could lead us to repeat the unfortunate events from the 60s. We must not forget that "classic" psychedelics, despite being pharmacologically safe substances at the physiological level, can pose great risks at the psychological level, if they are administered without prior screenings that can rule out a propensity for psychosis or bipolarity, or without prior preparation, or in a context without adequate control by professionals, or without subsequent integration of the experience.

Our modern societies are not yet used to handling these substances, just as there are other societies that may be used to them, but may not be used to, let's say, alcohol. Whenever a new psychoactive substance enters a society that is unaware of it, the risk potential is much greater than when it is already part of that culture and its handling is known by the majority of the population.

The Rise of a New Industry

The relationship of psychedelic substances with Silicon Valley and with the great centers of technological innovation is nothing new, and in this sense, another event that contributed to resurrecting these substances in the field of technological innovation was the report that Steve Jobs, the most important technological entrepreneur in history and creator of the most valued company, Apple, had declared:

> *Taking LSD was a profound experience, one of the most important things in my life. LSD shows you that there is another side to the coin, and you can't remember it when it wears off, but you know it. It reinforced my sense of what was important – creating great things instead of making money, putting things back into the stream of history and of human consciousness as much as I could.*

When Apple started working for the U.S. government in the 1980s, Steve Jobs had to be investigated by the Department of Defense, and underwent a background check, to obtain a top-secret security clearance (recently declassified and published) in which he also defended the positive contribution of psychedelics to his life.

Along these same lines, at the end of 2021, Elon Musk, CEO of Space X, Tesla, and the richest man in the world, declared at an event:

> *I think, generally, people should be open to psychedelics. A lot of people making laws are kind of from a different era, so I think, as the new generation gets into political power, we'll see a greater receptivity to the benefits of psychedelics.*

The use of psychedelic substances aimed at improving creativity, productivity and work in general, is also currently

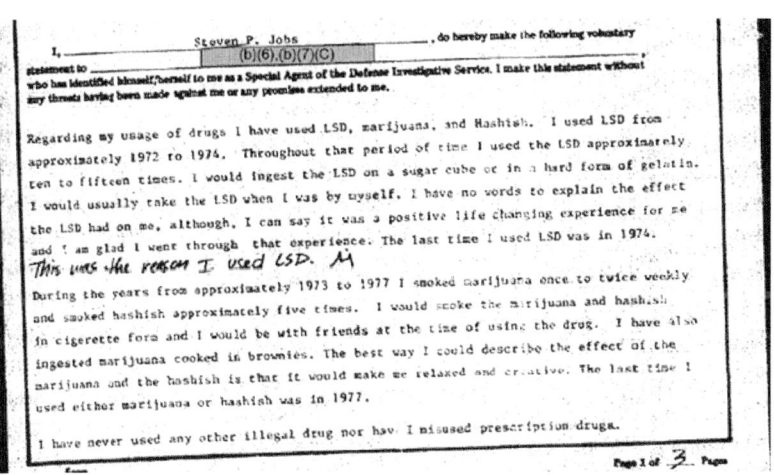

I used LSD from approximately 1972 to 1974. Throughout that period of time I used the LSD approximately ten to fifteen times. I would ingest the LSD in a sugar cube or in a hard form of gelatin. I would usually take the LSD when I was by myself. I have no words to explain the effect the LSD had on me, although, I can say that it was a positive life-changing experience for me and I am glad that I went through that experience.
(Via https://www.wired.com/2012/06/steve-jobs-security-clearance/).

trending – changing the stereotype of the user from "hippie" to "yuppie"- An exponent of this trend is the emergence of some practices that do not seek transformative experiences, but rather integrate the potential of psychedelics with the workplace, as is the case of *microdosing*, an apparently popular practice in Silicon Valley and other innovation ecosystems, which consists of taking small, minimal, sub-perceptual doses[27] of psychedelics on a regular basis to go to work or perform creative activities, with some people reporting they improve productivity, mood, habits and relationships[28]. Despite the fact that it has not yet been proven to be better than a placebo, it is a practice the media has reported as very common (there has even been a high-level dismissal related to it), and it already has some resources dedicated exclusively to it as The Third Wave, although it still has very little evidence and there are still many unknowns about its real effectiveness compared to placebo[29].

That is why there is often talk of a paradoxical evolution of the stereotype of the person who consumes psychedelics, from the image of the hippie of the 1960s, associated with spiritual, ecological and human development, to the "yuppie" of today, with a professional drive to improve creativity and productivity.

But there not only an interest in its use associated with work and creativity – psychedelics themselves represent the emergence of a new industry. Although the therapeutic model of psychedelic-assisted psychotherapy may seem less exploitable compared to other models in the traditional pharmaceutical industry, due to the fact that the psychedelic substance is only administered a couple of times throughout the treatment (as opposed to the daily use of common treatments with antidepressants or anxiolytics), and with fewer opportunities for

---

[27] Below the minimum detectable amount.

[28] Aylet Waldman, *A Really Good Day: How Microdosing Made a Mega Difference in My Mood, My Marriage, and My Life* (Anchor, 2017).

[29] Balázs Szigeti et al., "Self-blinding citizen science to explore psychedelic microdosing", *eLife* 10 (March 2, 2021).

patenting (because most classic psychedelics are natural or off-patent), this has not prevented the emergence of innovative *startups* and new pharmaceutical companies in recent years (such as Compass Pathways, MindMed, Cybin, Atai, Numinus, Havn Life or Mydecine Innovations). These, in addition to supporting clinical research in the field, are even achieving great results on Wall Street and other exchanges, obtaining billions of dollars in financing, which is clear evidence of the interest in the subject and of its future development, which some analysts predict will exceed 10,000 million dollars in the next 5 years.

However, more research is still needed, together with better regulation and financing of these treatments, as well as deepening the debates on the future coexistence of regulated and medicalized commercial models with the ancestral cultural practices of the use of psychedelics that some societies still maintain. The Western pharmaceutical development of these substances is not without some controversy or ethical debates.

"Psychedelic tourism", and tradictional healing centers, managed by small initiatives of traditional use, like the Takiwasi Center or the Temple of the way of Light (both in Peru), or large companies such as Synthesis, and groups that offer retreats with ayahuasca and other psychedelic compounds or the possibility of participating in ceremonies, are now very accesible in every Western city. Its services are demanded by many people with various profiles, from people with a simple curiosity, to those seeking self-exploration, spirituality, therapy, and even *celebrities* and CEOs. Modern clinics that already worked with ketamine legally have also been established in Western countries and offer their services in a highly professional manner, as is the case with Field Trip Health , while awaiting authorization for medical use of other psychedelic substances.

In short, this new industry and its various ramifications are trending and seem to have a promising future, especially in the clinical and pharmaceutical fields, but also in the sociocultural field. Although it will take some time to see all the aspects and enduring developments of this psychedelic renaissance, it is very likely that many advancements will continue to appear in all these areas in the coming years.

How Psychedelics Work

It is not the purpose of this book to delve much into the mechanisms of action of psychedelics, a subject widely addressed in other books in this collection. It would also require us to explain, in much greater depth, the functioning of the brain.

Instead, I will give a global and simplified idea of the effects and mechanisms that underlie an altered state of consciousness induced by psychedelic substances. This will make it easier to fully understand the psychotherapeutic potential of these substances and how they can change us – temporarily or lastingly.

Although we still cannot fully detail all the mechanisms of action of these compounds in the human brain, new research is published almost every month that improves our understanding of the brain under the influence of psychedelics and their potential clinical applications, so the evolution in this field is the order of the day.

Mechanisms at the Neuroreceptor Level

As we have seen before, psychedelic compounds (also known as "hallucinogens" or "entheogens") are a specific group of psychoactive substances that come from various chemical families, both of natural origin (present in plants, fungi and even animals) and synthetic. They have the capacity to induce altered states of consciousness through, fundamentally, the activation of neuronal serotonin receptors (more specifically those of the 5-HT2a type).

Although some psychedelic substances may be "atypical" and produce these effects by different routes, for the purpose of explaining their brain mechanisms I will stick to the classic psychedelics (psilocybin, LSD, DMT, etc.), which share their direct action on this neuroreceptor of the serotonin system precisely because they resemble this neurotransmitter in some areas and "fit" into its locks.

Serotonin, Psilocybin, DMT and LSD. Molecules with psychedelic effects resemble serotonin, and therefore fit into its neuroreceptors, particularly 5-HT2a.

We know the importance of the 5-HT2a receptor because numerous studies that have been carried out in animals and humans[1] show that the substances with the greatest affinity for the 5-HT2a receptor are the ones that produce the greatest

---

[1] Katrin H. Preller et al., "Changes in global and thalamic brain connectivity in LSD-induced altered states of consciousness are attributable to the 5-HT2A receptor," *eLife* 7 (October 25, 2018).

psychedelic effect, while, antagonistic substances (blockers) of this receptor (such as ketanserin), can eliminate the effect of any psychedelic substance.

These 5-HT2a receptors are mostly in the cerebral cortex, the outer layer of the brain (which humans have proportionally larger than any other animal). This layer is responsible for high-level cognitive functions, such as analytical, abstract and associative thinking, among others. The proportion of the number of 5-HT2a receptors activated by a psychedelic in the cortex is directly correlated to the intensity of the psychedelic experience in a person, seeing approximately more than 60 % of these receptors activated when the psychedelic effects with the most therapeutic interest begin to occur, such as "ego dissolution", "mystical experiences[2]", etc. In short, the more 5-HT2a receptors are activated in the cerebral cortex, the greater the psychedelic effects that will be produced; and for most of the therapeutic effects to be produced, a threshold has to be exceeded, which will trigger transient but profound changes in brain connectivity.

Mechanisms at the Brain Level

Before, I mentioned that one of the factors that is making this psychedelic renaissance possible is a better understanding of their mechanisms of action, thanks, among other things, to modern neuroimaging techniques such as PET or fMRI.

When scientists began to look at the brain under the influence of psychedelics like psilocybin or LSD, they expected to find that they activated different cortical regions. Instead, they found that they produced a decrease in activity in only certain brain regions, specifically in a network known as the

---

[2] A mystical experience is a very personal introspective experience in which some kind of universal unity or transcendence of time and space is described.

Temporary decrease in blood flow and activation in certain brain regions after psilocybin. Regions shown are those that had a significant decrease when exposed to psilocybin compared to placebo. *(Taken from Carhart-Harris et al., "Neural correlates of the psychedelic state as determined by fMRI studies with psilocybin." Proceedings of the National Academy of Sciences, 109(6), 2138-2143). With permission from RCH, first author)*

Default Neural Network (DMN) and that this decrease in activity affected the way the rest of the brain worked. They also noticed that this was highly correlated with the psychedelic effects perceived by the individual (ego dissolution, synesthesia, etc.). For this reason, they hypothesized that the DMN was the main area in the brain where psychedelics exerted their action.

Based on these observations, work began on a theory explaining why these effects occur when reducing DMN activity and what this tells us about brain function. One of the most current and complete theories on these effects is the unified model "REBUS and the anarchic brain[3]" (Relaxed

---

[3] R. L. Carhart-Harris and K. J. Friston, "REBUS and the anarchic brain: Toward a unified model of the brain action of psychedelics", *Pharmacological Reviews* 71, n. 3 (July 2019): 316-44.

Beliefs Under pSychedelics), built upon a revised version of the "entropic brain theory[4]" by Robert Carhart-Harris[5], and the "free energy principle[6]" by Karl Friston. I will not delve into them, but they will be the basis on which I will support a very simplified explanation of the mechanisms of action of these substances at the brain level.

How Does the Brain Work? Hierarchical Predictive Coding

Our brain works like a machine to reduce the uncertainty of the world around us. It does this not only by continuously interpreting our changing environment, in order to give quick answers that guarantee our survival, but also by constantly making predictions based on models[7] and beliefs created by past experience – always using as little sensory information as possible – in order to save energy and time. Then, it compares those predictions with the reality that comes through the senses and see if they match.

Thus, it can build complex stories about the world that surrounds us with little sensory information, less consumption of resources, and saving time, by generating predictions in advance, which increases our probability of survival and adaptation. This is called predictive coding.

---

[4] Robin L. Carhart-Harris et al., "The entropic brain: A theory of conscious states informed by neuroimaging research with psychedelic drugs", *Frontiers in Human Neuroscience* 8 (February 3, 2014): 20.

[5] Robin L. Carhart-Harris, "The entropic brain - revisited," *Neuropharmacology* 142 (November 2018): 167-78.

[6] Karl Friston, "The free-energy principle: A unified brain theory? *Nature Reviews. Neuroscience* 11, n. 2 (February 2010): 127-38.

[7] A model is a simplified version of something. The brain needs models to work efficiently and effectively, and not be overwhelmed by all the sensory input it continually receives.

The brain improves in this task of prediction as it becomes an adult and develops and tests its models better against reality, learning the world around it and elevating these "confirmed" models in the hierarchy of brain processes. The problem is, in exchange for this efficiency, our thinking becomes "rigid" by creating models of fixed predictions ("automated" and efficient) based on past experiences that are very powerful, but which, in turn, limit us and influence our experience of the present outside reality.

These models and beliefs are like the colored lenses through which we see the world. There comes a time when these models that we build become so powerful that they also control the information (external and internal) that reaches them: they filter it out and prevent us from "seeing" some things, so we begin to perceive a reality that is highly influenced by our beliefs and experiences, one that can be very far from objective reality. If our predictive models become maladaptive and show us a world that is too negative or difficult, it can sometimes make it hard to live a healthy and happy life.

In other words, when we are born, we do not have models, beliefs or patterns about how the world works around us, but, since we need them to be able to adapt to the environment and survive, our brains begin to develop and structure themselves based on the information coming in during that stage. As this task is slow and very costly energetically, if we remained in this state of experimentation and constant observation we would not survive long, so the brain learns and automates what it is able to verify, that is, it creates models with what it sees, feels and experiments, and starts to make predictions based on those models. At first, these predictions fail a lot, but they improve with the accumulation of experience and end up being established as our models of the world.

All this psychological process is also neurological and morphological, and, as it progresses, our brain is "carved", creating structures and hierarchies. Neural networks with superior functions emerge that impose their operation and their learned models (their "world view") on networks with more basic functions, such as sensory ones, which are limited to receiving information. And even though this information is more objective, it is too abundant to continuously process all of it in real time. The function of these networks of superior hierarchy and their models is very important, since without them, we could not go from contemplating the world with fascination as a child to anticipating it and acting on it as an adult.

When we reach adulthood, our brain is a structure of hierarchical networks, both morphologically and functionally. This means that we have high-ranking neural networks that control, modulate or limit the action of other hierarchically "inferior" neural networks, filtering their information and deciding what is relevant and what is not, anticipating what might happen, planning and acting accordingly. We call this hierarchical predictive coding.

For example, at the base of this hierarchy are the sensory circuits that bring us information from the senses, from the outside world, with hardly any processing; and at the top would be networks such as the Default Neural Network, which is considered the seat of the ego, and which is activated when we are not doing any external tasks and we wander through our minds absorbed in our plans, memories or concerns.

Many optical illusions are based on deceiving these models and their predictions, such as the classic hollow mask illusion: where we are presented with a hollow mask, and because we ignore which side is facing us, our brain will interpret and predict, based on the models it has established throughout our lives, that the mask is facing us when in fact it could be facing away and we could be looking at its hollow interior.

With the limited ambivalent sensory information the brain is receiving, it makes a prediction based on our years of experience identifying faces, which are always oriented towards us. So it interprets that the mask is facing us, confirming the

Video of the hollow mask illusion, showing us how we are conditioned by our learning to make predictions about reality, sometimes erroneously, instead of simply interpreting all the information that comes to us from the outside world, which would be overwhelming to do continuously.

validity of the sensory information that corresponds to this idea as opposed to the one that does not, filtering and discarding that information because it contradicts what we have been seeing for years. Furthermore, it is not able to change that prediction until the mask starts to rotate and, after a few tenths of a second of confusion, the sensory information contradicting our pre-established model becomes undeniable, and our brain finally "listens" to it and reformulates its prediction: what we were looking at was actually the concave side of this hollow mask.

In an infant state, before we have these top-tier predictive models built and in place, this optical illusion doesn't work[8], and we are able to see the mask as it really is: concave.

But it also doesn't work in a psychedelic state, or in other altered states of consciousness that can occur, for example, in schizophrenia. In these states, the hollow mask does not deceive the brain. The sensory information prevails over the pre-established high-level models and beliefs that would normally modulate and filter its activity (imposing its learned predictions against the reality that it receives through the senses), but that in these states are diminished or absent.

---

[8] Aki Tsuruhara et al., «The Hollow-Face Illusion in Infancy: Do Infants See a Screen Based Rotating Hollow Mask as Hollow?», *i-Perception*, 2011.

Formerly, it was thought that psychedelic substances opened our "doors of perception" by removing the filters through which we experience the reality that our senses perceive, but today we know that this concept, although it may be somewhat accurate, is much broader and more complex. In essence, psychedelics temporarily dismantle this hierarchical pyramid structure in charge of filtering our senses and predicting the world, making the adult brain more like that of a child: open, perceptive, flexible, imaginative, creative, fanciful... giving us a window of opportunity to change some things. Now we will see how they do it.

How Do Psychedelics Affect our Brain Function?

As we have mentioned before, when someone takes a psychedelic, the activation of the 5-HT2a neuroreceptors (mainly) of the cortical neurons of their brain reduces the activity of one of those high-ranking neural networks, known as the default neural network (DMN). This area of the brain is considered the seat of the ego or "I", and it normally controls, filters and constrains other lower neural networks (such as the sensory neural networks responsible for collecting all the information from the senses). This neural network is by default a great communication center of the brain and acts as an orchestra conductor or as a traffic cop, coordinating communication and traffic between different areas of the brain and deciding which messages rise to our consciousness and which do not, filtering a good part of the subconscious cognitive flow and suppressing messages from other more primitive or less hierarchical areas of the brain.

In the absence of the control exerted by the DMN, the normal neuronal activity of the brain is destabilized and the lower hierarchical level networks that were limited, filtered or controlled by it, become disorganized and lose their habitual structured

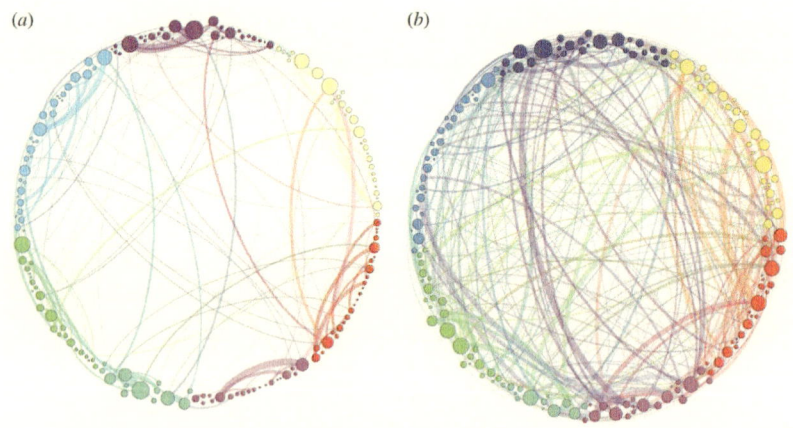

This representation shows the functional connectivity of different regions in a brain that has taken a placebo (a) versus a brain that has taken a dose of psilocybin (b).(*G. Petri, P. Expert, F.Turkheimer, R. Carhart-Harris, D. Nutt, PJ Hellyer, and F.Vaccarino, CC BY-SA 4.0 <https://creativecommons.org/licenses/by-sa/4.0>, via Wikimedia Commons*).

functioning patterns. The hierarchy of brain function ceases to be so pyramidal and becomes more horizontal. It dissolves, and various neural networks in the brain stop communicating with each other as independent clusters and begin to do wholly, with all its regions, so that the functional connectivity of the brain as a whole increases and diversifies, it becomes interconnected. The brain begins to function in a more unified way, as we can see in the following image[9].

The usual "highways" between specialized and compartmentalized areas of the brain disintegrate, while the brain, as a whole, integrates, becomes more globally interconnected and unified, more uniform and less specialized. It goes from using a few highways with few origins and destinations, to using many, many smaller highways with many

---

[9] G. Petri et al., «Homological Scaffolds of Brain Functional Networks», *Journal of the Royal Society, Interface / the Royal Society* 11, n. 101 (December 6, 2014): 20140873.

more origins and destinations, allowing regions of the brain that normally don't communicate with each other to do so, creating synesthesias[10], hallucinations, novel connections, new ideas, creativity, etc...

An analogy to understand this effect is to imagine neural signals as cars and neural pathways as highways. Under normal conditions, most traffic would circulate on highways to reach their usual destination faster, following the "usual" route and without looking at the landscape too much. But if we temporarily limit traffic on those usual highways with roadworks and make them more difficult to navigate, many cars will prefer to move on other secondary roads for some time. This will help rediscover new and old places (new restaurants, new landscapes, new paths), giving life to some towns that had been abandoned for years... and, even though traffic may return to normal after a few hours, some of those secondary roads and their towns will have been brought back to life, with some drivers preferring to continue traveling through them. There will have been a lasting change in those models or routes, because the knowledge of this temporary experience will last for a long time, thanks to, among other things, an increase in neuroplasticity[11], also induced by these substances.

Another widely used analogy is to compare a psychedelic experience to what happens when you shake a snow globe. For a while that "snow" will be in a state of chaos, but it will settle again, although in a different way than it was at the beginning, which can be a great therapeutic opportunity.

---

[10] Synaesthesia is the blending of senses: hearing a color, tasting a sound.
[11] Neuroplasticity is the flexibility of the brain's neural networks to adapt to changes, forming new connections (synapses) between neurons or modifying existing ones. Learning or memory are forms of neuroplasticity. Neuroplasticity is a capacity that decreases as the brain ages.

Imaging studies showed how LSD (right) increases connectivity between brain regions that do not communicate with each other under normal conditions (left). (Beckley/Imperial Research Program, from Carhart-Harris, R. L., Muthukumaraswamy, S., Roseman, L., Kaelen, M., Droog, W., Murphy, K., ... & Nutt, D. J., "Neural correlates of the LSD experience revealed by multimodal neuroimaging," Proceedings of the National Academy of Sciences, 113, n. 17 (2016): 4853-4858.) & Nutt, DJ (2016). Neural correlates of the LSD experience revealed by multimodal neuroimaging. Proceedings of the National Academy of Sciences, 113(17), 4853-4858). With permission from RCH, first author)

By silencing the DMN, psychedelics act on our fundamental beliefs, allowing them to be influenced by lower hierarchies that are temporarily freed from the limitations imposed by the DMN. Sensory or memory areas (inferior to the DMN) are now able to send information without it being discarded by the "filter" of our beliefs and models, as infant brains do. In this process, the DMN becomes more malleable and, with this new information, can undergo lasting change, thereby effecting change to our models of the world. This puts the brain in what is known as a "pivotal mental state" (like a bifurcation on the road, a crossroads), in which a change occurs that, depending on the conditions and the context of our mental state, may choose a a path towards lasting change.

What Happens at the Psychological Level?

Although at the cerebral level psychedelics "turn off" some regions and interconnect others, generating temporary chaos in the structures of the brain, the subjective phenomenology a person lives through during the psychedelic experience is enormously varied, creative and subjective. It does not only depend on the psychedelic that has been consumed and its dose, but, above all, on who the person is, their previous life experiences, mental and emotional state, present context, their intentions and expectations, etc. In short, on their "set and setting" at the specific moment of ingestion. That is why no two psychedelic experiences are the same, and why the variables of person and context are so important when working with psychedelics, because the final experience and its results will depend on them.

The most characteristic psychological effects are significant changes in sensory perceptions, cognition, and consciousness.

In this informative chaos due to the absence of the DMN, the brain fluctuates between three options: allow the unfiltered passage of sensory information from neural networks hierarchically lower, also known as *bottom-up* (like looking at the hollow mask without interpreting that it is looking at us, that is, allowing uncertainty); impose its predictions based on its models (or *top-down*), risking being wrong, which would create predictive errors (hallucinations like seeing faces in the clouds) by trying to eliminate uncertainty at all costs; or simultaneously both processes, which supposes an overload of unfiltered information which the brain tries to make sense of through inaccurate predictions, returning to a primitive state of consciousness based more on "magical thinking."

Changes in sensory perceptions can manifest visually, with color enhancement, distortions in the shapes and movements of things, or colorful kaleidoscopic visions with closed eyes. Synesthesia (blending of the senses, like "smelling colors" or "seeing sounds"), increased tactile, thermal or tingling sensations may appear. Hearing disturbances can lead to an increased appreciation of music and sounds. Also, there may be a noticeable increase in tactile, olfactory or taste sensations. All of these symptoms can lead a person to laugh, achieve a state of wonder, confusion or anxiety.

Cognitive alterations can be perceived as positive and pleasant or negative and difficult, and it is common for psychedelic experiences to include good stages and more difficult moments during the same session, which is why they are called "trips." It is common for biographical and personal content to emerge, as well as relationships with people who are significant to the subject or thoughts and concerns they may have at the time.

In general, the reduction of the ego or "death of the ego" (as it has been called) that occurs after the deactivation of the DMN, softens or erases the limits of our body, facilitates an experience of fusion with the environment, of unity, of connection with everything, of love. Consciousness expands beyond the usual constrictions. Sensory perception and mental states are greatly amplified, allowing information normally "filtered" by our models and beliefs of the world, located in the DMN, to rise into our consciousness. Not surprisingly, the term "psychedelic" derives from Latin roots *psyche* (mind) and *delos* (manifest), referring to its ability to "manifest the mind" or the underlying mental processes. Psychedelics make the unconscious conscious, make the invisible visible. If we were to imagine our mind as an iceberg with the tip being the conscious mind and the submerged part being the unconscious, the psychedelic would lower the water level so that a greater percentage of our mental processes become conscious.

Furthermore, when the ego dissolves, we stop being the center of our universe, we see things from another perspective, without preconceptions, and feelings of connection and deep universal love for everything can emerge, accompanied by well-being and joy. But feelings of anxiety or fear can also appear in the face of what can be perceived as a loss of identity, existence or even sanity.

This state of expanded consciousness is characterized by a feeling of being in the present and connection with what surrounds us or is within us at that moment, like a child who lives in the now, full of spontaneity. This contrasts with the adult ego state, which lives in the past or in the future, characterized by feelings of separation between us and what surrounds us, giving rise to fears, anxieties, remorse, repentance, defense, haste, etc. Many psychedelics can reduce the activity of the amygdala, the center of the brain related to fear and fight or flight responses, and therefore induce a positive bias in the perception of ourselves and our environment.

At high doses, the experience can rise to the level of what is known as a "mystical experience," which is a deeply introspective and personal experience of ego and identity dissolution, including "numinous feelings," a deeply positive emotional state, of internal unity, transcendence of time and space, ineffability and sensation of unity and interconnection with all things, along with oceanic-type feelings and universal love. This can be lived as experiences of death and rebirth, of surrender and acceptance, new purposes, senses and meanings for life and the elements that make it up (relationships, work, spirituality, goals, etc.).

All this subjective experience develops according to a specific narrative, which is what gives psychedelic experiences the name of "trips." That is why each trip is different, because it does not depend so much on the substance as on what reaches our brain from the senses and from our own subconscious. Psychedelics temporarily open doors, but what passes through them depends greatly on the variables of person and context.

Why do we have these 5-HT2a Receptors and Psychedelic Experiences?

There is much speculation about the original evolutionary role of the 5-HT2a neuroreceptor in particular and its possible function. We know that serotonin is released, for example, in response to stress, just as endorphins are released in response to pain. Therefore, it is logical to think that serotonin plays a role in this type of situations, and the activation of the 5-HT2a receptor, among others, does too.

Serotonin is closely related to our sensitivity to context, to the conditions in which we find ourselves, whether social (as numerous experiments with MDMA on humans and even octopuses have shown) or otherwise. This serotonin 5-HT2a system is usually active in our childhood development, but it is much less so when we reach maturity. So, it is speculated that it could be related to the establishment and progressive rigidity of our beliefs, models and way of thinking, which become more effective and efficient but less flexible with age and experience. We become more "efficient" in our predictions of the world, but we lose the ability to "see" and learn freely from what surrounds us, and we filter the world through our lenses built from experience, applying our bias to reality.

Therefore, psychedelics make us extremely sensitive to our environment, be it our internal environment (*set*: thoughts, concerns, intentions, expectations, ideas, memories, subconscious) or the external physical and social context (*setting*: people, music, sounds, smells, images).

Likewise, the activation of the 5-HT2a receptor seems to increase brain plasticity, neuroplasticity, synaptogenesis, the growth of new "branches" in neurons, and facilitate the acquisition or elimination of maladaptive learning (such as phobias), that is, changing and updating our models with information from our particular *set and setting*. Once the system enters this mode of learning and neuroplasticity, it becomes very sensitive to internal and environmental conditions. You will relearn from them like a child, you will become more likely to doubt your own previous beliefs-models and you will be able to modify them in favor of new learning, being more open to change and adaptation.

One possibility that has been speculated is that the activation of these receptors acts as a *reset* button or as an update to our models that can be activated in extreme situations when we have to accelerate our adaptation to the environment, as would happen when we expose ourselves to any kind of stressful situation, like a near-death experience. In fact, we know that in animals, such experiences produce a marked increase in serotonin in the brain, as well as in DMT (a powerful psychedelic substance that is present in minute amounts in the brains of all mammals). This would be in line with some of the ideas laid out by Rick Strassman in his book *DMT: The Spirit Molecule*[12], where he proposed its release in extreme situations, with an adaptive function – although this field is still quite speculative.

How Can Psychedelics Help With Mental Health Disorders or Other Maladaptive Conditions?

Many mental health disorders (such as depression, addictions, OCD) are correlated to over-activity in the default neural network (DMN). In other words, our higher models of the world have become so rigid and maladaptive that they become pathological, excessively filtering and controlling the functioning of our brain, our behavior, our thinking and our vision of the world. This disconnects us from the reality that surrounds us, pushing us to repeat patterns, constantly ruminate on thoughts in the first person, making it difficult for us to change and reinforcing our convictions and models, even if they are being harmful to us.

---

[12] Rick Strassman, *DMT: The Spirit Molecule: A Doctor's Revolutionary Research into the Biology of Near-Death and Mystical Experiences* (Inner Traditions / Bear & Co, 2000).

Changing those models, beliefs, or thought patterns is a very arduous and time-consuming task. However, during a psychedelic experience, these models and patterns break down, become more flexible, their hierarchy dissolves or becomes less pronounced, making it easier for abstract concepts to mix with sensory information and vice versa, and thus, "updating" these models within a therapeutic context.

Psychedelic substances act in the brain in such a way that they allow us to doubt those beliefs or high-ranking models, making them more flexible and reshaping them, "updating" them with external information coming from the senses or with internal information coming from our memory or from other neural networks of lower hierarchy than the DMN. This allows us to see new perspectives of things, remember things that we had forgotten, detect "blind spots" in our way of thinking that could be harming us and that are normally filtered by the DMN and its models, discover and correct subconscious patterns, etc.

It is as if taking a psychedelic temporarily "softens" a brain in a solid state and full of rigid pathological thought patterns and models, allowing it to be reshaped before it solidifies again and its hierarchical structure reappears, but this time maybe slightly improved .

Another simile of this process would be to imagine the hierarchy of the brain as a highly stratified social class system with a bad government that maintains a status quo that does not work well (DMN), hardly listening to the working classes (sensory networks and others) and oppressing them. In this scenario, the psychedelic experience would be the equivalent of a social revolt that seeks to break the system of hierarchies, social classes and change the government, and even if it only achieves a temporary collapse of the system (and social stratification), the government that is established again later will be something different from what it was before, it will have learned from what it has lived and listened to social demands.

It could be said that psychedelics expand consciousness by erasing the borders that our own ego imposes on us and allowing our models of the world to mix and update with what surrounds them at that moment, hence the paramount importance that these experiences are carried out with a clear intention, in controlled contexts and with adequate preparation of the patient. Hence the importance of taking good care of the set and setting.

The reduction of activity in the DMN and the dissolution of the ego also reduce rumination, which is very present in most disorders, making it easier for us to stop being the center of the universe and for our problems to be relativized. We are then able to see them from a distance, with perspective, like an astronaut looking onto Earth and the insignificance of their problems from the immensity of space.

This is combined with a subjective experience, which in good therapeutic conditions, can be full of revelations, epiphanies and new points of view. Since properly prepared psychedelic experiences allow us to facilitate new perspectives of the world and our problems, we can see them from afar, with fresh eyes, finding new meanings to things, new answers to the most basic questions related to our existence or the universe (such as the meaning of life), new purposes in life, which are often concealed under mental disorders such as depression or anxiety. Likewise, they allow us to review autobiographical content of a traumatic nature from a new perspective that allows it to be reprocessed, making great advances in the therapeutic process of various disorders such as PTSD or addictions.

In the words of Robin Carhart-Harris, former director of the Center for Psychedelic Research at Imperial College London:

> The effect of successful psychedelic therapy is often a revelation or epiphany. People talk about witnessing the "big picture," putting things into perspective, accessing deep insight into themselves and the world, releasing pent-up mental pain, feeling physically and emotionally recalibrated, clear-sighted, and level-headed. This is very different from people's descriptions of the effects of SSRIs (the most common antidepressants today), where a feeling of emotional numbness is not uncommon[13].

Many of these revelations may not have great therapeutic value later, but some do, and in order to reinforce and implement these new insights and insights into life, in combination with this psychedelic-induced temporary neuroplasticity "window," it is important to follow a process of psychological integration afterwards, as we will see later.

What many studies are finding is that living a mystical experience is what best predicts improvement in a disorder, in other words, that the mystical experience is an important part of the therapeutic process. If two people get exactly the same dose, but one goes through that kind of experience and the other doesn't, the one who does is much more likely to have a lasting therapeutic result than the other.

Of course, all this will depend a lot on the person's *set* and *setting* their intentions, etc., and there is always the possibility of living a difficult experience, with anxiety and fear. This, although it does not usually last longer than a few hours, could produce negative changes if it is not well managed.

---

[13] Robin Carhart-Harris, «We can no longer ignore the potential of psychedelic drugs to treat depression», *The Guardian*, June 8, 2020, http://www.theguardian.com/commentisfree/2020/jun/08/psychedelic-drugs-treat-depression.

Present and Future of Clinical Research with Psychedelic Drugs

Psychedelic-Assisted Psychotherapy

As we have mentioned before, when we talk about psychedelic treatments, in most cases we are actually referring to a model known as "psychedelic-assisted psychotherapy." Within the different models of psychedelic therapies, this is the one that currently seems to be offering the greatest therapeutic efficacy, safety, and efficiency.

This model combines classic elements of psychotherapy with some specific pharmacological interventions ("sessions") of psychedelics under direct therapeutic supervision, and a post-session integration process that allows subjects to continue working on those experiences. This model does not require the use of psychedelic substances on more than one or very few occasions, and its therapeutic effects are very long lasting.

There are several different ways in which psychedelic-assisted psychotherapy can be structured and it will depend on many factors, such as the psychedelic substance to be used. At present, the most effective and efficient format to work with each substance and condition is not yet fully optimized, so it is possible that in the future this therapeutic model will evolve along with the findings and the accumulation of new evidence that will maximize its results and safety, while also minimizing its cost in each case. These days, the most commonly used approach in the clinical research context is an intervention divided into three blocks: "screening and preparation", "administration" and "integration and follow-up", the administration and integration may be repeated within a certain period of time.

- Screening: therapy usually begins with a screening or evaluation in which it is sought to rule out patients who may not be suitable for psychedelic treatment. Patients with a propensity for some psychiatric illnesses, such as bipolarity, psychotic disorders, schizophrenia, or borderline personality disorder, or a family history of these, are excluded. Also, heart problems, or general physical health that can bring about complications in the event of an emotionally intense experience.
- Preparation: once it has been verified that the person does not have a condition that could be especially dangerous for the consumption of psychedelics, work is carried out during a number of sessions to evaluate and prepare the patient for the psychedelic experience. In order to properly prepare the psychedelic experience, it is very important to work on the expectations for it, define an intention that serves as a guide during the session, strengthen the trust and bond between patients and the therapists who will accompany them during the administration of the psychedelic (usually a man and a woman), as well as preparing for possible psychological difficulties that may occur during the session with relaxation and coping techniques (for example, not running away from what frightens us, but facing it and asking: "What have you come to teach me?").

- Administration: when the patient is ready, the administration session is scheduled. Depending on the pathology and the psychedelic substance to be used, you can proceed in various ways, but the most common is for sessions to start in the morning. The accompanying therapists (normally a man and a woman) and the patient go into a room that has been prepared and set for the session. In it, one last conversation is had, reminding the participant of the instructions ("Trust, let go and be open") and the intention for that session. The patient ingests the psychedelic and lies down to relax while waiting for its effects to start.

   Sessions are designed to invite introspection and, to promote this, patients are asked to wear an eye mask. They also wear headphones with specially selected music to accompany them throughout, thus facilitating the different phases of the session. The experience of mystical experiences[1] is usually correlated with better therapeutic results, so it is desirable.
- Integration: During the integration phase, the patient and psychotherapist work on all the material that has emerged during the administration session. Sometimes, if the protocols of the study contemplate it (remember that most psychedelic-assisted psychotherapy work carried out today is in the context of clinical trials), the administration and integration sessions can be repeated after a few weeks, depending on how many are planned in the treatment. The most common approach is to have two: one with a medium dose and another with a high dose.

---

[1] A mystical experience is a very personal introspective experience where some kind of universal unity or transcendence of time and space is described.

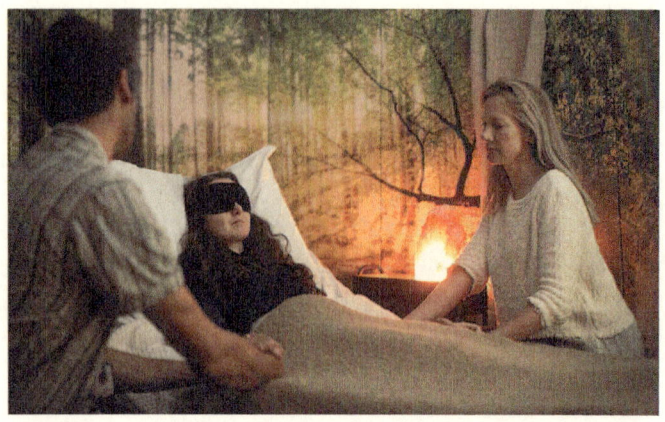

Recreación de un ensayo clínico con psicodélicos con los doctores Jonny Martell, Roberta Murphy y Rosalind Watts enel Centro Imperial para la Investigación Psicodélica.*(Thomas Angus, Imperial College London, CC BY-SA 4.0 <https://creativecommons.org/licenses/by-sa/4.0>, via Wikimedia Commons).*

- Follow-up: this is a phase that occurs mostly in clinical research, and its function is to evaluate if the changes and improvements produced during the administration session and integration work last and for how long. It also allows for detecting any relapses and guiding the subject if necessary.

During the session, which can last more or less depending on the psychedelic used, interactions between therapists and patients are commonly limited to support if requested by the latter, holding hands and other comforting gestures, or accompanying them to the bathroom.

In the specific case of MDMA-assisted psychotherapy work, which is mostly applied in post-traumatic stress disorder, there is more freedom to interact with the patient and psychotherapy work can be performed during the administration sessions (there are usually three or four).

Let's briefly see the results that this therapeutic intervention is having in different mental health conditions:

Post-Traumatic Stress Disorder (PTSD)

One of the areas in which substances with psychedelic effects, and more specifically MDMA (ecstasy), are showing greater efficacy, is in the treatment of *Post Traumatic Stress Disorder* (PTSD), which is already in Phase III clinical trials in the U.S. USA (the last phase before it is authorized for medical use) an initiative backed by MAPS. There is also some Phase II research exploring the use of other psychedelics such as psilocybin for this disorder (like those from Mydecine Innovations and COMPASS Pathways).

Post-traumatic stress disorder is a mental health problem that develops in a person after experiencing or witnessing a traumatic event (war, assault, rape, accident, kidnapping, etc.). After having experienced this event, it is normal for the body to go into "alert mode", characterized by fear reactions, release of certain hormones and creating "fight or flight" responses like increased blood pressure, increased heart rate, rapid breathing, pupil dilation, etc. This response lasts for a while, even after the threat has already disappeared.

Normally, this reaction decreases over time so the person can return to a normal life, with the traumatic event gradually subsiding from present memory, without it becoming a stumbling block in their life. But there are also cases in which the person continues to suffer, reliving this event and reacting very intensely to it in the absence of the threat, even decades later, having enormous difficulties in resuming a normal life or a good quality of life. These people who remain chronically affected by trauma may be diagnosed with post-traumatic stress disorder.

The most common symptoms usually include re-experiencing the trauma in the form of flashbacks, nightmares, intrusive thoughts, avoidance strategies (such as avoiding places or objects that remind the event), being hypervigilant (insomnia, tension, anxiety, easily startled) and reactive. Also, some people may show cognitive or mood symptoms, such as feelings of guilt, problems with memory, concentration, loss of interest in things, etc.

Currently, this disorder affects many millions of people in the world, it occurs especially among those who have experienced natural disasters, violence, war, abuse, rape, accidents, etc. It is estimated that 7-12% of the population suffers from it to a greater or lesser extent, and that 60% of men and 50% of women have experienced at least one traumatic event in their lives[2].

The successful treatment of this pathology is especially important, given that traumas are at the base of many mental illnesses, and that they are responsible for much disability, suffering and deaths by suicide every year in the world.

Currently, this disorder is treated with psychotherapy combined with pharmacological interventions based on antidepressants (like the famous selective serotonin reuptake inhibitors, SSRIs, such as Prozac) and anxiolytics (like the well-known benzodiazepines, such as Orfidal), or with therapies such as EMDR. Unfortunately, a significant percentage of people who suffer from this disorder do not manage to recover through these treatments and become chronic "treatment resistant" patients. It is in this type of patients that treatments with MDMA-assisted psychotherapy are being tested the most.

In this disorder, MDMA-assisted psychotherapy is proving to be extremely effective in patients who have not been able to recover through classic psychotherapy treatments combined with antidepressants and anxiolytics.

As we have seen in the previous chapter, there are many ways in which MDMA is a suitable substance for this. In addition to its psychedelic effects, MDMA reduces the activation of the amygdala, which is the area of the brain responsible for

---

[2] Lukoye Atwoli et al., "Epidemiology of Posttraumatic Stress Disorder: Prevalence, Correlates and Consequences", *Current Opinion in Psychiatry* 28, n. 4 (July 2015): 307-11.

fear and the fight-flight response that accompanies it, allowing the patient to remember the traumatic event from a safe place, without suffering an excessive negative emotional response or fear. In addition, given its empathogen-entactogen effect, it helps the patient feel safe, trusting and sharing their experience more easily with the therapist. It also facilitates self-compassion, eliminating the feelings of guilt or responsibility often associated with this type of trauma. Likewise, the neuroplasticity derived from the activation of the 5-HT2a neuroreceptors allows this new way of understanding and evaluating the traumatic event to be established more easily, as if fear were unlearned.

Several clinical trials have been conducted in recent years exploring this. Some examples include:

MDMA-Assisted Therapy for Severe PTSD: A randomized, Double-Blind, Placebo-Controlled Phase III Study[3]

Double blind[4], placebo-controlled[5] clinical trial to test the efficacy and safety of MDMA-assisted therapy for the treatment

---

[3] Jennifer M. Mitchell et al., "MDMA-Assisted Therapy for Severe PTSD: A Randomized, Double-Blind, Placebo-Controlled Phase 3 Study", *Nature Medicine* 27, n. 6 (June 2021): 1025-33.

[4] Neither researchers nor patients know who receives MDMA and who receives a placebo, until the end of the study.

[5] A placebo is a substance that lacks pharmacological action for the treatment of a pathology, but can produce an effect by suggestion if the person taking it is convinced that it is really a drug. Normally clinical trials are done by comparing the effect of the future drug with a placebo, for which it is necessary that neither patients nor therapists know which is the placebo and which is the active drug (this is called "double blind") until the end of the study, for which both have the same appearance, taste, shape, etc; if both turn out to have similar effects or effectiveness, it is that the drug is not really doing anything beyond the placebo effect itself and therefore its effectiveness and pharmaceutical development is discarded.

of patients with severe PTSD. After three preparation sessions, 90 PTSD patients (suffering from the condition for an average of 14 years) received MDMA or placebo therapy, followed by nine integration sessions.

PTSD symptoms (measured with the CAPS-V PTSD Scale), and functional impairment (measured with the Sheehan Disability Scale, SDS), were assessed at baseline and 2 months after the last experimental session. MDMA was found to induce a significant and robust attenuation in the CAPS-V score compared to placebo and significantly reduce the total SDS score. The mean change in CAPS-V scores in participants who completed treatment was −24.4 points in the MDMA group versus −13.9 points in the placebo group.

Graph representing the results of the study in the treatment group versus the control group. (MAPS).

Sixty-seven percent of participants who received three sessions of MDMA-assisted psychotherapy no longer met diagnostic criteria for PTSD (vs. 32% achieved by placebo therapy), and 88% experienced a clinically relevant reduction in symptoms (vs. 62% who improved with placebo therapy).

MDMA did not induce adverse events of abuse potential, suicidality, or heart problems.

These data indicated that, compared to normal therapy combined with an inactive placebo, MDMA-assisted therapy is highly effective in people with severe PTSD and the treatment is safe and well tolerated, even in those with comorbidities.

Long-Term Follow-up Outcomes of MDMA-Assisted Psychotherapy for Treatment of PTSD: A Longitudinal Pooled Analysis of Six Phase II Trials[6]

The aim of this study was to examine the long-term change in PTSD symptoms in 100 patients who underwent MDMA-assisted psychotherapy (from 6 different trials) and to assess whether there was additional benefit or harm 12 months after completing the experimental treatment.

Participants received two to three active doses of MDMA (75 to 125 mg) in therapy sessions, with additional non-substance therapy sessions. PTSD symptoms were assessed using the PTSD Scale (CAPS-IV) at baseline, 1 to 2 months after the last active MDMA session (end of treatment), and at least 12 months after the last MDMA session. Changes in CAPS-IV total severity scores were assessed.

---

[6] Lisa Jerome et al., "Long-Term Follow-up Outcomes of MDMA-Assisted Psychotherapy for Treatment of PTSD: A Longitudinal Pooled Analysis of Six Phase 2 Trials." *Psychopharmacology* 237, n. 8 (August 2020): 2485-97.

There was a significant reduction in CAPS-IV total severity scores from baseline to the end of treatment. CAPS-IV scores continued to decline from the end of treatment to the 12-month follow-up.

Out of 100 participants, the percentage no longer meeting criteria for PTSD two months after completing MDMA-assisted psychotherapy treatment was 56%, but increased to 67% out of the 91 participants interviewed 12 months after having finished the treatment. Most participants reported benefits, including improved relationships and well-being, with a minority (4%) reporting their condition worsened in the 12 months after treatment ended.

Breakthrough for Trauma Treatment: Safety and Efficacy of MDMA-Assisted Psychotherapy Compared to Paroxetine and Sertraline[7]

Paroxetine and sertraline (SSRIs) are approved treatments for the treatment of PTSD but analyses of pharmacotherapies for PTSD found only small to moderate effects compared to placebo.

The primary efficacy evaluation of six Phase II trials regarding the change from baseline to primary endpoint using CAPS-IV *Total Severity* indicated a significant effect of MDMA over the comparison group, with a large effect size between groups equivalent to approximately twice that of paroxetine and three times that of sertraline. Compared with the mean change in total CAPS scores, placebo subtraction scores for sertraline ranged from 6.8 to 9.8 units, for paroxetine from 6 to 14 units, and for MDMA they reached 26. 2 units,

---

[7] Allison A. Feduccia et al., "Breakthrough for Trauma Treatment: Safety and Efficacy of MDMA-Assisted Psychotherapy Compared to Paroxetine and Sertraline." *Frontiers in Psychiatry / Frontiers Research Foundation* 10 (September 12, 2019): 650.

with the improvement in MDMA treatment also being much faster (significant after 3-5 days) than in SSRIs, which can take between 2 and 12 weeks. In addition, the effects of MDMA-assisted psychotherapy last for at least 12 months. Sertraline was only shown to be statistically significant in women and not in men, whereas MDMA has been effective for both men and women with no difference in measured response.

Comparing data used for the approval of paroxetine and sertraline and pooled data from Phase II studies, MAPS showed that MDMA-assisted psychotherapy is a substantial improvement over available pharmacotherapies in terms of safety and efficacy. The MDMA-assisted psychotherapy studies had lower dropout rates compared to the sertraline and paroxetine trials. Since MDMA is only administered under direct observation for a limited number of sessions, there is little chance of protocol deviations, accidental or intentional overdose, or withdrawal symptoms upon discontinuation.

Depression and Anxiety

Depression and anxiety are two of the conditions for which substances with psychedelic effects (especially "pure" or "classic" psychedelics such as psilocybin) are showing greater efficacy and are closer to being authorized for medical use. In fact, there are several companies currently studying them in Phase II-III clinical trials with psilocybin (COMPASS Pathways, Usona Institute, Braxia, Cybin, etc.), the Compass Pathways trials being already well underway. But there is also a lot of research into the use of esketamine (a purified form of ketamine), which has already been licensed for the treatment of depression and is marketed under the name Spravato.

Depression is a mental illness that can be attributed to various causes (psychological, genetic, environmental, biological) but that usually manifests as a deep feeling of emptiness, sadness, lack of motivation and interest, fatigue, anhedonia (lack of pleasure), trouble sleeping or excessive sleepiness, loss of or excessive appetite, and, in more severe cases, may be accompanied by the desire to disappear and suicidal ideations.

Currently, major depressive disorder is a disease that affects more than 300 million people in the world, being the leading cause of disability, increasing the relative risk of death by 1.7 times compared to the general population. in the US In the U.S., approximately 10 % of the adult population has been diagnosed with depression in the last year, and its annual cost is estimated at around 210,000 million dollars.

Nowadays, it is treated with psychotherapy combined with pharmacological interventions such as antidepressants and anxiolytics, but these substances have limited efficacy and side effects that make it difficult for some patients to adhere to treatment. Although this treatment reduces depressive symptoms and even achieves remission in many patients, approximately 30 % to 50 % do not respond at all, and 10 % to 30 % do not obtain more improvement than if they were given a placebo,8 which means they are not obtaining benefits from the pharmacological treatment.

In this disorder, psychedelic-assisted psychotherapy is proving to be quite effective in patients who have not managed to recover through classical treatments, like psychotherapy combined with antidepressants and anxiolytics.

As we have seen in the previous chapter, there are many reasons why psychedelics are suitable substances for this and, unlike SSRI (Selective Serotonin Reuptake Inhibitors) antidepressants, they do not focus on covering up symptoms or reducing emotions. Rather, they allow the person to confront the underlying cause(s) of their condition, also allowing a window of neuroplasticity that can facilitate lasting changes in the perception of oneself and the world.

---

[8] Bradley N. Gaynes et al., "What Did STAR*D Teach Us? Results from a Large-Scale, Practical, Clinical Trial for Patients with Depression", *Psychiatric Services* 60, n. 11 (November 2009): 1439-45.

Likewise, they help patients with terminal illnesses to accept their illness, lose the paralyzing fear of death and find meaning and enjoyment in their last months or years of life, even declaring that they feel: "greater clarity and confidence about their personal values and priorities, and a renewed or enhanced recognition of the intrinsic meaning and value of life[9]."

In recent years, the results of several clinical trials exploring these therapeutic uses of psilocybin have been published, including the following:

Trial of Psilocybin versus Escitalopram for Depression[10]

A double-blind, randomized, controlled trial involving 56 patients with moderate to severe, long-standing major depressive disorder, comparing psilocybin treatment with escitalopram, with psychological support, over a 6-week period. They were divided into two groups without knowing it:
- Psilocybin Group: Patients received two separate doses of 25 mg of psilocybin 3 weeks apart, plus 6 weeks of daily placebo.
- Escitalopram group: They received two separate 1mg doses of psilocybin11 3 weeks apart, plus 6 weeks of daily oral escitalopram.

---

[9] Ira Byock, "Taking Psychedelics Seriously", *Journal of Palliative Medicine* 21, n. 4 (April 2018): 417-21.

[10] Robin Carhart-Harris et al., "Trial of Psilocybin versus Escitalopram for Depression", *The New England Journal of Medicine* 384, n. 15 (April 15, 2021): 1402-11.

[11] 1 mg of psilocybin is an imperceptible dose, and in this case it is used as a placebo. A common way to measure the placebo effect without lying to patients is to tell them that they will receive psilocybin, but giving a very low dose, so the placebo placebo effect can be measured and compared with the active dose.

The primary outcome assessed by the study was the change in the QIDS-SR-16 Rapid Inventory of Depressive Symptomatology score (scores range from 0 to 27, with higher scores indicating greater depression) between baseline and week 6.

Mean scores on the QIDS-SR-16 test at baseline were 14.5 in the psilocybin group and 16.4 in the escitalopram group. Mean changes in scores from baseline to week 6 were −8.0 points in the psilocybin group and −6.0 in the escitalopram group, with a between-group difference of 2.0 points.

There was a greater than 50 % reduction in QIDS-SR-16 score in 70 % of patients in the psilocybin group versus 48 % in the escitalopram group, with a between-group difference of 22 percentage points in favor of psilocybin.

Remission (measured as a QIDS-SR-16 score less than 5) occurred in 57 % of participants in the psilocybin group versus 28 % of participants in the escitalopram group, with a between-group difference of 28 percentage points in favor of psilocybin. The incidence of adverse events was similar in both trial groups.

The primary outcome of this study (change in QIDS-SR-16 depression scores at week 6) showed a slight difference in favor of psilocybin, but unfortunately not significant. The rest of the results could show a clearer difference in favor of psilocybin, but the study was not designed to focus on their measurement, so larger and longer trials are required to compare psilocybin with established antidepressants.

Effects of Psilocybin-Assisted Therapy on Major Depressive Disorder: A Randomized Clinical Trial[12]

In this Johns Hopkins University study, a group of 24 people who had been suffering from depression for an average of more

---

[12] Alan K. Davis et al., "Effects of Psilocybin-Assisted Therapy on Major Depressive Disorder: A Randomized Clinical Trial", *JAMA Psychiatry* 78, n. 5 (May 1, 2021): 481-89.

than 20 years, with no history of psychotic disorder, suicide attempts or serious hospitalization, were given two doses of psilocybin, a first of 20mg and a second of 30mg.

After the first psilocybin session, 71 % of patients reported decreases of more than 50 % in their depression symptoms.

After the second psilocybin session, 71 % of patients reported decreases of more than 50 % in their depression symptoms.

After the first week, 58 % of the participants were in remission (their symptoms were so reduced that they no longer met diagnostic criteria for depression).

At 4 weeks, the patients were followed up, and 54% of the participants were still in remission (their symptoms were greatly reduced).

The conclusion of this study is that psilocybin-assisted psychotherapy produces large, rapid and persistent antidepressant effects over time in patients with chronic depression resistant to conventional treatment. Adverse effects that were reported were not serious and were transient, such as mild to moderate headache and challenging emotions, which were limited to the time of the session.

However, there were some limitations of this study like the small number of participants, the absence of a placebo group (although there was a control group) or the exclusion of participants with more severe forms of the disease that included previous suicide attempts.

Psilocybin Produces Substantial and Sustained Decreases in Depression and Anxiety in Patients with Life-Threatening Cancer: A Double-Blind Randomized Trial[13]

---

[13] Roland R. Griffiths et al., "Psilocybin produces substantial and sustained decreases in depression and anxiety in patients with life-threatening cancer: A randomized double-blind trial", *Journal of Psychopharmacology*, 2016.

In this Johns Hopkins University study, 51 life-threatening cancer patients with depression or anxiety were given 20 to 30 mg of psilocybin or a dose of placebo (in this case, a sub-perceptual dose of psilocybin between 1 and 3 mg). Participants, staff, and community observers rated participants' moods, attitudes, and behaviors throughout the study.

High doses of psilocybin produced large decreases in measures of depression and anxiety self-reported by the patient and the physician, along with increases in quality of life, meaning of life, and optimism, and reductions in death anxiety. At 6 months from the end of the treatment, these changes were maintained and about 80 % of the participants continued to show clinically significant decreases in depressed mood and anxiety.

Participants reported improvements in attitudes about life and about themselves, mood, relationships, and spirituality from the high-dose experience, with more than 80 % expressing a moderate or greater increase in well-being and life satisfaction. Ratings from observers in their communities confirmed these changes.

Mystical experience on the day of the session measured the effect of psilocybin dose on therapeutic outcomes.

There were no serious or persistent adverse events attributed to psilocybin administration. The most common adverse effects were transient and limited to psychological discomfort, anxiety, and headaches, but were resolved before the end of the session.

At 12 months, a follow-up was published as *Efficacy and safety of psilocybin-assisted treatment for major depressive disorder: Prospective 12-month follow-up*[14] and large decreases were observed from baseline in GRID-HAMD scores at 1, 3, 6,

---

[14] Natalie Gukasyan et al., "Efficacy and Safety of Psilocybin-Assisted Treatment for Major Depressive Disorder: Prospective 12-Month Follow-Up", *Journal of Psychopharmacology* 36, n. 2 (February 2022): 151-58.

and 12-month follow-ups. At 12 months after completion of treatment, treatment response (measured as a reduction in GRID-HAMD score of more than 50 %) was maintained in 75 % of participants and remission in 58 % of the participants. There were no serious adverse events considered to be related to psilocybin in the long-term follow-up period, and no participants reported psilocybin use outside the study context. Participants' ratings about the personal significance, spiritual experience, and mystical experience after the sessions predicted greater well-being at 12 months but did not predict improvement in depression.

These findings demonstrate that the strong antidepressant effects of psilocybin-assisted therapy can last in many patients for at least 12 months after occasional interventions.

Rapid and Sustained Symptom Reduction Following Psilocybin Treatment for Anxiety and Depression in Patients with Life-Threatening Cancer: A Randomized Controlled Trial[15]

In this double-blind, placebo-controlled, crossover trial, 29 patients with cancer-related anxiety and depression received treatment with a single dose of psilocybin (0.3 mg/kg) or niacin (a placebo), along with psychotherapy on both cases. Primary outcomes were the assessment of anxiety and depression between groups before crossover at 7 weeks.

Psilocybin produced immediate, substantial, and sustained improvements in anxiety and depression and led to decreased cancer-related lack of motivation and hopelessness, as well as improved spiritual well-being and higher quality of life. At follow-up 6.5 months after completing treatment, psilocybin

---

[15] Stephen Ross et al., "Rapid and sustained symptom reduction following psilocybin treatment for anxiety and depression in patients with life-threatening cancer: a randomized controlled trial", *Journal of Psychopharmacology*, 2016.

was associated with long-lasting anxiolytic and antidepressant effects (approximately 60 % to 80 % of participants continued to have clinically significant reductions in depression or anxiety), benefits were sustained in existential anguish and quality of life, as well as better attitudes towards death. Psilocybin-induced mystical experience impacted the therapeutic effect of psilocybin on anxiety and depression.

Thus, it can be said that, along with psychotherapy, psilocybin in a single moderate dose produced rapid, robust, and long-lasting anxiolytic and antidepressant effects in patients with cancer-related psychological distress.

At 4.5 years, the people who had participated in the study were followed up and results published as "*Long-term follow-up of psilocybin-assisted psychotherapy for psychiatric and existential distress in patients with life-threatening cancer*[16]" It was observed that the reductions in anxiety, depression, hopelessness, lack of motivation and death anxiety were maintained. Effect sizes within the group were considerable. At 4.5 years, approximately 60-80 % of participants continued to meet criteria for clinically significant antidepressant or anxiolytic responses. Nearly all participants attributed positive life changes to the psilocybin-assisted therapy experience, calling it one of the most meaningful experiences, both personally and spiritually, of their lives.

These findings suggest that psilocybin-assisted psychotherapy holds promise for long-term relief of cancer-related psychiatric distress. However, limited conclusions can be drawn regarding the efficacy of this therapy due to the crossover design of the original study.

---

[16] Gabrielle I. Agin-Liebes et al., "Long-Term Follow-up of Psilocybin-Assisted Psychotherapy for Psychiatric and Existential Distress in Patients with Life-Threatening Cancer", *Journal of Psychopharmacology* 34, n. 2 (February 2020): 155-66.

In 2019, esketamine was approved in the U.S. and Europe for the treatment of depression, becoming the first substance with psychedelic properties to be authorized for therapeutic use in mental health, in combination with the use of classic antidepressants.

For example, one study that showed its therapeutic potential was:

<u>Efficacy and Safety of Intranasal Esketamine Adjunctive to Oral Antidepressant Therapy in Treatment-Resistant Depression: A Randomized Clinical Trial</u>[17]

In this Phase II, double-blind, placebo-controlled study, 67 patients with depression resistant to conventional treatment were randomly assigned to groups with placebo, esketamine 28 mg, 56 mg or 84 mg, administered twice weekly. Participants continued their existing antidepressant treatment during the study. The primary efficacy endpoint was the change from baseline to day 8 in the Montgomery-Åsberg Depression Rating Scale (MADRS) total score.

The change in MADRS total score in the 3 esketamine groups was greater than the placebo group, and was significantly greater with a higher ketamine dose (28 mg: −4.2; 56mg: − 6.3, 84mg: −9.0). The improvement in depression symptoms appeared to be sustained (−7.2) despite the reduction in dosing frequency in the final phase of the study. 4 out of the 56 patients (7%) treated with esketamine had adverse events that led to their withdrawal from the study (syncope, headache, dissociative syndrome and ectopic pregnancy).

---

[17] Ella J. Daly et al., "Efficacy and Safety of Intranasal Esketamine Adjunctive to Oral Antidepressant Therapy in Treatment-Resistant Depression: A Randomized Clinical Trial", *JAMA Psychiatry* 75, n. 2 (February 2018): 139-48.

The antidepressant effect was rapid onset and dose-related. The response appeared to persist for more than 2 months despite a lower dosing frequency. The results support further investigation in larger trials.

Addictions

The use of psychedelic substances for the treatment of addictions is currently being explored. These are mainly for substance addictions ("Substance Use Disorders"), although they may also show potential for behavioral addictions. In the treatment of addictions to substances such as alcohol, tobacco, heroin or cocaine, the psychedelics that are being explored the most are psilocybin, ibogaine, MDMA, DMT (normally in the form of ayahuasca) and LSD.

Addictions, whether to substances or behavioral (gambling, sex, social networks, shopping, food, etc.) represent a huge public health problem today. Substance use disorders affect hundreds of millions of people globally, accounting for the loss of more than 130 million DALYs (disability-adjusted life years) in 2016. Today, it is one of the main causes of the 11.8 million annual deaths related to alcohol, tobacco and other drugs.

The diagnostic manual of mental disorders, in its latest edition (DSM-5), defines substance use disorder as a pathological pattern of behaviors related to the persistent use of drugs (including alcohol) despite substantial harm and adverse consequences. The essential feature of substance use disorders is the association of cognitive, behavioral and physiological symptoms that indicate that the person continues to use the substance despite significant problems related to it. The diagnosis can be made on 10 classes of substances that have been included in the DSM-5, except for caffeine. "For some substances, these symptoms are less conspicuous, and not even all symptoms occur (e.g., withdrawal symptoms are not specified in phencyclidine, other hallucinogen, or inhalant use disorder). An important feature of substance use disorder is the underlying change in brain circuits that persists after detoxification, and that occurs especially in people with severe disorders. The behavioral effects of these brain changes are shown in repeated relapses and intense cravings when the person is exposed to drug-related stimuli." This definition could be expanded in the coming years by the inclusion of criteria for addictions without substance or smoking, which would drastically increase the number of people who would meet its diagnostic criteria.

Unfortunately, current mental health treatments do not achieve sufficient efficacy rates to counteract or alleviate this increase in prevalence, and their majority model is in question. It is especially in the field of addictions where there are more populations of chronic patients resistant to such treatments or with difficulties in adherence. The effectiveness of these treatments involves a high consumption of economic, health and human resources, a cost that in many cases is assumed by the public health systems and by the patients themselves, together with the great productivity loss caused by the disorder. In addition, these are treatments with multiple side effects and health risks derived from the chronic use of psychotropic drugs such as antidepressants, anxiolytics or antipsychotics; without forgetting the complex pharmacological interactions with other drugs, often toxic, as well as the risk of using these substances for suicide purposes.

These conventional therapies, which have hardly evolved in recent decades, are proving insufficient to contain this mental health epidemic, while other areas of medicine and health have experienced a very important and exponential evolution in recent years.

Addictions, like depression or PTSD, manifest psychologically through rigid patterns of thought and behavior, and it is common to find that they developed as a response to voids or traumas. That is why they are a strong candidate for psychedelic-assisted psychotherapy. In fact, this model of treatment emerged precisely in the work with people with alcoholism problems in the late 1950s.

In recent years, several clinical trials have been carried out exploring this field:

Pilot Study of the 5-HT2AR Agonist Psilocybin in the Treatment of Tobacco Addiction[18]

Pilot study in which moderate (20 mg/70 kg) and high (30 mg/70 kg) doses of psilocybin were administered within a structured program of cognitive behavioral therapy for 15 weeks to stop smoking. Participants were 15 psychiatrically healthy smokers, with a mean of six prior quit attempts and smoking a mean of 19 cigarettes per day for a mean of 31 years at the start of the study.

Using self-reports and biomarkers, it was shown that after experimental therapy, 12 out of 15 participants (80 %) quit tobacco and remained abstinent for at least 6 months.

The observed smoking cessation rate substantially exceeds commonly reported rates for other behavioral or pharmacological therapies (typically less than 35 %).

Although the open-label design did not allow definitive conclusions to be drawn about the efficacy of psilocybin, these findings suggest that psilocybin may be a

---

[18] Matthew W. Johnson et al., "Pilot Study of the 5-HT2AR Agonist Psilocybin in the Treatment of Tobacco Addiction", *Journal of Psychopharmacology* 28, n. 11 (November 2014): 983-92.

potentially effective adjunct to current smoking cessation treatment models.

At 12 and 16 months, a follow-up of the participants in the study was published as "<u>Long-term follow-up of psilocybin-facilitated smoking cessation</u>[19]" and found that, at 12 months, 67 % of the participants were still smoke-free, and at 16 months it was confirmed that 60 % were still smoke-free. 86.7 % of the participants rated their experiences with psilocybin among the five most personally and spiritually significant experiences of their lives. Thus, these results suggest that, in the context of a structured treatment program, psilocybin holds great promise for promoting long-term tobacco abstinence.

<u>Cessation and Reduction in Alcohol Consumption and Misuse after Psychedelic Use</u> [20]

An anonymous, online survey of people with prior Alcohol Use Disorder (AUD), but who reported cessation or reduction of use after psychedelic use in non-clinical settings.

343 people completed the survey. Participants reported a median of seven years of problematic alcohol use (72 % met retrospective criteria for severe AUD) prior to the psychedelic experience, to which they attributed the reduction in alcohol use. Most reported a significant reduction after taking a moderate or high dose of LSD (38 %) or psilocybin (36 %).

After the psychedelic experience, 83 % no longer met diagnostic criteria for AUD, the disorder had remitted. Participants rated their psychedelic experience as highly significant and

---

[19] Matthew W. Johnson, Albert Garcia-Romeu, y Roland R. Griffiths, "Long-Term Follow-up of Psilocybin-Facilitated Smoking Cessation", *The American Journal of Drug and Alcohol Abuse* 43, n. 1 (January 2017): 55-60.

[20] Albert Garcia-Romeu et al., "Cessation and Reduction in Alcohol Consumption and Misuse after Psychedelic Use", *Journal of Psychopharmacology* 33, n. 9 (September 2019): 1088-1101.

"insightful", and for 28 % it was the changes in life priorities or values associated with the psychedelic experience that facilitated the reduction in alcohol misuse. A higher psychedelic dose, the sensation of insight, mystical-type effects and the personal meaning of these experiences were the elements that were related to a greater reduction in alcohol consumption, facilitating the control of previous consumption and associated distress.

Although the results of an *on-line*survey are unable to prove causality or rule out a placebo effect, they suggest that psychedelic use could lead to cessation or reduction of problem drinking, supporting further investigation of psychedelic-assisted treatments for AUD.

Psilocybin-Assisted Treatment for Alcohol Dependence: A Proof-of-Concept Study[21]

Single-arm proof-of-concept study to quantify the acute effects of psilocybin in alcohol-dependent participants and to provide preliminary outcome and safety data. Following therapy sessions devoted to the preparation and information regarding the psilocybin sessions, 10 alcohol-dependent volunteers, according to DSM-IV, received orally administered psilocybin in one or two supervised sessions, in addition to motivational enhancement therapy.

Withdrawal did not increase significantly in the first 4 weeks of treatment (when participants had not yet received psilocybin) but did increase significantly after administration of the substance. The gains were largely maintained during follow-up up to 36 weeks.

---

[21] Michael P. Bogenschutz et al., "Psilocybin-Assisted Treatment for Alcohol Dependence: A Proof-of-Concept Study", *Journal of Psychopharmacology* 29, n. 3 (March 2015): 289-99.

The intensity of perceived effects in the first psilocybin session (at week 4) strongly predicted change in alcohol consumption during weeks 5 to 8, also predicting decreases in craving and increases in withdrawal during week 5.

There were no significant treatment-related adverse events. These preliminary findings provided a strong rationale for conducting controlled trials with larger samples to investigate efficacy and mechanisms.

Lysergic Acid Diethylamide (LSD) for Alcoholism: Meta-Analysis of Randomized Controlled Trials[22]

Meta-analysis of randomized controlled trials to assess the clinical efficacy of LSD in the treatment of alcoholism. Six trials meeting all criteria were included, with a total of 536 participants.

Of the patients who took LSD as part of their treatment, 59 % had less alcohol abuse compared to 38 % of those who received placebo. Those people who took LSD also reported greater alcohol withdrawal.

This effect was maintained at six months after treatment, but after a year, the difference between those who had taken LSD and those who had not taken LSD was no longer significant.

A single dose of LSD, in the context of various alcoholism treatment programs, was associated with decreased alcohol abuse.

---

[22] Krebs y Johansen, "Lysergic Acid Diethylamide (LSD) for Alcoholism: Meta-Analysis of Randomized Controlled Trials."

Neurodegenerative Diseases or Neurorehabilitation

The research field of possible psychedelic use for the treatment of neurodegenerative diseases, such as dementia, Alzheimer's or Parkinson's, or to accelerate learning or rehabilitation, is still in the field of speculation and in the phase of preliminary studies.

Neurodegenerative diseases, and especially those associated with age, are becoming more frequent in our societies, as a result of increased life expectancy and various environmental and cultural factors related to modern life.

In recent years, it has been discovered[23] that many substances with psychedelic properties have the ability to induce neuroplasticity (facilitate the neural networks of the brain to change, adapt and thus facilitate learning), synaptogenesis (the formation of new synapses or connections between neurons) and also neurogenesis (the formation of new neurons in specific areas of the brain). In addition, psychedelics have been shown to increase several neuronal growth factors, such as Brain-Derived Neurotrophic Growth Factor (BDNF) or Nerve Growth Factor (NGF).

These findings open the door to the investigation of possible psychedelic use in neurodegenerative diseases, which are characterized by the death of neurons, or also in situations that require the need to accelerate the readaptation of the brain, such as neurorehabilitation or learning processes in situations of neural difficulty.

Titles from study publications that showed promise in this regard and that can open the door to future trials in humans include:

---

[23] Cato M. H. deVos, Natasha L. Mason, y Kim P. C. Kuypers, "Psychedelics and Neuroplasticity: A Systematic Review Unraveling the Biological Underpinnings of Psychedelics", *Frontiers in Psychiatry / Frontiers Research Foundation* 12 (September 10, 2021): 724606.

The Alkaloids from Banisteriopsis caapi, the plant source of the Amazonian hallucinogen ayahuasca, stimulate adult neurogenesis in vitro[24]

N,N-dimethyltryptamine compound found in the hallucinogenic tea ayahuasca, regulates adult neurogenesis in vitro and in vivo[25]

A single dose of psilocybin increases synaptic density and decreases 5-HT receptor density in the pig brain[26]

Psilocybin induces rapid and persistent growth of dendritic spines in the frontal cortex in vivo[27]

Low doses of LSD acutely increase BDNF blood plasma levels in healthy volunteers[28]

---

[24] Jose A. Morales-García et al., "The Alkaloids of Banisteriopsis Caapi, the Plant Source of the Amazonian Hallucinogen Ayahuasca, Stimulate Adult Neurogenesis in Vitro", *Scientific Reports* 7, n. 1 (July 13, 2017): 5309.

[25] Jose A. Morales-Garcia et al., "N,N-dimethyltryptamine compound found in the hallucinogenic tea ayahuasca, regulates adult neurogenesis in vitro and in vivo", *Translational Psychiatry*, 2020.

[26] Nakul Ravi Raval et al., "A Single Dose of Psilocybin Increases Synaptic Density and Decreases 5-HT Receptor Density in the Pig Brain", *International Journal of Molecular Sciences* 22, n. 2 (January 15, 2021).

[27] Ling-Xiao Shao et al., "Psilocybin Induces Rapid and Persistent Growth of Dendritic Spines in Frontal Cortex in Vivo", *Neuron* 109, n. 16 (August 18, 2021): 2535-44.

[28] Nadia R. P. W. Hutten et al., "Low Doses of LSD Acutely Increase BDNF Blood Plasma Levels in Healthy Volunteers", *ACS Pharmacology & Translational Science* 4, n. 2 (April 9, 2021): 461-66.

Behaviour Change

Another possibility that is speculated, based on several anecdotal reports, is to use psychedelics as tools to facilitate the change of habits, fundamentally those that may be more dangerous for health or society.

Through the combination of certain therapeutic interventions in improving habits, such as cognitive behavioral therapy or motivational interviewing, nowadays, the use of psychedelics could increase their efficacy and durability when it comes to promoting the improvement of diet, exercise, exposure to nature and also mindfulness or stress reduction practices, all of which can contribute to better health and physical and psychological well-being[29].

Couples Therapy and Conflict Resolution

An important potential use of psychedelics, fundamentally MDMA, is in the resolution of conflicts in various fields. This use was explored mainly in the field of couples therapy in the 70s and 80s. There is clinical experience and some studies on the subject.

In therapeutic contexts, MDMA facilitates communication, empathy, understanding, forgiveness, reduces the negative interpretation of ourselves and others, the processing of negative emotions, also reducing the reactivity and the defenses that can arise during a conflict.

---

[29] Pedro J. Teixeira et al., "Psychedelics and Health Behaviour Change", *Journal of Psychopharmacology* 36, n. 1 (January 2022): 12-19.

In this regard, preliminary clinical studies, both specific and in combination with other diagnoses, especially post-traumatic stress disorder[30]. have been carried out with promising results[31]. Likewise, its use is being explored in the context of other conflicts, such as the Palestinian-Israeli one, where some studies are obtaining very interesting results[32].

Microdosing

In recent years, a practice has become popular that champions the use of psychedelics in very low doses and repeatedly throughout the week, following different dosage models that I will explain below. According to its advocates, it can improve well-being, creativity, concentration, mood, and even symptoms of depression, anxiety, PTSD, attention-deficit/hyperactivity disorder (ADHD), obsessive-compulsive disorder (OCD) and more.

Microdosing became popular after the publication of Jim Fadiman's book *The Psychedelic Explorer's Guide*[33], 2011. In this book, he spoke of this practice, which consists of taking very low doses in the range of one tenth of the normal active dose of a psychedelic (the usual range of these microdoses is usually

---

[30] Candice M. Monson et al., "MDMA-Facilitated Cognitive-Behavioural Conjoint Therapy for Posttraumatic Stress Disorder: An Uncontrolled Trial", *European Journal of Psychotraumatology* 11, n. 1 (December 7, 2020): 1840123.
[31] Anne C. Wagner et al., "Relational and Growth Outcomes Following Couples Therapy With MDMA for PTSD", *Frontiers in Psychiatry / Frontiers Research Foundation* 12 (June 28, 2021): 702838.
[32] Leor Roseman et al., "Relational Processes in Ayahuasca Groups of Palestinians and Israelis", *Frontiers in Pharmacology* 12 (May 19, 2021): 607529.
[33] James Fadiman, *The Psychedelic Explorer's Guide: Safe, Therapeutic, and Sacred Journeys* (Simon and Schuster, 2011).

between one twelfth and one eighth) at the start of the day, as if it were coffee, and then carrying out normal daily activities.

For example, in the case of LSD, the conventional active dose is 100 µg. When microdosing, a dose would fall in the range of 8 to 12 µg, normally 10 µg.

This practice is not practiced daily, but rather in the form of a scheduled protocol. There are several, but the most popular are:
- The Fadiman protocol, which alternates one day of intake with two days of rest.
- The "two days a week" protocol, which is similar to the previous one but sets the intake on two specific non-consecutive days of the week (for example, Monday and Thursday).
- The "alternate day" protocol, which proposes taking a microdose every other day (for example Monday, Wednesday and Friday).
- The Stamets protocol, which consists of consuming a combination of a microdose of psilocybin with Lion's Mane mushroom and niacin (vitamin B3) for 4 days, and then resting for 3 days, taking only Lion's Mane.

To date, there have been no well-constructed clinical trials to evaluate this practice. While studies to date have shown that people who believe they are microdosing improve in some ways, they have not been able to strongly demonstrate that microdosing is better than placebo. There was one study that found small differences but attributed them to the design of the study itself[34], so it is possible that said improvement effect could be the result of autosuggestion. Still, it is a field in which much remains to be investigated.

---

[34] Szigeti et al., "Self-Blinding Citizen Science to Explore Psychedelic Microdosing."

What has been observed is that small doses of LSD, even in this microdose range, produce BDNF release in humans[35], which might potentially be very interesting for neuroplasticity and even for neurogenesis, although this release is not something exclusive to psychedelic substances.

Unfortunately, trying it for long periods of time is not peril-free, as there are (at least in theory) potential risks[36] for the heart when consuming psychedelics on a daily basis. Although it is true that at such low doses it is not known whether they can represent a real danger or not, some researchers have already warned that it might be possible.

OTHER LINES OF RESEARCH FOR POSSIBLE FUTURE APPLICATIONS:

- Creativity.
- Learning disorders.
- Obsessive-compulsive disorder.
- Language disorders such as stuttering or dyslexia.
- Social anxiety in people with autism.
- Anorexia.
- Tinnitus.
- Phobias.
- Palliative care.
- Chronic pain.
- Grief.
- Others.

---

[35] Hutten et al., "Low Doses of LSD Acutely Increase BDNF Blood Plasma Levels in Healthy Volunteers."

[36] Hutten et al.; Joshua D. Hutcheson et al., "Serotonin Receptors and Heart Valve Disease--It Was Meant 2B", *Pharmacology & Therapeutics* 132, n. 2 (November 2011): 146-57.

THE DIFFERENT PSYCHEDELIC SUBSTANCES

PSILOCYBIN ("MUSHROOMS")

DEFINITION, COMPOSITION AND ORIGIN

Psilocybin (also called 4-PO-DMT or 4-phosphoryloxy-N,N-dimethyltryptamine), formerly marketed as Indocybin®, is a naturally occurring psychedelic substance from the tryptamine chemical family (they have similarities to serotonin). It is found in up to 180 varieties of fungi, distributed throughout all continents, but especially in tropical and subtropical forests. The most common and popular species of psilocybin mushrooms are: *Psilocybe cubensis*, *Psilocybe subcubensis* and *Psilocybe semilanceata*, commonly known as "Magic Mushrooms" or "Liberty Caps."

Although these mushrooms usually also contain other active ingredients, such as psilocin (4-HO-DMT) and baeocystin (4-HO-NMT), psilocybin is considered their main active ingredient, since it is the one with the greatest presence and chemical stability, which makes it the most abundant in mushrooms when consumed. Paradoxically, it is not the psilocybin that ultimately acts on the brain. When it enters the body it is converted into psilocin and it is this psilocin that is responsible for most of the final psychoactivity.

Applications

Throughout history, psilocybin mushrooms have had various religious, ritual and shamanistic uses, in fact, there are prehistoric artistic representations on practically every continent. In the Aztec language, these mushrooms were called *Teonanacatl*, or "meat of the gods."

Currently, it may be associated with recreational use, with self-exploration self-knowledge, spiritually and, therapeutically, it is being investigated for the treatment of depression, anxiety, post-traumatic stress disorder, addictions, obsessive-compulsive disorder, etc., making it the most studied psychedelic substance today, along with MDMA and ketamine.

Like other tryptamines, it has also been successfully used for the treatment of cluster headaches.

Forms and Routes of Administration

Psilocybin is commonly ingested orally as a component of a mushroom or truffle, both of which can be found fresh or dried. These mushrooms and truffles can be purchased from a drug supplier or grown at home with one of the many home

Psilocybe cubensis "Golden Teacher" mushrooms (Mädi, CC BY-SA 3.0 <https://creativecommons.org/licenses/by-sa/3.0>, via Wikimedia Commons).

grow kits available today. They can also be found in the field but given the huge variety of similar mushrooms in nature, many of them poisonous, this practice can be very risky for non-experts. The consumption of psilocybin orally is done by chewing the dried or fresh mushrooms, or by preparing a tea, with water or lemon, known as a "lemon tek[1]." The latter method has some advantages, such as reducing the nausea usually experienced when eating raw mushrooms, improving absorption, and speeding up the onset of effects.

In clinical research, psilocybin is often used in pure, isolated, synthetic form, typically manufactured to GMP (Good Manufacturing Practices) pharmaceutical standards. It is usually administered orally isolated in capsules, but has also been administered intravenously, especially in neuroimaging studies.

Pharmacology and Effects

After mushrooms or truffles are ingested, eaten raw or in tea form, psilocybin is absorbed by the stomach, enters the blood, and begins to convert to psilocin within the body through a process called dephosphorylation. This psilocin, which is responsible for the psychoactive effects, reaches the brain and

---

[1] Preparation of squeezed lemon juice with crushed or powdered mushrooms that, after soaking for a few minutes, is strained and drunk.

activates the 5-HT2a serotonin neuroreceptors (like most psychedelic substances) and the 5-HT1a receptors in the neurons of the brain, triggering the psychedelic effects that we have described in previous chapters.

The physical effects of psilocybin are few, mainly dilation of the pupils and a slight increase in heart rate and blood pressure, especially in high doses and in direct relation to the psychological effects the person is experiencing.

The psychological effects of psilocybin are numerous and highly dependent on variables like dose, person, and context. The most characteristic are major changes in sensory perceptions, cognition, and consciousness.

Changes in sensory perceptions can manifest visually, with color enhancement, distortions in the shapes and movements of things, and colorful kaleidoscopic visions with closed eyes. Synesthesia (blending of senses, such as "smelling colors" or "seeing sounds") and increased tactile, thermal and tingling sensations may appear. Hearing disturbances can lead to an increased appreciation of music and sounds.

Cognitive alterations can be perceived as positive and pleasant or negative and difficult, and it is common for psychedelic experiences to include good stages and more difficult moments, which is why they are called "trips."

They commonly bring up biographical and personal content, like relationships with significant people in your life. In high doses and controlled contexts, psilocybin can induce mystical experiences, with the dissolution of personal and ego boundaries, and oceanic feelings, which can be experienced with great peace and transcendence, but can also generate anxiety and even fear.

Psilocybin can reduce the activity of the amygdala, the center of the brain related to fear, and therefore induce a positive bias in the perception of ourselves and our environment. It can also produce a lot of laughter.

It also tends to produce a feeling of physical tiredness that is less conducive to movement or exploration than other psychedelics as LSD.

Dosage

Mushrooms, when dried, lose about 90 % of their weight, which was in the form of water, so, in general terms, each gram of dried mushroom is equivalent to 10 g of fresh mushroom.

Although some psychoactive substances are dosed taking into account the weight of the person receiving the substance, in the case of psilocybin this does not seem to have much influence on the final effect, which is why fixed doses are typically used[2]. The dose of pure psilocybin used in research is around 20-25 mg, which would be equivalent to about 2.5-3 g of dried psilocybe mushrooms (about 15 or 20 g of fresh psilocybe mushrooms), if we consider the contribution of the small amounts of psilocin that accompany it, especially if they are fresh.

Those who consume it in microdoses look for a tenth of the active dose, equivalent to about 2 mg of psilocybin or 250-300 mg of dried psilocybe mushroom.

The concentration of psilocybin in a mushroom or truffle will depend on many factors, such as its species, its exposure to light, its growth and harvest time, its level of drying, the specific part of the mushroom, its age and its conservation (psilocybin, like other compounds, tends to degrade over time after harvesting and drying.) Therefore, it is very difficult to know the concentration of psilocybin, psilocin and baeocystin in a sample of mushrooms without doing an analysis of it, but some approximate average concentrations per species collected in the literature[3] are:

---

[2] Albert Garcia-Romeu et al., "Optimal dosing for psilocybin pharmacotherapy: Considering weight-adjusted and fixed dosing approaches", *Journal of Psychopharmacology* 35, no. 4 (April 2021): 353-61.

[3] Paul Stamets, *Psilocybin Mushrooms of the World: An Identification Guide* (Random House Digital, Inc., 1996).

Species	% Psilocybin by Weight of Dried Mushroom
Psilocybe azurescens	1.78 %
Psilocybe semilanceata	0.98 %
Psilocybe cubensis	0.63 %
Psilocybe cyanescens	0.85 %
Psilocybe tampanensis (truffles)	0.68 %
Panaeolus cyanescens / Copelandia cyanescens	2.51 %

As for the doses, various levels can be established depending on the intention of consumption: microdoses (below the threshold of the minimum psychoactive dose) for those seeking imperceptible effects; low doses or medium doses for a first approach to the substance or "recreational" use, and high doses for therapeutic work or mystical experiences.

Doses	Dried Psilocybe Cubensis Mushrooms - Oral	Psilocybin - Pure
Microdose	< 0.25 g	< 2.5 mg
Minimal Psychoactive	0.25 - 0.5 g	3 - 6 mg
Low	0.5 - 1 g	6 - 10 mg
Medium	1 - 2.5 g	10 - 20 mg
High	2.5 - 5 g	20 - 35 mg
Very High (higher risks)	> 5 g	> 35 mg

DURATION

The following table shows some approximate times for both the total duration of the experience and the duration of the different phases. The absorption/latency phase is the time that passes from when the substance is ingested until its effects begin to be noticed. The rise phase (or come-up) is the time between the appearance of the initial effects until its maximum intensity is reached. The plateau phase (or peak) is the time of maximum "stable" psychoactive effects of the substance, in which the majority of the psychedelic experience takes place. The descent phase (or come-down) is the time when these effects fade until they become insignificant, and the brain gradually returns to normal. The residual phase or afterglow refers to the later time, in which psychological normality has already returned, but there are still some slight sensations in the background, usually positive.

Duration of Effects	Psilocybin - Oral
Total Duration	4 - 7 hours
Absorption / Latency	15 - 60 minutes
Rise	15 - 30 minutes
Plateau	2 - 4 hours
Descent	1 - 3 hours
Residual / "Afterglow"	6 - 12 hours

Specific Risks

Like other classic psychedelics, psilocybin has a very low level of toxicity and no addictive potential. However, it presents risks on a psychological level, especially in people with latent psychiatric disorders or a propensity for them.

All psychedelics can produce feelings of dizziness or nausea at the onset of their effects, but psilocybin mushrooms can be especially prone to this, especially if eaten raw (and not in tea form) and on a full stomach. In addition, a full stomach can also greatly attenuate the desired effects of psilocybin, which is why it is usually consumed when fasting for at least 4–6 hours. To reduce nausea and speed absorption, some people prepare "lemon tek."

There is a risk of using the wrong mushroom or consuming others that may be toxic, especially if they are collected in the wild.

Despite a well prepared "set & setting", sometimes you could encounter difficult experiences (commonly called "bad trips") when you may feel anxiety, fear, paranoia, confusion, agitation, space-time disorientation, a feeling of "going crazy." But they are usually transient and rarely last beyond the pharmacological effect of the substance. Eating small amounts may help reduce these effects. There are also strategies described in the section called "Bad trip management and other psychedelic emergencies," in the "Psychedelic Risk Reduction" chapter of this book, that can help.

At the psychiatric level, the consumption of psilocybin by people with a propensity for psychosis, bipolarity, schizophrenia or a family history of any of these, can increase the risk of triggering episodes. In very rare cases it can cause "flashbacks" or hallucinogen persisting perception disorder (HPPD).

LSD ("Acid")

Definition, Composition and Origin

LSD (German initials for Lysergic Acid Diethylamide) and known on the street as "acid" or "blotter", formerly marketed as Delysid®, is a semi-synthetic substance with psychedelic effects from the chemical family of tryptamines (they have similarities with serotonin). They are derived from lysergic acid and are present in various plant and fungal species, such as the well-known ergot (*Claviceps purpurea*).

APPLICATIONS

LSD began to be used as a psychotomimetic, but it was soon discovered that it had great therapeutic potential to help people with alcoholism overcome their addiction, and terminal cancer patients lose their fear of death and come to terms with their life.

Also, like other tryptamines, it has been used successfully in the treatment of cluster headaches.

Since its prohibition at the end of the 1960s, its visible use has been eminently recreational or in *underground* therapy. Now, it is being investigated again clinically for the treatment of various psychological disorders such as depression, anxiety and various addictions. Although given its long duration of effects and less tendency to induce introspection, it has less clinical interest compared to psilocybin.

FORMS AND ROUTES OF ADMINISTRATION

LSD is a salt, but its active doses are so minimal (in the order of micrograms, that is, millionths of a gram) that they are almost invisible to the human eye and, therefore, dosage using a scale is very difficuldt. For this reason, it is normally dosed by diluting it in water or another solvent, such as ethyl alcohol, and administering that solution directly orally in the form of drops; or placed on a blotting paper (or any other porous, transportable material), and allowed to dry, leaving the dose of LSD "trapped" inside and ready to transport or consume. It is usually sold in thick blotting papers pre-cut into small squares, and with elaborate designs known as *blotters* or "sheets."

LSD blotter with 5 doses (Motorbase, CC BY-SA 3.0 <https://creativecommons.org/licenses/by-sa/3.0>, via Wikimedia Commons).

Many people collect these beautifully designed blotters, usually empty, but also sometimes laced with LSD.

LSD is usually taken orally, although research has also used it intravenously. There is a myth that it is consumed applied directly to the eye, but it is frankly unlikely that this practice will go beyond the anecdotal.

Pharmacology and Effects

LSD reaches the blood through the digestive system and gains access to the brain. Once there, it binds to several serotonergic receptors, in particular the serotonin 5-HT2a receptor, considered to be the main responsible for its psychedelic effects. It also binds to other receptors such as 5-HT1a, 5-HT2b, 5-HT2c, and 5-HT6, but its effects are less well understood.

Unlike other serotonergic psychedelics, LSD has some effect on dopamine and norepinephrine receptors, with a small contribution to the psychedelic experience that may be somewhat more uplifting and energetic than that induced by psilocybin.

The physical effects of LSD are few, mainly dilation of the pupils and a slight increase in heart rate and blood pressure, especially in high doses.

As in other psychedelic substances, the psychological effects of LSD are numerous and highly dependent on the variables of dose, person and context. The most characteristic are significant changes in sensory perceptions, cognition and consciousness.

Desired effects of this substance include (but are not limited to): euphoria, laughter, sense of perception, enlightenment, synesthesia, new ways of thinking about oneself and others, deep feelings of love and well-being, changes in the perception of time and space, spiritual experiences, visual hallucinations (but generally distinguishable from reality), etc.

Changes in sensory perceptions can manifest visually, with color enhancement, distortions in the shapes and movements of things, and colorful kaleidoscopic visions with closed eyes. Synesthesia (blending of senses, like "smelling colors" or "seeing sounds") and increased tactile, thermal and tingling sensations may appear. Hearing disturbances can lead to an increased appreciation of music and sounds.

Cognitive alterations can be perceived as positive and pleasant or negative and difficult, and it is common for psychedelic experiences to include good stages and more difficult moments, which is why they are called "trips."

It commonly brings up biographical and personal content, like relationships with significant people in your life. In high doses and controlled contexts, LSD can induce mystical experiences, with the dissolution of personal limits and the ego, with oceanic feelings, which can be experienced with great peace and transcendence, but can also generate anxiety and even fear.

Compared to psilocybin, it is considered a more energetic, outgoing, and highly visual experience.

Dosage

LSD is such a powerful molecule that the active dose is almost invisible to the naked eye, so proper dilution is the only way to dose it with less risk of error. On the other hand, when it is sold already dosed in *blotters*, chemical analysis is the only way to know the potency and purity of a given batch.

On the market, *blotters* can contain a wide variety of dosages, but they are usually between 80 and 150 µg, which would be an average dose, very common in recreational or experimental contexts of use.

Sex, body weight, sensitivity to psychedelics and previous tolerance are factors that would determine the final potency of the effects.

Doses	LSD – Oral
Microdose	< 12 µg
Minimal Psychoactive	15 – 25 µg
Low	25 – 75 µg
Medium	75 – 150 µg
High	150 – 250 µg
Very high (higher risks)	> 250 µg

Duration

The effects of LSD are very long lasting, ranging between 8 and 12 hours, but can reach 16 hours in very high doses. In any case, an experience never has the same intensity throughout, and it is considered that most of its effects are concentrated in the first 4-6 hours after ingestion.

Duration	LSD – Oral
Total Duration	8 – 12 hours
Absorption/Latency	15 – 30 minutes
Rise	45 – 90 minutes
Plateau	3 – 5 hours
Descent	3 – 5 hours
Residual / "Afterglow"	12 – 48 hours

Specific Risks

Like other classic psychedelics, LSD has a very low level of toxicity and no addictive potential. However, it presents risks on a psychological level especially in people with psychiatric disorders or propensity to them.

Like other tryptamines, LSD does not have much interaction with the cardiovascular or respiratory systems, or others. It dilates the pupils (mydriasis), and, at high doses, it can slightly raise heart pressure, heart rate and body temperature, but it does not generally do so in a magnitude of risk, except in cases of people with previous hypertensive disease.

Despite a well prepared "set & setting", sometimes you could encounter difficult experiences (commonly called "bad trips") when you may feel anxiety, fear, paranoia, confusion, agitation, space-time disorientation, a feeling of "going crazy", but they are usually transient and rarely last beyond the pharmacological effect of the substance. In any case, there are also strategies described in the section called "Bad trip management and other psychedelic emergencies," in the "Psychedelic Risk Reduction" chapter of this book, that can help.

At the psychiatric level, the consumption of LSD by people with a propensity for psychosis, bipolarity, schizophrenia or a family history of any of these, can increase the risk of triggering episodes. In very rare cases it can cause flashbacks or hallucinogen persisting perception disorder (HPPD).

DMT / Ayahuasca

Definition, Composition and Origin

DMT (abbreviation for N,N-DiMethylTryptamine, also called the "Spirit Molecule") is a psychedelic tryptamine, from the chemical family of tryptamines (it has similarities to serotonin), and of natural origin. It can be found in a wide variety of plants (such as acacias, mimosas or chacruna (*Psychotria viridis*) and even in small amounts in the mammalian brain[4].

Applications

Although the physiological role of endogenous DMT is unknown, DMT has been used for centuries as one of the main psychoactive ingredients in ayahuasca, for ritualistic, religious and therapeutic use.

Although in Western countries the use of DMT has been associated with recreational contexts (especially in the form of pure DMT crystals that are vaporized), currently, the ritual, spiritual and therapeutic use of this Amazonian potion is also experiencing great growth and popularity in Western countries. The use of this drink in recreational or non-ceremonial contexts is practically non-existent at the moment.

Likewise, research on its therapeutic potential is booming, with studies of its use, both in the form of oral ayahuasca and intravenous injection of pure DMT, for the treatment of depression, anxiety or addictions and for its potential for neurogenesis and neuroplasticity.

---

[4] Jon G. Dean et al., "Biosynthesis and extracellular concentrations of N,N-dimethyltryptamine (DMT) in mammalian brain," *Scientific Reports*, 2019.

Extraction of DMT in crystallized form (DM Trott, CC BY-SA 4.0 <https://creativecommons.org/licenses/by-sa/4.0>, via Wikimedia Commons).

FORMS AND ROUTES OF ADMINISTRATION

DMT is usually found isolated in the form of crystallized salts that are extracted through a process of dissolution and filtration from the dried and pulverized bark of plants such as the *Mimosa hostilis*. These salts are vaporized in a glass pipe or electronic vaporizer and inhaled, the effects are very intense and take a few seconds to appear.

DMT is also found as one of the two main active ingredients that make up the sacred Amazonian drink ayahuasca (or "yagé"), known as "medicine" in traditional consumption contexts. This drink also contains substances that allow DMT to be active orally, because otherwise the human body contains enzymes called monoamine oxidases that destroy DMT if it were ingested alone. These substances, called beta-carbolines, come from "yagé" (*Banisteriopsis caapi*) and act as monoamine oxidase inhibitors (MAOIs), canceling these enzymes and allowing DMT to reach the brain and exert its pharmacological effect.

Inspired by the combination of DMT with MAOIs for oral consumption, other westernized versions of Amazonian ayahuasca have appeared, such as "mimosahuasca", which

Ayahuasca ingredients before being cooked. (Awkipuma, CC BY 3.0<https://creativecommons.org/licenses/by/3.0>, via Wikimedia Commons).

combines the DMT of a mimosa with the MAOIs present in the Mediterranean harmala (*Peganum harmala*), or the "farmahuasca", which combines DMT with MAOIs for pharmaceutical use[5].

There is also a smokeable vegetable preparation known as "changa" that combines DMT with MAOIs on some herbs, in such a way that it prolongs the effects of DMT compared to it being vaporized alone, but it is quite exotic and difficult to find.

PHARMACOLOGY AND EFFECTS

Whether vaporized or taken orally accompanied by MAOIs, DMT reaches the blood and crosses the blood-brain barrier to

---

[5] Although MAOIs were used as a treatment for tuberculosis, they later began to be used as the first antidepressants, and today they continue to exist in the pharmacopoeia and are still commercialized.

reach the brain, where it exerts its pharmacological action by binding to the 5-HT2a serotonin neuroreceptor, as well as to 5-HT1a and 5- HT2c.

There has been much speculation about whether the DMT produced by our body has a specific function, with theories relating it to dreams, neuroplasticity, psychological change or near-death experiences, but there is much speculation on this subject and still few certainties.

Psychedelic experiences with vaporized DMT are extremely fast and intense, very visual. The person is immersed in a trance during which they lie down with their eyes closed and without much interaction with the environment.

The experience combines intense kaleidoscopic images, to the point of feeling as if they are astral travelling through galaxies, encountering other "entities," which can

Ayahuasca ceremony at the Takiwasi center, Peru (Takiwasi, CC BY-SA 4.0 <https://creativecommons.org/licenses/by-sa/4.0>, via Wikimedia Commons).

manifest in various forms and appearances. A good example of these images are the paintings and designs of the artist Alex Grey.

Instead, oral ayahuasca experiences are more similar to those that psilocybin can induce, except for a greater tendency to nausea and differences in intensity and duration of effects. The ceremonial context in which the consumption of ayahuasca is carried out also endows the experience with a spatial imaginary.

Dosage

Without a chemical analysis, the dosage of ayahuasca is very complicated to predict, because it is not a "standardized" preparation – there are many different preparations, with different concentrations of DMT, and its potency is also greatly influenced by its concentration of MAOIs.

On the other hand, if it is pure vaporized DMT, its dosage is easier to establish. Nevertheless, it will also depend a lot on the efficiency of the vaporization process, in which, depending on the temperature applied, the molecule may not be able to vaporize at all or it could burn.

Doses	DMT - Vaporized
Minimal Psychoactive	2 mg
Low	10 mg
Medium	20 mg
High	40 mg
Very high (higher risks)	> 60 mg

There are many plants that contain DMT, below a list of some of them and their concentrations:

Plant DMT Content	% DMT in Dry Weight
Jurem (*Mimosa hostilis*)	1.7 % in root bark
Chacruna (*Psychotria viridis*)	0.1 % to 0.6 % in leaves
Yopo (*Anadenanthera spp.*)	0.16 % DMT in the pods, along with 7.4 % bufotenin and 0.04 % 5-MeO-DMT
Giant reed (*Arundo donax*)	0.0057 % DMT along with 0.0023 % 5-MeO-MMT, 0.026 % bufotenine and 5-MeO-NMT
Bundleflower (*Desmanthus illinoensis*)	0.34 % DMT in the root bark
Chagropanga (*Diplopterys cabrerana*)	1.3 % DMT, and trace amounts of 5-MeO-DMT, bufotenine, and methyltryptamine
Harding grass (*Phalaris aquatica*)	0.1 % DMT, 0.2 % 5-MeO-DMT, and 0.005 % bufotenin.
Reed canary grass (*Phalaris arundinacea*)	0.12 % DMT
Phalaris tuberosa	0.02 % DMT
Salparni (*Desmodium gangeticum*)	0.057 % DMT in root and leaves

Duration

There are marked differences between the duration of effects of vaporized DMT compared to the oral route in the form of ayahuasca.

Durations	DMT - Vaporized	Ayahuasca - Oral
Total Duration	5 - 20 minutes	4 - 6 hours
Absorption / Latency	20 - 40 seconds	20 - 60 minutes
Rise	1 - 3 minutes	30 - 45 minutes
Plateau	2 - 8 minutes	1 - 2 hours
Descent	1 - 6 minutes	1 - 2 hours
Residual / "Afterglow"	10 - 60 minutes	1 - 8 hours

Specific Risks

In addition to the typical psychological risks of psychedelic substances that arise, fundamentally, from the context in which they are carried out and from the psycho-emotional state of the person who consumes them, ayahuasca tends to produce nausea and vomiting. It also presents additional physical risks related, especially, to its content of monoamine oxidase inhibitors (MAOIs), since these substances can cause sweating, palpitation, tremors, tachycardia, and serious symptoms such as hypertensive crises and hyperpyrexia (high fever).

This presence of MAOIs also makes it very dangerous to consume it if you are being treated with other medications, especially antidepressant psychoactive drugs; or combined with foods rich in tyramine such as mature cheeses, nuts, chicken liver, or fish such as herring and sardines, which can cause hypertensive crises. This is another reason why people who are going to take it undergo a diet before and after.

Despite a well prepared "set & setting", sometimes you could encounter difficult experiences (commonly called "bad trips") where you may feel anxiety, fear, paranoia, confusion, agitation, space-time disorientation, a feeling of "going crazy", but they are usually transient and rarely last beyond the pharmacological effect of the substance. In any case, there are also strategies described in the section called "Bad trip management and other psychedelic emergencies," in the "Psychedelic Risk Reduction" chapter of this book, that can help.

Although very rare, some deaths related to the consumption of ayahuasca have been reported, especially in people with other treatments or heart problems.

Aside from the risk of falls (and pipe burns), which makes consumption sitting or lying down safer, experiences with DMT can be so intense that they could be unpleasant for some people.

At the psychiatric level, the consumption of DMT or ayahuasca by people with a propensity for psychosis, bipolarity, schizophrenia or a family history of any of these, can increase the risk of triggering episodes. In very rare cases it can cause flashbacks or hallucinogen persisting perception disorder (HPPD).

5-MeO-DMT ("Toad")

Definition, Composition and Origin

5-MeO-DMT (abbreviation for 5-MetOxi-N,N-DiMethylTryptamine, also called the "God Molecule") is a psychedelic molecule, from the chemical family of tryptamines (they have similarities to serotonin) and of natural origin. It is found in some plants (such as *Anadenanthera peregrina*, "Yopo") and, along with bufotenin (5-HO-DMT) and others, in the glandular secretions of at least one species of toad, the Bufo Alvarius (*Incilius alvarius*), which inhabits the Sonoran desert region, in Mexico.

Applications

Its use, which has traditionally been ceremonial and religious although less so than that of plants, currently endures and has become very popular recently, given its potency and legal status in many countries, although it is still rare to see it in recreational environments, as it happens with extracted DMT.

At the moment, there is little clinical research on its possible therapeutic uses, but some observational studies have reported improvements in symptoms of depression and anxiety disorders among its users, and it has also been shown to stimulate brain neuroplasticity, which is encouraging the design of clinical studies with the substance.

Forms and Routes of Administration

5-MeO-DMT can be found pure, normally of synthetic origin, or accompanied by other substances, in the case of the natural glandular secretions of the *Bufo alvarius* toad.

Given the ecological problems involved in extracting 5-MeO-DMT from toad glands and its greater potential toxicity in this format, as it contains other bufotoxins,

Incilius alvarius toad, also known as *Bufo Alvarius* (Holger Krisp, CC BY 3.0 <https://creativecommons.org/licenses/by/3.0>, via Wikimedia Commons).

the consumption of synthetic or isolated 5-MeO-DMT is currently more and more widespread.

As with crystallized DMT, 5-MeO-DMT is usually vaporized and inhaled, although it can also be snorted.

Pharmacology and Effects

Whether vaporized or snorted, 5-MeO-DMT reaches the blood and enters the brain, where it binds primarily to serotonin neuroreceptors 5-HT2a and 5-HT1a. In addition, it has monoamine oxidase inhibitory action, which allows it to prolong its own action but could increase its risk profile.

As with DMT, the experience with 5-MeO-DMT is brief but very intense, more so than with DMT, to the point that this molecule is considered the most powerful of all psychedelics, also having a longer duration than DMT.

If DMT is known as the "Spirit Molecule," 5-MeO-DMT is considered the "God Molecule," although the latter term is often applied to both substances.

Dosage

The dosage will depend on the route of consumption, the doses being higher by snorting than by pulmonary route (vaporized).

Doses	5-MeO-DMT – Vaporized	5-MeO-DMT – Snorted
Minimal Psychoactive	1 - 2 mg	3 - 5 mg
Low	2 - 5 mg	5 - 8 mg
Medium	5 - 10 mg	8 - 15 mg
High	10 - 20 mg	15 - 25 mg
Very high (higher risks)	> 20 mg	> 25 mg

Duration

There is an important difference between snorting it and taking it via pulmonary route (vaporized).

Duration of Effects	Vaporized	Snorted
Total Duration	20 - 40 minutes	2 - 3 hours
Absorption / Latency	5 - 60 seconds	1 - 10 minutes
Rise	30 - 60 seconds	2 - 5 minutes
Plateau	5 - 15 minutes	10 - 40 minutes
Descent	10 - 20 minutes	30 - 60 minutes
Residual / "Afterglow"	15 - 60 minutes	1 - 3 hours

Specific Risks

The risks of 5-MeO-DMT vary if it is derived from the isolated molecule or the secretions of the toad, since the latter contains other substances, called bufotoxins, which can make its consumption more dangerous.

In addition to the typical psychological risks of psychedelic substances, which fundamentally arise from the context in which they are used and from the psycho-emotional state of the person who uses them, the bufotoxins of 5-MeO-DMT (from toad secretions), can be cardiotoxic, and some deaths have been reported due to this form of ingestion, especially in people with heart disease or who mixed it with other psychoactive substances or drugs.

Likewise, the 5-MeO-DMT molecule itself, both isolated and in its toad secretion form, has some inhibition effects on monoamine oxidase, so its combination with other psychoactive substances, such as stimulants, antidepressants or other psychoactive drugs, can be dangerous.

Aside from the risk of falls (and pipe burns), which makes consumption sitting or lying down safer, experiences with 5-MeO-DMT can be intense enough to be unpleasant. At the psychiatric level, the consumption of 5-MeO-DMT by people with a propensity for psychosis, bipolarity, schizophrenia or a family history of any of these, can increase the risk of triggering episodes. In very rare cases it can cause flashbacks or hallucinogen persisting perception disorder (HPPD).

MESCALINE ("CACTUS")

DEFINITION, COMPOSITION AND ORIGIN

Mescaline (3,4,5-trimethoxy-β-phenylethylamine) is a psychedelic substance of the chemical family of phenylethylamines (it has similarities with dopamine) and of natural origin (although very few psychedelics of this chemical family are of natural origin). It is found in several species of cacti, such as peyote (*Lophophora williamsii*, which also contains other psychoactives such as pellotine), San Pedro (*Echinopsis pachanoi*), the Peruvian Torch (*Peruvian Echinopsis*), and other cacti. It can also be found in some species of the legume family.

APPLICATIONS

Mescaline is a substance with a long history of ceremonial use, especially in Native American cultures, and was popular in some circles before the advent of LSD; but in today's Western World it does not have much presence and is viewed as exotic. It is credited with nearly 6,000 years of use and is considered one of the oldest psychedelic substances used by man.

Its therapeutic use was studied in the 1960s, along with those of LSD and psilocybin, but given its pharmacological characteristics, it did not generate a clinical interest as strong as other substances.

Currently, unlike other classic psychedelics, there is not much research on its clinical potential, but its use is still legal for Native Americans in the U.S. In the US its use is still legal for Native Americans.

FORMS AND ROUTES OF ADMINISTRATION

Mescaline can be found in the peyote and San Pedro cacti. Peyote can be eaten directly (it has edible "buttons") or prepared as a tea or other decoction. On the other hand, the San Pedro is a tall columnar cactus with a lower concentration of mescaline, so it is necessary to consume a larger portion, usually prepared in the form of a decoction of the outer part of its stem, called "wachuma." Both cacti can be dried, or dehydrated, and ground into a powder to make infusions.

Peyote cactus in bloom, Lophophora williamsii (Dav Hir, CC BY-SA 3.0 <https://creativecommons.org/licenses/by-sa/3.0>, via Wikimedia Commons).

Like most psychoactive substances, mescaline can be administered using different routes, but it is mainly ingested orally in the form of peyote or San Pedro, eaten raw, fresh or dried, or in tea form or mixed in a smoothie; usually on an empty stomach to prevent nausea and maximize its absorption and effects.

The San Pedro cactus and the Peruvian Torch (a similar cactus, also containing mescaline) are very easy to find in gardens or for sale in nurseries, florists and garden stores.

Given its long maturation period, the consumption of home-grown peyote is even less common than that of San Pedro, although there are grafting techniques that allow the accelerated growth of peyote on the tip of a San Pedro cactus.

Mescaline can also be found isolated from the cactus, or synthetically, in the form of a salt, both as mescaline sulfate and mescaline hydrochloride. However, it is quite an unusual substance to find and requires large doses compared to other psychedelics.

Pharmacology and Effects

Like most psychedelics, mescaline enters the blood through the digestive tract and reaches the brain, where it binds to various serotonergic receptors, but in particular to the serotonin 5-HT2a receptor, which is considered to be primarily responsible for its psychedelic effects. It also binds to other receptors such as 5-HT2c, and interacts with dopaminergic receptors in a special way, due to its phenethylamine structure, different from that of other classic psychedelics such as LSD or psilocybin, but its effects on this system are even less well known.

The physical effects of mescaline are few, mainly the dilation of the pupils and the increase in heart rate and blood pressure, especially in high doses.

The psychological effects of mescaline are numerous and highly dependent on variables such as dose, person, and context. The most characteristic are significant changes in sensory perceptions, cognition and consciousness.

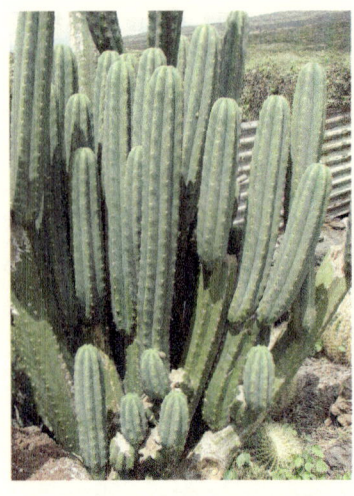

San Pedro cactus Echinopsis pachanoi (Forest & Kim Starr, CC BY 3.0 <https://creativecommons.org/licenses/by/3.0>, via Wikimedia Commons).

Changes in sensory perceptions can manifest visually, with color enhancement, distortions in the shapes and movements of things, and colorful kaleidoscopic visions with eyes closed. Synesthesia (blending of senses, such as "smelling colors" or "seeing sounds") and increased tactile, thermal and tingling sensations may appear. Hearing disturbances can lead to an increased appreciation of music and sounds. There can also be a lot of laughter.

Cognitive alterations can be perceived as positive and pleasant or negative and difficult, and it is common for psychedelic experiences to include good stages and more difficult moments, which is why they are called "trips."

Desired effects of this substance include (but are not limited to): euphoria, sense of perception, enlightenment, synesthesia, new ways of thinking about oneself and others, deep feelings of love and well-being, changes in the perception of time and space, spiritual experiences, visual hallucinations (but generally distinguished from reality), etc.

It commonly brings up biographical and personal content, including relationships with significant people in your life. In high doses and controlled contexts, mescaline can induce mystical experiences, with the dissolution of personal limits and the ego, with oceanic feelings, which can be experienced with great peace and transcendence, but can also generate anxiety and even fear.

Mescaline is reputed to produce psychedelic experiences that are more pleasant or have fewer difficult stages than other psychedelics, and a more luminous, with oneiric[6] quality.

Dosage

Mescaline is not a very potent psychedelic, so doses are considerably large compared to others, hovering around a third of a gram (300 mg), but it is rarely taken in isolated or purified form, so amounts depend very much on the age of the peyote or how the San Pedro "wachuma" has been prepared. It is usually measured in number of glasses.

Cacti With Mescaline	% mescaline - fresh weight	% mescaline - dry weight
Peyote (*Lophophora williamsii*)	0.4 %	3 - 6 %
Lophophora decipiens	No data	3 %
San Pedro (*Echinopsis pachanoi*)	0.12 %	0.33 - 4 %
Peruvian torch (*Peruvian echinopsis*)	No data	0.24 - 0.82 %
Bolivian Torch (*Echinopsis lageniformis*)	No data	0.56 %
Echinopsis puquiensis	No data	0.11 % - 0.50 %
Echinopsis cuzcoensis	No data	0.14 % - 0.22 %
Echinopsis schoenii	No data	0.14 % - 0.22 %

---

[6] Pertaining to dreams.

Dosages for pure mescaline or cactus mescaline typically fall within these ranges:

Doses	Mescaline - Oral
Microdose	< 25 mg
Minimal Psychoactive	50 - 100 mg
Low	100 - 200 mg
Medium	200 - 400 mg
High	400 - 600 mg
Very high (higher risks)	> 600 mg

DURATION

Duration Of Effects	Mescaline - Oral
Total Duration	8 - 14 hours
Absorption / Latency	45 - 90 minutes
Rise	60 - 120 minutes
Plateau	4 - 6 hours
Descent	2 - 3 hours
Residual / "Afterglow"	6 - 36 hours

These times are approximate and will depend largely on the particularities of the dose, purity, person and context.

SPECIFIC RISKS

Like other classic psychedelics, mescaline has a very low level of toxicity and no addictive potential, it could have a greater risk of elevating blood pressure than other classic psychedelics, but this risk is low in healthy people. However, it presents risks on a psychological level, which arise fundamentally from the context of use (setting) and the psycho-emotional state of the person (set). They are especially high in people with psychiatric disorders or propensity to them.

All psychedelics can produce sensations of dizziness or nausea at the onset of effects, but cacti with mescaline can be especially prone to it, especially if they are eaten raw (and not as a tea) and on a full stomach, which is why it is usually consumed fasting for at least 4-6 hours.

Despite a well prepared "set & setting", sometimes you could encounter difficult experiences (commonly called "bad trips") where you may feel anxiety, fear, paranoia, confusion, agitation, space-time disorientation, or feel like you're "going crazy", but they are usually transitory and rarely last beyond the pharmacological effect of the substance. Eating small amounts can help reduce these effects. In any case, there are also strategies described in the section called "Bad trip management and other psychedelic emergencies", in the "Psychedelic Risk Reduction" chapter of this book, that can help.

Mixing psychedelics with other psychoactive substances increases psychological risks and can add physical risks. This is especially true for mescaline, which has more interactions, especially with stimulants, MAOIs, and other drugs.

At the psychiatric level, the consumption of mescaline by people with a propensity for psychosis, bipolarity, schizophrenia or a family history of any these, can increase the risk of triggering episodes. In very rare cases it can cause flashbacks or hallucinogen persisting perception disorder (HPPD).

IBOGAINE

Definition, Composition and Origin

Ibogaine (12-Methoxybogamine) is a substance with psychedelic and dissociative properties, from the chemical family of tryptamines (they have similarities with serotonin) and of natural origin. It is found in plants of the family *Apocynaceae* as the *Tabernanthe iboga, african voacanga* and *Tabernaemontana undulata*. In its natural form, it is usually accompanied by other alkaloids such as ibogaline and ibogamine.

Applications

It has a long history of traditional ritual and religious use in Africa, most notably in the Bwiti region, in Gabon.

Some uses of ibogaine have included the treatment of asthenia, as a stimulant, and for the treatment of depression, fatigue, and recovery from infectious diseases.

It is a very rare substance in Western countries, where there are no known uses in the recreational field, although it is being investigated for its therapeutic uses in the treatment of addictions with very promising results. This has been an ongoing interest since the 1960s, when it was shown to have properties to treat physical and psychological addiction to opiates (heroin, morphine, fentanyl, etc.)

Forms and Routes of Administration

Ibogaine is usually consumed orally, using the bark of the iboga root (*Tabernanthe iboga*), a tree that grows in West Africa, and is traditionally used in rituals and ceremonies. Ibogaine, in its natural state, is usually accompanied by other substances with psychoactive effects that add to its own, as is the case with almost all natural sources of psychedelics, such as mushrooms, ayahuasca, etc. In fact, the root bark of the *Tabernanthe iboga* contains the alkaloids ibogaine, ibogaline and ibogamine.

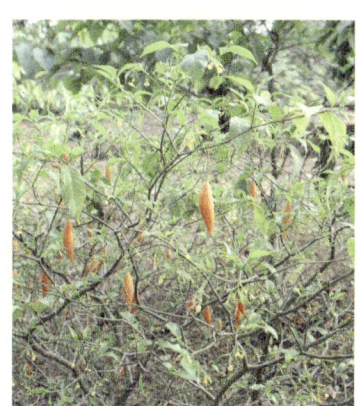

Tabernanthe iboga bush (Marco Schmidt[1], CC BY-SA 2.5 <https://creativecommons.org/licenses/by-sa/2.5>, via Wikimedia Commons).

PHARMACOLOGY AND EFFECTS

Ibogaine is absorbed through the digestive system and reaches the blood, where it is slowly metabolized in the liver, transforming into noribogaine and other metabolites[7], some of which may be psychoactive. Noribogaine enters the brain, where it acts on numerous receptor systems, including the dopaminergic, serotonergic (5-HT2A neuroreceptor, among others), nicotinic, GABAergic, and muscarinic systems. Some studies have found evidence that ibogaine can interrupt opioid dependence mechanisms.

Unlike most classic psychedelics, ibogaine's effects are both psychological and physical, since they also manifest in the cardiovascular system.

On a psychological level, it combines stimulating effects with psychedelic effects at high doses.

In addition to the typical psychedelic effects, it induces a greater dreamlike and floating sensation, reevaluation of memories, etc.

---

[7] Substances that are generated in the body's process of transformation or elimination of a substance.

Iboga (DM Trott, CC BY-SA 4.0 <https://creativecommons.org/licenses/by-sa/4.0>, via Wikimedia Commons).

Dosage

Ibogaine typically accounts for 1 % of the dry weight of the root bark of the iboga tree (*Tabernanthe iboga*).

Ibogaine is just an alkaloid from the iboga plant and is used almost exclusively in medical settings to treat addiction. A typical dose is 15 to 20 mg per kg of the person's weight, which is logically much less than in its natural unextracted version.

It is a substance that has not yet been studied extensively and, therefore, it is very difficult to know its exact dosage, but based on reports of use, these would be its approximate dosage levels:

Doses	Ibogaine - Oral
Minimal Psychoactive	100 mg
Low	200 - 400 mg
Medium	400 - 600 mg
High	600 - 800 mg
Very high (higher risks)	> 800 mg

Duration

It is considered a very long-lasting natural psychedelic, with reports of high doses lasting for up to 24 hours.

Duration Of Effects	Ibogaine - Oral
Total Duration	8 - 12 hours
Absorption / Latency	45 - 120 minutes
Rise	60 - 120 minutes
Plateau	2 - 4 hours
Descent	4 - 6 hours
Residual / "Afterglow"	12 - 24 hours

Specific Risks

As with most psychedelics, its risks are fundamentally psychological, closely related to the variables of the context in which it is consumed (*setting*) and the psycho-emotional state of the person (*set*). However, unlike other classics such as psilocybin or LSD, ibogaine does have cardiovascular risks, since it can cause a decrease in heart rate (bradycardia) and prolong cardiac QT intervals. Therefore, it should be avoided by people with a history of arrhythmias, heart attacks, heart operations, murmurs, etc., and why it is advisable to undergo an electrocardiogram and stress test before consuming it, avoiding very high doses, to reduce risks as much as possible.

It can have pharmacological interactions with foods or drugs that are metabolized by the CYP450 enzyme, so its consumption should be avoided with any substance or food of this type, as it could pose additional risks.

Despite a well prepared "set & setting", sometimes you could encounter difficult experiences (commonly called "bad trips") where you may feel anxiety, fear, paranoia, confusion, agitation, space-time disorientation, or feel like you're "going crazy", but they are usually transitory and rarely last beyond the pharmacological effect of the substance. In any case, there are also strategies described in the section called "Bad trip management and other psychedelic emergencies," in the "Psychedelic Risk Reduction" chapter of this book, that can help.

At the psychiatric level, the consumption of ibogaine by people with a propensity for psychosis, bipolarity, schizophrenia or a family history of any of these, can increase the risk of triggering episodes. On very rare occasions it could produce flashbacks or hallucinogen persisting perception disorder (HPPD).

MDMA ("Ecstasy")

Definition, Composition and Origin

MDMA (abbreviation for 3,4-MethyleneDioxy Met Amphetamine), better known as "ecstasy", "Molly", "X", "E", "hug drug" or " love drug." It is a synthetic psychoactive substance with entactogenic-empathogenic, stimulant and atypical psychedelic effects, from the chemical family of phenylethylamines (which structurally resemble dopamine).

Applications

Since its popularization in the early 1980s, MDMA has had psychotherapeutic use (which was interrupted and forced underground by its prohibition in the mid-1980s) and recreational use, closely associated with the rave culture.

It is currently a very popular recreational drug, especially in clubs, music festivals and in the electronic music scene. But also in more intimate settings, among couples and friends.

Research into its therapeutic properties in the context of MDMA-assisted psychotherapy is very promising and growing, with a Phase III study for its use in PTSD treatments being successfully piloted in several countries, and very close to being accepted for medical use, and many other potential uses in research such as: alcoholism, couples therapy, social anxiety in people with autism, etc.

FORMS AND ROUTES OF ADMINISTRATION

MDMA is usually found in two main forms: pills or crystal (known as "molly").

Like most drugs, MDMA could be consumed via different routes, but it is mainly taken orally, in the form of crystal or designer pills, or inhaled in powder form.

In Europe, the purity of these crystals is usually around 80 % MDMA by weight, making it a fairly pure substance. Outside of Europe, purity tends to be lower and may appear mixed with some psychoactive adulterants.

Ecstasy pills (MDMA) (Photo via ravejungle.com).

As for its presentation in the form of pills, they usually come in different colors and shapes, with different logos, but with a highly variable concentration of MDMA. In recent years, their average MDMA content has increased considerably, currently exceeding 150 mg in many cases and 200 mg in some, which makes it more dangerous to consume them whole, being less risky to consume them in quarters or halves.

In some contexts, MDMA is snorted to accelerate its onset of effects, and even injected, like in Chemsex[8] contexts sometimes, although this greatly increases its risks and changes its effect profile.

Pharmacology and Effects

Whether taken orally or snorted, MDMA reaches the blood and gains access to the brain. MDMA acts mainly as a serotonin, norepinephrine and dopamine releasing agent in the brain, increasing their concentration in neuronal synapses, and also acts as a reuptake inhibitor of these three neurotransmitters, especially serotonin, facilitating their accumulation. It also increases the concentration of the hormonal neurotransmitter oxytocin, related to bonding, trust or sociability.

MDMA also has weak agonist activity at serotonin 5-HT1 and 5-HT2 receptors, the latter closely related to its mild psychedelic effects, which are more noticeable at high doses but fall short of a psychedelic classic like psilocybin or LSD, which is why it is considered a semi-psychedelic or atypical psychedelic.

At a systemic level, these effects increase the activation of the prefrontal cortex (responsible for executive functions, among other things) and reduce the activation of the amygdala (the brain's fear response center), activating reward pathways.

These mechanisms promote feelings of happiness, love, emotionality, and positivity, along with increased empathy,

---

[8] Leisure practice that combines long sessions of sex with high drug use, sometimes intravenously, notably increasing the risks that may be associated when both practices are done separately.

self-esteem, and self-acceptance. The desired effects of this substance also include euphoria, relaxation, tactile pleasure, music appreciation, sexual arousal, energy, etc.

DOSAGE

There are several ways to dose crystal/powder MDMA, but the general rule of thumb is to take between 1 and 2 mg per kilo of the person's weight, with 1 mg per kilo being a low dose, 1.5 mg per kilo a medium dose, and 2 mg per kilo a high dose. For example, the dose for a 70kg person would range from 70 mg (low dose), 100 mg (medium dose), to 140 mg (high dose), depending on your prior tolerance and the intensity of experience you seek.

But, as a general rule, the doses that best balance the positive effects against the risks are in the range of 80-120 mg, with 120 mg being the usual dose used in MDMA-assisted psychotherapy in highly controlled settings.

Doses	Pure MDMA - Oral
Minimal Psychoactive	25 mg
Low	25 – 75 mg
Medium	75 – 125 mg
High	125 – 150 mg
Very high (higher risks)	> 150 mg

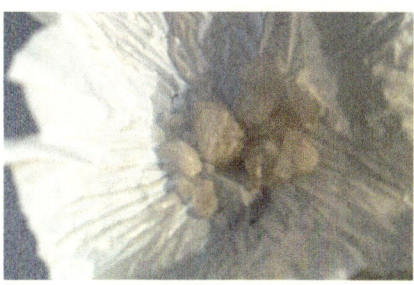

MDMA in crystals (AnonymousUnknown author, Public domain, via Wikimedia Commons).

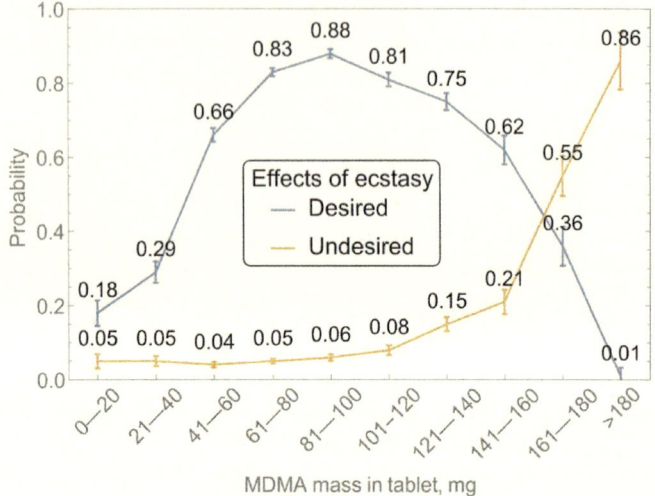

The dosage of MDMA that maximizes the positive effects, without greatly increasing the risks, is around 80–100 mg. (Linking the pharmacological content of ecstasy tablets to the subjective experiences of drug users. Brunt T. M., Koeter M. W., Niesink R. J., van den Brink W., CC BY-SA 4.0 <https://creativecommons.org/licenses/by-sa/4.0>, via Wikimedia Commons).

If you take MDMA in pill form, due to the high dosage of modern pills (over 150 mg in many cases, and over 250 mg in some cases), it is always less risky to try a quarter and wait for the effects before deciding whether to take another quarter.

DURATION

If taken orally, its effects take 30 to 60 minutes to appear (or longer, depending on stomach contents), peak in 1.5 to 2.5 hours, and last for a total of 3 to 6 hours, depending very much on the dose consumed, the body characteristics and the tolerance of the user. If snorted, all of these times are shortened, but the subjective effects are generally considered less positive.

Duration Of Effects	MDMA – Oral
Total Duration	3 - 6 hours
Absorption / Latency	30 - 60 minutes
Rise	15 - 30 minutes
Plateau	90 - 150 minutes
Descent	60 - 90 minutes
Residual / "Afterglow"	12 - 48 hours

Specific Risks and Risk Reduction Strategies

Although at moderate doses and in physically and psychologically healthy people, MDMA (ecstasy) is considered quite safe and generally produces very positive experiences, it has more bodily risks than classic psychedelics, given its stimulating profile. At high doses or in people with health problems, it can pose cardiovascular risks (such as heart attacks, strokes, arrhythmia, tachycardia, high blood pressure), dehydration, hyperthermia (even heatstroke), stimulant psychosis, hyponatremia[9], and others that may derive from the combination with other substances.

Specifically, the risks to watch out for are:
- Dehydration: preventable if you consume water (or isotonic drinks) on a regular basis, avoiding the consumption of other dehydrating agents such as alcohol.
- Hyperthermia: due to its stimulating properties, the effects on the serotonergic system and the increase in the metabolic rate, the body temperature could increase a lot, generating a risk of heatstroke in adverse conditions.

---

[9] Hyponatremia is a medical emergency, related to a drop in sodium in the body, which occurs very rarely, and can be prevented by avoiding excessive consumption of water and drinking electrolyte drinks.

- Hyponatremia: Drinking too much water can affect the balance of sodium and other minerals in the body, and in large amounts, water can be toxic and even deadly.
- Hangover, "crash" or "mid-week blues": If high doses are used, MDMA hangovers could present as a form of low mood, tiredness, irritability, sadness, strokes, etc. It usually comes on after two or three days (that is why it is called "mid-week blues"), and usually lasts no more than a day or two, but it could last longer depending of the person and dose consumed. Some people use nutritional supplements with 5-HTP (or other serotonin precursors) when the effects of MDMA wear off, to mitigate these hangovers.
- Previous psychiatric disorders: the use of MDMA by people with a propensity for psychosis, bipolarity, schizophrenia or a family history of any of these, can increase the risk of triggering episodes.

Given its markedly positive effects, the risk of having a "bad trip"-type experience is even lower than those of classic psychedelics, hardly ever negative, although in high doses, in unprepared people and in inappropriate contexts, episodes of anxiety, dizziness or discomfort can sometimes occur.

The long-term risks of repeated use of MDMA depend largely on the frequency and doses consumed. A high frequency or high doses can cause psychological disorders, neurotoxicity, cardiovascular diseases and even addiction. The main risks include:
- Depression: Although infrequent, the most common psychological disorder of long-term, repeated high-dose MDMA abuse is depression.
- Neurotoxicity: It has long been debated whether MDMA produces relevant neurotoxicity[10], since its consumption seems to be neurotoxic for serotonergic

---

[10] Many psychoactive substances, both legal and illegalized, can produce neurotoxicity, but usually at low levels in sporadic use of moderate doses.

neurons and induces indirect excitotoxicity[11] on mammalian brains – although the extent of this phenomenon and its long-term impact on human cognition remains unclear. The intake of some antioxidant nutritional supplements together with ecstasy (such as alpha-lipoic acid (ALA), n-acetylcysteine (NAC), acetyl-L-carnitine (ALCAR), vitamins C and E, magnesium, etc.) seem to potentially reduce this risk of neurotoxicity, at least in animals.

- Addiction: Although not on the same level as other pure stimulants, long-term abuse of MDMA may present some risk of psychological and physical addiction.

Due to the high purity of MDMA in recent years (mainly in Europe, the main world productor) there is a risk of overdosing, but there are also risks due to its adulteration in some markets (mainly in the American continent and Australia). So, if you are going to consume MDMA acquired on the black market, it is highly recommended to perform chemical drug testing before consumption. This can be done by a colorimetric reagent test[12], or contacting drug testing services for risk and harm reduction, such as those offered globally by Energy Control[13], DrugsData[14] (formerly EcstasyData) or other local harm reduction organizations.

Mixing MDMA with other psychoactive substances increases its risks. Mixing it with other stimulants (caffeine, cocaine, amphetamines) can be problematic because it can exacerbate their stimulant properties. It can also be risky to mix it with depressants (such as GHB, benzodiazepines, ketamine or cannabis) as they could mask its stimulant effects, which

---

[11] Toxicity that occurs due to the overexcitation of neurons, caused by many stimulants.
[12] Sold *on-line*, especially Marquis, Mecke and Mandelin reagents.
[13] https://energycontrol-international.org/.
[14] https://www.drugsdata.org/.

could lead to an overdose of both – with all the effects, risks and increased amnesia associated to them. Mixing MDMA with alcohol increases its thermal and dehydration risks, as well as being unpleasant, especially at first, with dizziness and nausea, despite being short-lived side effects.

The effects of MDMA can take a long time to kick in (up to 90 minutes or more), especially if taken on a full stomach (not recommended), so it's risky to get impatient and, thinking it is not working, redose before noticing the effects of the first dose. It is a common mistake, and you may discover that you have taken too high a dose when the effects finally kick in, but by then it's too late to change the course.

It's important to be aware of the body temperature and stay cool, especially if dancing. Stimulants in general, but MDMA in particular, can sometimes increase body temperature to dangerous levels. To prevent this and an eventual heatstroke, it is advisable to stay well hydrated with isotonic drinks or water (without overdoing it). Avoid exposing yourself to the sun or wearing too much clothing indoors; take breaks to rest, hydrate and refresh yourself if dancing for long hours, and check from time to time for signs of excessive body temperature. Elevated body temperature also increases the potential for excitotoxicity of stimulants.

In the case of MDMA like other substances, it is important to avoid using it very regularly. Potential harm increases with dose and frequency of use, and tolerance and the risk potential addiction increase as well. In general, it is stated that to reduce the long-term risks of MDMA, it should never be taken more than once a month, and ideally less than once every three to four months. With MDMA and other psychoactive substances, "less is more."

Both snorting and injecting MDMA increase the damage potential of the substance. If snorted, it is important to reduce the dose, powder the substance well to reduce damage to the nose, use a clean tube (avoiding rolled-up bills) and not share it to avoid contagion of respiratory diseases or hepatitis, and finish by cleaning the inside of the nose with saline water.

Very high blood pressure or heart rate, muscle stiffness, very high body temperature, confusion, hallucinations, psychosis, extreme agitation, despondency or unconsciousness... these are all signs of an overdose.

MDMA overdoses are rare, and when they do occur, it is usually moderate, but may be fatal. So, when in doubt, it is always safest to collect as much information as possible about what the person has taken and about any other health conditions they may have, and call emergency services to take care of the situation. But if this is not possible, or while they arrive, it is important to stop the person from taking any other substance, keep them in a safe, cool, calm environment, hydrate them and cool them down if necessary.

If the person is unconscious, it is important not to give them liquids or food, to avoid choking, and keep them in recovery position[15]. If they stop breathing, resuscitation (CPR) should be started. There is no specific antidote for an MDMA overdose, so the general treatment is to monitor the person while the MDMA content in the blood decreases, keeping body temperature in a safe margin or using blood pressure lowering drugs if necessary.

KETAMINE

---

[15] The recovery position, easy to see in any internet search, allows an unconscious person not to choke on their own vomit, if the situation arose.

Definition and Origin

Ketamine (also known as "*Special-K*", "KitKat", "K", or Ketalar®) is a synthetic substance in the psychoactive class of semi-psychedelic or atypical psychedelic dissociatives, and the chemical family of arylcyclohexylamines. It is a synthetic compound that can be sold as a powder or dissolved in liquid in pharmaceutical vial form.

Applications

Since its approval in 1970, it has been widely used as a human and veterinary anesthetic and sold under the brand name Ketalar®, among others. Its recreational use also became popular in the *rave* scene of the 1980s.

Today, ketamine is still widely used in medicine. It is included in the World Health Organization's "Essential Medicines List", a list of the most effective medicines that should be available in any modern health system. The use of ketamine as an anesthetic or analgesic is very common in veterinary medicine, as well as in outpatient emergency medicine or with patients who are at risk with more conventional anesthesia, such as neonates or children. When used as an anesthetic or analgesic, it is usually administered together with a benzodiazepine to minimize its psychedelic effects.

Thanks to being an approved medicine, it was possible to conduct extensive research and use it as an *off-label* medication (drugs prescribed by healthcare providers for non-approved conditions) in various psychedelic-assisted psychotherapy treatments. Recently, a purification of the molecule called esketamine has been authorized for use in the treatment of depression in the form of a nasal spray under the trade name of Spravato®, becoming the first substance with psychedelic effects to be authorized for the treatment of mental disorders.

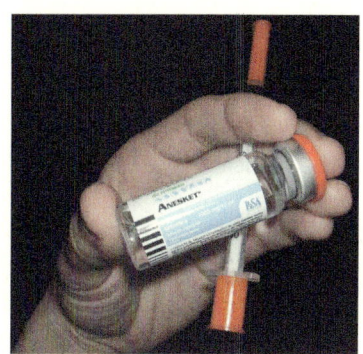

Ketamine vial, in this case for veterinary use (Psychonaught, CC0, via Wikimedia Commons).

FORMS AND ROUTES OF ADMINISTRATION

Ketamine is often found diluted in vials of Ketalar® or other brands for hospital use, or as a bright white powder on the black market.

Like most drugs, ketamine could be consumed via different routes, but in recreational use it is mainly consumed by insufflation or orally, although in clinical settings it is most commonly injected. The new esketamine medication called Spravato® is a nasal spray that is inhaled, similar to snorting it.

Crystallized ketamine (Coaster420, Public domain, via Wikimedia Commons).

Powdered ketamine is often obtained by drying a diluted pharmaceutical preparation, in a process that many people call "cooking", although it is more like "drying."

Pharmacology and Effects

Whether taken orally, through the nose or via injection, Ketamine first enters the bloodstream and then reaches the brain, where it blocks NMDA glutamate receptors (leading to loss of sensation, difficulty moving, and eventually the notorious state known as "K- hole"), and acts on many other neuroreceptors at different doses. Since it does not appear to have any relevant action on the 5-HT2a receptor, it is considered an atypical psychedelic substance.

It is a substance with a wide range of effects depending on the dose consumed, but in general terms the desired effects of this substance include (but are not limited to): dissociation, depersonalization, derealization, distortion of time and space, relaxation, insight, hallucinations, euphoria, sensation of floating, visual distortions, etc.

Ketamine in high doses induces psychedelic-like experiences, called "falling into a k-hole" (or simply "k-hole"), which could be treated in a similar way to a psychedelic experience, taking into account the loss of tactile sensitivity and motor control, very present in the specific case of ketamine. The experience of a "k-hole" can be desired and pleasant for some people but very unpleasant for others.

Dosage

Unlike what happens with classic psychedelics, the dosage of this substance is very delicate since its effects can be highly variable, making it a very important issue to take care of.

Doses	Ketamine - Snorted	Ketamine - Oral
Minimal Psychoactive	5 mg	50 mg
Low	10 - 30 mg	50 - 100 mg
Medium	30 - 60 mg	100 - 200 mg
High	60 - 100 mg	200 - 300 mg
Very high (higher risks)	> 100 mg	> 300 mg

DURATION

Taken orally, its effects take 10 to 30 minutes to become noticeable (depending on the contents of the stomach), with peaks reached in 45 to 90 minutes and a total duration of effects of 2 to 2.5 hours, depending very much on the dose consumed. Snorted, its effects take 5 to 10 minutes to become noticeable, peaking at 30 to 60 minutes and a total duration of effects of 1 to 1.5 hours, depending largely on the dose consumed.

Duration Of Effects	Ketamine - Snorted	Ketamine - Oral
Total Duration	1 - 1.5 hours	2 - 2.5 hours
Absorption/Latency	2 - 5 minutes	10 - 30 minutes
Rise	5 - 10 minutes	5 - 20 minutes
Plateau	30 - 60 minutes	45 - 90 minutes
Descent	3 - 6 hours	3 - 6 hours
Residual / "Afterglow"	2 - 12 hours	4 - 8 hours

SPECIFIC RISKS

Similarly to classic psychedelics like LSD or psilocybin, ketamine has very low toxicity even at high doses, and is in fact widely used in medicine at these doses. Therefore, physical and physiological safety is generally not a concern at medium doses, unless the person has accidentally taken a very high dose that could affect breathing. Certain activities that require coordination and reflexes such as moving about, driving, moving things, etc., should also be avoided under its effects, as the risk of falling or having an accident increases.

Likewise, because it causes a slight increase in blood pressure and subjects may undergo intense experiences that can generate anxiety, people with a history of cardiovascular disease should refrain from using it.

The possibility of having a difficult experience or bad trip does exist, although it can be greatly minimized with a carefully prepared "set and setting." Long-lasting psychological difficulties from such an experience (negative trauma, anxiety or long-lasting fear) are very rare, but could occur especially if the substance is taken in high doses, for the first time and in highly uncontrolled environments, without adequately preparing their "set and setting."

Although the risk of psychiatric complications is low, the use of ketamine by people with a propensity for psychosis, bipolarity, schizophrenia, or a family history of any of these, can increase the risk of triggering episodes, especially at high doses. It can be difficult to know if someone is at risk of a psychotic reaction, especially if you are still very young, which is one of the reasons that the use of psychedelics is generally less risky in older and more mature people. In very rare cases it can cause flashbacks or hallucinogen persisting perception disorder (HPPD).

Although the long-term risks of ketamine use depend largely on the frequency of use and the doses consumed, there are some specific risks such as addiction[16], urinary and bladder problems, neurotoxicity and withdrawal syndrome. Taking it despite underlying mental conditions such as psychosis,

---

[16] Of the psychedelic substances, ketamine is the one with the greatest addictive risk.

bipolarity, or psychotic disorders could worsen the course of these disorders and contribute negatively to long-term outcome.

The neurotoxicity of ketamine is still debated, but it appears that it could produce some indirect excitotoxicity at very high doses and frequency of use. However, no long-term cognitive impairments from this seem to have been found, and short-term cognitive impairments seem to recover when use of ketamine is stopped. But it is always a good thing to follow the "precautionary principle" and avoid prolonged use or high doses.

Psychedelic Risk & Harm Reduction Strategies

Risks and Harm Reduction

The use of drugs, whether legal (such as alcohol), controlled for medical use (such as amphetamines) or illegalized (such as ecstasy), always carry health risks – ALWAYS. These risks can be higher or lower depending on many variables and, although the only way to completely avoid them is to not consume them, this does not mean that this is the only option, or that there aren't ways of using them with less risk. Therefore, there are strategies that reduce these risks as much as possible for those who are going to consume them.

Harm reduction (also called risk reduction) is an approach that accepts that, despite the laws and public health campaigns, drug use (of legal or illegalized psychoactive substances) is present in our society, so instead of judging it, offers a set of information materials, practices and tools to reduce as much as possible the risks associated with drug use, for people who use them.

So far, we have mainly talked about the use of psychedelics in clinical therapeutic contexts and under professional control, but we must not forget that today the majority of people who use psychedelic drugs or any other class (whether legal, medicinal or illegalized), are doing it outside of the realm of clinics and laboratories.

Although they expose themselves to risks, as with any other drugs, it is not because they seek to harm their health, but rather because they obtain some benefit from their use (pleasure, fun, therapeutic benefit, self-knowledge, evasion,

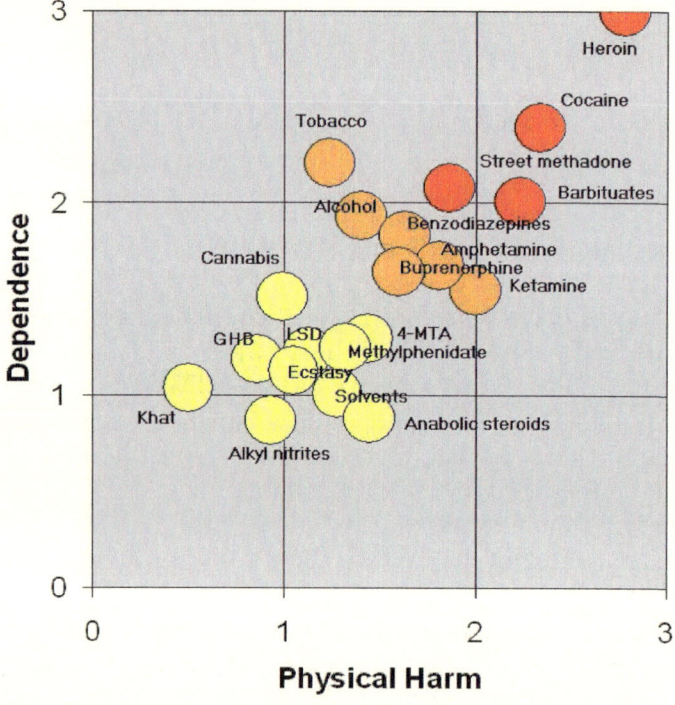

Comparative table of the risks of different substances due to their physical damage and addictiveness, most psychedelics are in the lower part of both. (*A rational scale to assess the harm of drugs. Data source is the March 24, 2007 article: David Nutt, Leslie A. King, William Saulsbury, Colin Blakemore. "Development of a rational scale to assess the harm of drugs of potential misuse," The Lancet 2007; 369:1047-1053.) (Apartment2, Public domain, via Wikimedia Commons).*

socialization, etc.), and, in their opinion, these benefits are worth the risk. Although propaganda has led us to believe for years that any drug use that is not legal or medicinal is "bad," science is showing that this is not always the case, and in some cases the potential benefits may indeed outweigh the risks. Furthermore, putting all psychoactive substances in the same bag is a big mistake. Not only are their effects (and potential uses) very different, but their risk profiles are also quite dissimilar, even opposite, and therefore they deserve a more individualized evaluation, as we could see in the previous table of risks of addiction and toxicity.

In addition, many of the dangers of the use of psychoactive substances are not intrinsic to the substance itself but are usually linked more to the lack of information about the risks and the strategies used to reduce them, and the context of its use. This is because many of these substances are considered a social taboo and, unfortunately, this type of information about their risks is not usually provided, as it is for pharmaceutical drugs in the form of patient information leaflets. What the evidence shows us[1] is that, if a well-informed person freely decides to consume a substance (whether legal or illegalized), and they have access to all the information and tools available to reduce those risks, without necessarily giving up on the effects they seek with consumption, the person will generally apply these strategies and they will work, even though this is a field in which there is still much to be researched.

To give an example from a recreational standpoint, a person that is well-informed would not be exposed to the same risks when taking MDMA (ecstasy) at a music festival as a person who is not. The first person would take it only once a year, with trusted friends, analyzing the purity of

---

[1] Alison Ritter and Jacqui Cameron, "A review of the efficacy and effectiveness of harm reduction strategies for alcohol, tobacco and illicit drugs," *Drug and Alcohol Review* 25, no. 6 (November 2006): 611-24.

the substance to adjust the dose and avoid toxic adulterants, consume a moderate dose according to their body weight, hydrate themselves, not mix it with alcohol or other drugs, not redose[2] and would take breaks from dancing to allow their body to cool down. The second person would take high doses of the substance, no previous analysis, mixing it with alcohol and other drugs, surrounded by complete strangers, redosing several times throughout the night, spending hours in the sun, taking no breaks from dancing, and doing it several times a month. Although in both cases they expose themselves to risks, there is a huge difference between the level of risk present in the first case compared to the second. Unfortunately, most uninformed recreational ecstasy users match the second profile more than the first.

There is no doubt that all drugs have risks, but that does not mean that they always cause harm, and in this sense, they can be more dangerous or less dangerous (coffee does not have the same risk as methamphetamine). However, as Paracelsus said: "the dose makes the poison," so all substances, psychoactive or not, can be harmful, and even lethal, depending on the dose or the context, and also on the person taking it. Whether they finally are or not will depend on a series of factors that we are now going to see in this chapter in relation to psychedelics. The damage caused by different drugs, to individuals and to society, does not only come from the substance itself (reflected in the previous graph) but also from the context of consumption. Note that ecstasy and classic psychedelics are usually in the lowest levels of harm of any psychoactive drug, legal or illegalized.

Although risk reduction is considered a part of harm reduction, they are also considered two ends of the same

---

[2] Redosing is taking a second, subsequent dose of the same substance.

spectrum. Risk reduction encompasses strategies that can reduce risk and prevent harm from occurring in populations with occasional or experimental use of psychoactive substances (adequately prepared and controlled psychedelic experiences need not produce any physical or psychological harm), while harm reduction is more focused on the population with "problematic" use, where harm is already occurring, but tries to minimize it (such as syringe exchange programs among the population that regularly consumes intravenous heroin, generally with associated harm, but in order to prevent the spread of infectious diseases).

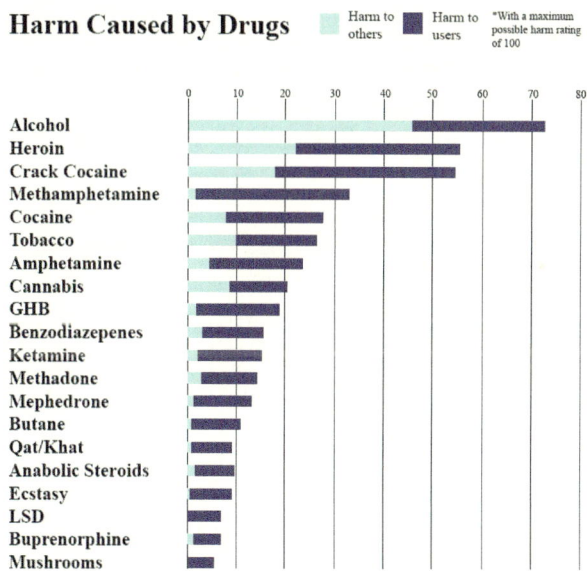

Ranking of the damage caused by the different drugs to the individual and to society in Europe. Note that ecstasy and psychedelics are at the bottom. (Jan van Amsterdam et al., "European rating of drug harms", Journal of Psychopharmacology 29, no. 6 (June 2015): 655-60).

There are many examples of publications[3], tools, materials and organizations[4] that can help with risk and harm reduction, but the main basic element to be able to reduce any risk is information and knowledge. This information, to be useful, must be based on scientific evidence and not on moral dogmas or beliefs, and it must avoid judgment.

In this sense, there are strategies of enormous impact, such as knowing our state of physical and mental health, the context, learning as much as possible about a substance before consuming it (its doses and its risks), planning consumption in advance, always start with the minimum dose before moving on to a higher dose, not doing it on days when you are psycho-emotionally unwell, always staying adequately hydrated and nourished, not mixing it with other drugs or medications, spacing consumption over time, and, as much as possible, avoiding substances that are not analyzed or that come from dealers unfamiliar to you.

In this sense, another tool that has been shown[5] to be effective in reducing risks is drug analysis, also known as drug testing or drug checking. It is a tool that not only allows for the monitoring of drug markets from a public health perspective, but provides, together with advice, a way for people who have decided to consume a drug of illegal origin to detect if it is adulterated with substances that may be toxic. Therefore, they can decide to rule out its consumption, or adjust the dose to reduce risks if the level of purity of the drug they have acquired is not what they expected. The implementation of these information and counseling services on risk reduction

---

[3] Eduardo Hidalgo Downing, *Sustainable Hedonism* (Amargord, 2011).

[4] Some are mentioned in the "Resources" section of this book.

[5] Nazlee Maghsoudi et al., "Drug checking services for people who use drugs: A systematic review," *Addiction*, November 2, 2021.

The risks and results of the consumption of a psychoactive substance can be classified into three contexts: Drug, individual and environment. This model is known as "Zinberg's Triangle".

and drug analysis[6] in music festivals, nightclubs, and other entertainment venues and events, is a practice that has been growing for some decades in Europe, and is also increasingly widespread in North America, South America, and Australia.

Now that we have detailed the concept of risk, its multiple factors and its variability, let's look into the main risks and reduction strategies in the use of psychedelic drugs. For this, I will divide them according to their origin into three categories: risks related to the substance (*drug*), to the person (*set*) or to the context (*settings*), a model known as the "Zinberg Triangle[7]."

These three variables greatly influence the risks of using any drugs. But it does not stop there, as they also influence the

---

[6] Some of these organizations and drug testing services are mentioned in the "Resource" section of this book.
[7] Norman E. Zinberg, *Drug, Set, and Setting: The Basis for Controlled Intoxicant Use*, 1986.

results of the experience itself, the effects the substance will cause (especially in the case of psychedelics, as we will see below) and, therefore, the result of consumption. But to be specific, let's see some examples of the variables to which I refer:

Dimensions	Variables
The substance	Type, dose, frequency of consumption, route of administration, purity, adulterants, combinations or interactions...
Person (*set*)	Mental and emotional state, tolerance, allergies, illnesses, sensitivity, expectations, information, preparation...
Context (*setting*)	Environment, other people, music, lights, smell, driving, unevenness of the terrain, legal status, calendar appointments or other responsibilities...

That said, and given that the use of psychedelics outside the clinical context is a social reality today, let's see how some of the most important elements are applied to reduce their associated risks:

Person & Context (*Set & Setting*)

As we have seen throughout the text, most of the risks of classic or typical psychedelics are on the psychological level, and that is why the psychological variables of person and context are especially crucial to make this type of experiences carry the least possible risk.

Since psychedelics greatly amplify what we perceive happening within us and around us (even things that are already present, but we are not giving our full attention to), it is crucial that the person properly prepares themselves and their context to maximize the possibilities of having a positive and constructive experience, minimizing those that could cause a negative or unpleasant one. That said, it is worth mentioning that, in certain therapeutic contexts, sometimes the objective is not to seek a "pleasant" experience, but rather a valuable or revealing one. Even if this implies facing moments of difficulty (which do not necessarily imply something negative). In many cases, reports have associated these difficult experiences or bad trips with good long-term therapeutic results. This does not mean that anyone should look to have a bad trip, but it does mean that they can be a valuable part of the psychotherapeutic work and not necessarily be "bad" but rather "difficult" as explained before.

A good graphic representation of the most relevant aspects to take into consideration would be the following infographic from plantamaestras.net.

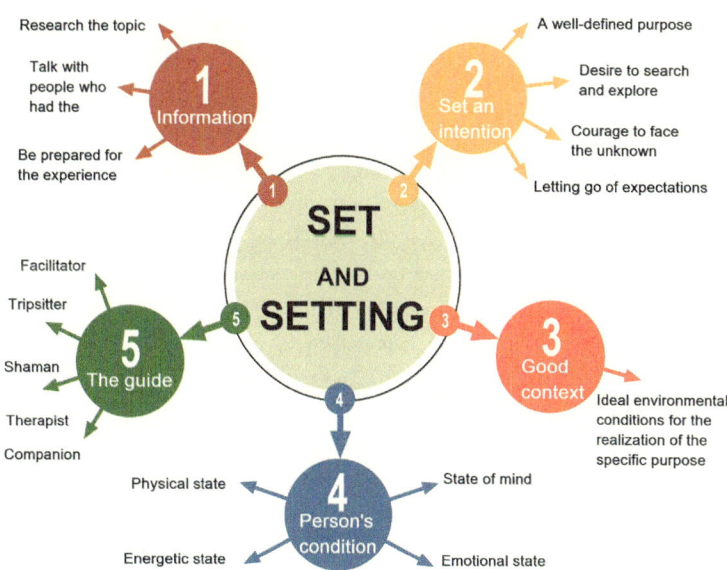

Breakdown of different variables of *set and setting* which should be carefully considered to reduce the risks when using a psychedelic. Jose Luis López Delgado at https://plantasmaestras.net/el-set-and-setting-en-la-experiencia-con-psicodelicos/.

Let's see the practical components in which all this translates.

Set

It is made up of the person and what they bring to the experience: their beliefs, expectations, mental and emotional state, concerns, intentions, state of physical and mental health, personality, fears, etc.

To minimize the risks in this area, it is advisable to:
- Learn about the substance and the experience very well, visiting risk reduction websites, reading books, watching videos, etc. Some helpful materials are available in the resource section of this book.
- Find out if you have any type of family history of psychosis, bipolarity, schizophrenia, and if you have ever suffered an episode. These conditions are very dangerous, and the use of psychedelics should be avoided at all costs if you suffer from any of them.
- Know your personality well and anticipate what your reactions might be in uncertain situations; if you have difficulty relaxing and letting go, if you tend to get anxious and need to be in control, if you try to analyze and understand everything, etc.
- Learn tools and exercises to control anxiety, such as breathing, meditation, visualizations of quiet places, yoga, etc.
- Be aware of your own emotional state before starting a psychedelic trip, and try to start from a place of calm, well-being and trust. It helps a lot to have a positive mindset[8] and choose a day when you feel especially well.

---

[8] Eline CHM Haijen et al., "Predicting responses to psychedelics: A prospective study", *Frontiers in Pharmacology* 9 (November 2, 2018): 897.

- Define a clear intention for the experience, but also know how to surrender to it and be open to what may come. Do not fight the experience, resist or run away, as this often makes it more difficult or negative.
- Forget the routine concerns of the outside world, don't bring them along on the trip; you have to disconnect to be able to immerse yourself in the experience. It is important to have plenty of time for the experience and its subsequent integration, without having to worry about the duration or upcoming commitments.
- Be able to accept and surrender to the experience, whatever it may bring. You have to "trust, let go and be open" to whatever comes, "turn off your mind, relax and float downstream."
- Be patient with everything: with the preparation, the ascent, the experience and the subsequent integration. Rushing can greatly spoil the experience and turn into anxiety.
- Stay hydrated and nourished. During the experience, you may not feel thirsty or hungry, but the body still needs to drink and eat, so it is better to drink water and eat light meals, such as fruits, nuts, juices, etc., keeping in mind that food can decrease psychedelic intensity, especially with psilocybin.

Setting

The setting is made up of the physical, social, and cultural environment in which the psychedelic experience occurs. Like the set, it has a huge influence on its outcome and its risks. Therefore, it is just as important to pay close attention to the following:
- Choosing a physical environment that is consistent with the intention of the experience. A recreational experience may be easier in a beautiful forest, while an introspective experience may be easier on a bed with eyes closed and headphones on.

- The physical environment must be safe, controllable and predictable. Better to avoid too many stimuli. Public places, with a multitude of strangers, noise and other variables that cannot be controlled, are not a conducive *setting* for a good experience. Instead, a house, a garden or private spaces where things are controlled are much safer, controllable and predictable.
- The physical environment should be pleasant, comfortable, positive and welcoming. Closely linked to the above, it is better to choose pleasant and positive spaces, which transmit good vibes, since uncomfortable or unwelcoming places can make negative sensations magnify enormously.
- Plan the session well in advance, leaving room for improvisation, but having everything you need close at hand (water, food, headphones, music, paper, notebook and pencils, paints) so you don't have to move around too much during the experience, since changes in space can totally alter the experience and not necessarily for the better. It's also a good idea to pre-test the psychedelic substance at a risk reduction testing service.
- Music is a crucial element in providing the experience with a positive and relaxing atmosphere. Changes in musical style can greatly affect the experience, so it is advisable to choose music that generates positivity and relaxation, such as the many *playlists* for psychedelic experiences available on Spotify, YouTube, etc.
- Surround yourself with people you know well, trust and whose good intentions you do not question, who are knowledgeable about psychedelics and do not make you feel judged. Any distrust, any suspicion or feeling of judgment can be magnified during a psychedelic experience and ruin it. In this sense, large groups are not usually a good idea, nor is consuming

- a psychedelic alone (especially the first few times). Better to have a few trusted people (2-3) and preferably with experience and knowledge of psychedelics.
- When using with someone else, it's a good idea to have at least one person with psychedelic experience stay sober. That way they can look after the safety and well-being of the others and know how to help if someone has a difficult experience. The sober person who accompanies someone while they are in a psychedelic experience is known as a "*tripsitter.*"
- It is also important that there is some freedom so that each person can choose their space based on their experience; that other people do not force anyone to be in a place where they do not want to be or to do something they do not want to do; that the intentions of those who take psychedelics in the same space be the same, compatible or at least not get in the way. Ideally, you should be able to withdraw or remain silent if you don't feel like talking or interacting.
- If there is a guide or shaman, it is best to be attuned to their way of guiding or structuring the session. For example, if you are an atheist, a religious ceremony can be difficult.
- Under no circumstances should you drive, operate machinery, dangerous objects or carry out risky activities under the influence of a psychedelic.

But, if despite carrying out all these risk reduction measures, a difficult situation arises, how should you act?

TRIPSITTING FOR MANAGING "BAD TRIPS" AND OTHER PSYCHEDELIC EMERGENCIES

Bad trips or difficult experiences are rare if the person has an adequate set & setting, but they could happen anyway, and doesn't need to be too much of a concern if the person has only taken one psychedelic substance in not-so-high doses, is well accompanied and supervised, and if there are no other drugs, medical conditions, or other risks present. It should be remembered that the classic psychedelics (psilocybin, LSD, DMT, etc) are pharmacologically very safe and there are no known deaths from their use, but the atypical psychedelics (MDMA, Ketamine) can be dangerous at very high doses, in certain people or in combination with other substances.

People going through a difficult experience may feel very scared, anxious, confused, afraid of death, or afraid of going permanently insane. Start by reframing the "bad trip" as a "difficult experience" that can be resolved – it is more accurate and better for a person going through said experience.

A difficult experience can be deeply unpleasant, but if someone is going through it, the most important thing to remember is that no one should panic, not the tripsitter and not the person going through the experience. As the phrase says: "there is nothing to fear but fear itself." Keep in mind, these are only transitory experiences that do not usually pose a threat to the healthy individual, and with good management they can even be a good learning opportunity.

If the environment is not helping (noisy, messy, unfamiliar people, full of stimuli), it is a good idea to change it (quiet music, dim lights, fewer people, people who are trustworthy), or move the person to a better place, calmer and safer, with fewer stimuli. Avoid frightening the person by appearing nervous, scared or worried, since it is very easy to "infect" an emotional state to a person who is under the influence of psychedelics. It is advisable to convey confidence, that everything will be fine.

Remind the person that they have taken a psychedelic drug voluntarily with a certain intention, and that what is happening is only a transient phase of the experience, that it is totally normal, and that although they may feel confused or scared now, they will soon feel fine or normal. Remind them it is just a substance that their body is getting rid of, and the effects will not last long. In addition, these substances are almost not toxic, and no healthy individual has ever died yet just from consuming mushrooms, LSD or other classic psychedelics alone. All of it eventually ends.

Also remind them that they are not alone, nor will they be if they don't want to be, that you are by their side to take care of them and help them in everything they need. It is important that you do not touch the person without their consent, but if you do, it may help to hold their hand or rest your hand on their shoulder or a different part of their body that is not intimate or sexual.

It can be helpful to remind the person that their body is fine, that there is no threat, that things look fine from the outside and everything is temporarily in their head.

It is helpful to invite the person not to fight the experience, not to run away, but to surrender to it and flow with it, trusting themselves and the intention with which they took the psychedelic. Also invite them to shift their focus to positive things, to think of a beautiful place, for example, to help redirect the experience towards a better phase.

Suggest the person to focus on their breath. Relaxation breathing techniques are often very helpful in reducing fear and anxiety.

If there is paranoia towards others, it may be beneficial to give the person some space in a comfortable, safe and quiet area, but to check on them regularly.

If it is necessary to reduce the effects, a little light food may help, as long as there is no risk of choking. For example, psilocybin is removed from the body through glucuronidation, and this process is supported by foods and nutrients such as sugars, curcumin, resveratrol, grape seed extract, milk thistle, hawthorn, omega-3 fatty acids, magnesium, apples and kale. Consuming these can help speed up your body's ability to metabolize psilocybin.

In the event the situation does not improve through these psychological interventions, or it worsens, and the person poses a risk to himself or others, emergency services can be of great help, providing medication in extreme cases, or if the situation is simply taking a long time to improve. The medications that are usually administered in this type of situation are anxiolytics, such as benzodiazepines (alprazolam or lorazepam), and in high-risk cases atypical antipsychotics (such as risperidone or olanzapine), but avoiding haloperidol or other typical antipsychotics, since they can aggravate the situation.

The decision to call an ambulance or transfer someone to a hospital should be weighed carefully in the case of difficult experiences that are not showing relevant physical or physiological risks for the individual or their environment. An unnecessary transfer could greatly accentuate the negative experience (noise, lights, unknown people, ambulance, change of setting, a hospital, questions, etc.).

If there is any risk to the life or physical integrity of the person due to previous medical conditions, inadequate dosage of the substance, combination with other compounds, error, etc., or dangerous symptoms are manifested (tachycardia, hypertensive crisis, hyperthermia, coma or cardiorespiratory arrest), then emergency services should be immediately alerted, giving them the most precise information possible about the location, type of symptoms, substance that has been consumed, medication combinations, other illnesses, etc. In case of a purely psychological difficult experience, however, it is better to work psychologically first with some of the ideas mentioned above to see if things improve before making the decision to call an ambulance or go to the hospital.

In the hypothetical case that a person is unconscious, it is important to place them in recovery position and monitor their vital signs (breathing, pulse, blood pressure, temperature, etc.) while an ambulance arrives. If the person is not breathing, cardiopulmonary resuscitation (CPR) maneuvers should be initiated. Fortunately, these types of situations are almost non-existent in the informed use of psychedelics.

Substance

Dosage, Frequency of Consumption and Tolerance

Back in the 16th century, the great alchemist Paracelsus said: "The dose makes the poison." And he was not wrong. Despite the fact that there are many decisive factors that influence the result of consuming a substance, as we have discussed, the dose is one of the most important and controllable variables, being able to determine if the desired effect will be obtained (whether therapeutic, recreational or of a different nature), if there will be no effect at all or if there will be an excessive effect, which would enter the field of what is undesirable or even dangerous in some substances. An overdose, whether fatal or simply unpleasant, should be avoided at all costs.

But dosing psychoactive substances in general, and psychedelics in particular, is never an easy or risk-free task, because there are a lot of variables to take into account before deciding on the exact milligrams to use. Some of these substances are unpredictable, but most are controllable, although little known by people. And, because of this, it is not uncommon to see cases of people who have had problems from improper dosing that would have been easily preventable with better risk reducing dosing information.

Although most of the classic psychedelics (psilocybin, LSD, mescaline) do not present great risks to the body in high dosages, the chances of being exposed to a psychologically difficult or extremely intense experience do increase, as well as their psychiatric risks in people with predispositions.

For example, in the case of the consumption of recreational doses, if we pay attention to the safety guidelines that are usually given by risk reduction services, the optimal doses are those that maximize the pleasures with respect to the risks. However, the lower the number of redoses and total dose consumed, the lower the risks.

Likewise, we must not forget that some of the semi-psychedelic or atypical psychedelic substances exposed in this book (MDMA, ibogaine, ketamine, MAOIs) can pose a risk to the body in high doses.

The doses must be adapted to the purpose of consumption and the sensitivity or tolerance of the person. It should also be noted that not all drugs are 100% absorbed and reach the bloodstream. In fact, almost none are, unless administered intravenously. Therefore, the dose is also highly dependent on the type of substance and the route of administration (oral, snorted, vaporized-inhaled, or intravenous).

In addition to bodyweight, there are other factors that must be considered when further specifying the dose. For example, it is necessary to take into account what the objective of consumption is, because a music festival is not the same as a therapeutic session; if it is the first time consuming this substance, as it could feel more intense, making a lower dose more convenient; if you have tolerance to the substance or to other compounds of the same family, in which case the dose would have to be increased a little; the sex of the person, since women are more sensitive to the effects and require lower doses; if drugs (such as MAOIs, Tramadol, Ritonavir, etc.) or other legal (alcohol) or illegal (stimulants) drugs are being consumed, which would greatly increase the risks (be very careful with mixing substances); the route of administration, because non-oral routes, such as snorting, require much lower doses... But, above all, there is one very important variable to consider: purity.

Before consuming any substance that comes from the black market, the ideal would be to have it analyzed qualitatively and quantitatively by a risk reduction analysis service, such as DrugsData or Energy Control, and thus not only prevent the presence of toxic adulterants, but also know the percentage of purity of the compound to estimate the dosages in advance with precision. Yet, in the real world, this is not always possible, so when dosing any substance of unknown purity, it is always best to start small, with the lowest active dose, as if the purity of the substance were the highest possible. Especially if it is the first time that it is consumed or if it is from a new batch, it is better to wait and feel the effects before increasing the dose, or as the English would say: "Start low and go slow." Because it is always safer to fall short than to go over. There is always the possibility of taking more, if necessary, until obtaining the desired effect. However, if you start by taking too much or too quickly, there is no way to "untake" it. What's done cannot be undone.

In terms of frequency of use, the less frequent the use of any psychoactive substance, the lower the risk of exposure to addiction or long-term damage. Typical psychedelics are substances that produce very intense experiences and do not invite regular consumption (with the exception of atypical psychedelics such as ketamine and ecstasy, which have greater potential for abuse), so their frequency of use is usually very low, normally spaced in months. Very frequent use is not a common problem.

In the case of ketamine and MDMA, it is important that their consumption is consciously spaced out over time as much as possible, to minimize the risk of addiction, neurotoxicity or psychological problems that could occur with very frequent consumption or at high doses. Likewise, another element to avoid is the development of tolerance, which would indicate that a neuroadaptation to its effects is taking place.

Tolerance is the habituation of the body or the brain to a substance, which, when consumed regularly, produces an adaptation of the neurons to its effects and requires an increase in the dose to obtain the same effect, with the consequent risks that higher doses may bring. Classic psychedelics are not usually consumed regularly, but if they were, they would produce a very rapid tolerance, making their consumption on consecutive days difficult, since their effects are quickly and greatly diminished, and much higher doses are required to replicate them. In fact, it usually takes about a week to completely lose tolerance after a one-off use of a classic psychedelic.

Purity and Adulterations

Psychedelic substances, like most illegal drugs, come from self-cultivation or the black market. In both cases there is no control over the quality of the substance, which allows some substances to be adulterated, generally with the purpose of defrauding the buyer with a product of lower purity and cheaper than the one they think they are buying.

Adulteration is a fraud, but it can also be dangerous to health. However, not all types of adulteration are as common or dangerous as it is thought, it is convenient to make distinctions between subtypes of adulteration that occur in the market:
- Dilution or use of excipients: normally using substances that, at an organoleptic level (color, texture, smell, taste), resemble the substance they intend to imitate. But they do not usually have their own relevant pharmacological effects or potential toxicity, that is, they are usually done with pharmacologically inert substances, such as sugars, starch, creatine[9] and other fillers. The objective is to obtain more quantity or weight of a drug, lowering its potency, which brings in a greater profit from the sale. This type of adulteration is usually not very dangerous. An example would be the use of sugars or creatine for any drug that appears to be a white powder, such as ketamine or crushed MDMA.
- Psychoactive adulteration: the drug is mixed with other psychoactive substances (which may be legal or illegalized), the effects of which are similar and can deceive the consumer, making them believe they have

---

[9] A sports nutritional supplement that looks like a white powder.

purchased the intended product or that it has a higher purity than it really does. This type of adulteration is dangerous due to the health risks it may entail, since it involves a mixture of substances unknown to the consumer and modifies the psychoactive properties of the original drug. An example would be adding caffeine or cathinones to ecstasy.
- Substitution: basically, ripping someone off. A substance is sold as if it were a drug that it actually does not contain, but may have other psychoactive substances that are intended to imitate its effect. This type of fraud is one of the most dangerous, since these substances may have pharmacological properties unknown to the user. An example would be selling 25i-NBOMe (a psychedelic with high-dose toxicity) as LSD.
- Synthesis-related impurities: the purification of a drug after synthesis is not a process that is carried out systematically in the illegal production of drugs, so many substances may contain impurities typical of the synthesis process. This adulteration can be unintentional, but very dangerous in case of a bad synthesis.

Most Common Adulterations in Psychedelic and Semi-Psychedelic Substances are:

Ecstasy / MDMA: as a result of the ban on the substances used to synthesize it, and some major international seizures, there was a great shortage in 2009 that greatly motivated its adulteration and substitution. But since then, and after the discovery of new synthesis routes that made it abundant and cheap, its purity has risen a lot, especially in Europe, where its adulteration has been very infrequent, at least until the start of the COVID-19 pandemic, when some evidence showed it may be rising again. These are some of the most frequent adulterants:

- Caffeine: this easily accessible legal stimulant drug is generally used to adulterate any substance with a stimulant profile, since its effects are very noticeable by the consumer. But in high doses it can cause insomnia, tachycardia, anxiety, dehydration and increase the risks of ecstasy.
- m-CPP: meta-chlorophenylpiperazine has stimulant and psychedelic effects, similar to those of MDMA, but also the risk of inducing severe migraines, dizziness, vomiting and headaches. Fortunately, it hasn't been seen as an adulterant for years.
- New psychoactive substances (NPS): various new synthetic drugs have been sold as if they were MDMA, such as cathinones (methylone, mephedrone, 3-MMC, etc.) or benzofurans (such as 6-APB or 5-APB).

Ketamine: the purity of ketamine has been relatively stable, since it commonly appears diluted with pharmacologically inert or unpurified substances, but it does not usually appear adulterated with other psychoactive substances, if at all, maybe caffeine on occasion. That said, it is sometimes replaced by other dissociative-type NPS that can have similar effects, but pose a greater risk to those who are unaware, because they are of greater potency, duration, intensity, or are substances that have not yet been studied, such as methoxetamine or deschloroketamine.

LSD: LSD is not usually adulterated, but it can appear together with other products derived from its synthesis or degradation, such as iso-LSD. Sometimes there have been cases of substitution of LSD with psychedelic NPS that may be more dangerous if the user is unaware of it, because they present greater risks than those of LSD or have a pharmacological profile unknown to the user. Some examples include 25i-NBOMe or DOx (DOC, DOI, etc.).

In recent years, adulterations and substitutions with fentanyl (a very dangerous opioid that should always be avoided), have appeared very rarely in some psychedelic substances in North America. It seems anecdotal or even accidental, but caution must be always given.

In a deregulated market, without controls, standards or good information, where guile is rewarded, it is difficult to completely avoid adulteration, but there are some basic strategies that can greatly help reduce the risks of consuming an excessively adulterated product or contaminated with toxic adulterants:

- Analyze whenever possible: there is no better way to reduce the risks of an adulterated product than to analyze it first, preferably using a service specialized in risk reduction, such as Energy Control (which, in addition to offering the service free of charge at festivals and at its locations in Spain, has an international analysis service by mail) or DrugsData, in the U.S. But if you don't have access to these services, they also sell colorimetric reagent kits, or thin-layer chromatography (TLC), for at home testing. These kits mainly detect substitutions and some common psychoactive adulterants, although they do not quantify the purity of the substance.
- Buying from reliable and known sources: buying a substance at a festival or nightclub, from a stranger who you will never see again, increases the risk of receiving an adulterated, substituted or low-purity product, since no one will have to answer for it later.
- Do not trust appearances: if the substance does not resemble the one you seek it may be an indication that it, in fact, isn't. However, since everything is imitable (color, smell, texture, brightness, etc.), even if it does resemble it, it is still not proof of its good quality or purity.
- Trust the effects: in this sense, one of the best risk reduction strategies is to take a small test dose to assess the effects before deciding whether to consume the "normal" dose.

Routes of Administration

For drugs to exert their action, they have to reach the brain, and for that they have to access the bloodstream. The time it takes for a drug to reach the bloodstream to access the brain and the duration of its effects are determined by many factors, but one of the most important is its route of administration.

The greater the absorption of the route and the faster it enters the blood, the faster and more intense the effects will be. This can make the same drug more dangerous or easy to overdose (and even more addictive in some cases) depending on how it is ingested. It must also be taken into account that as soon as a substance enters the body, it begins to be metabolized (degraded), so the longer it takes to reach its target, the smaller the amount of the substance that will reach it.

Almost all psychoactive substances can be taken by almost any route, but outside of laboratories, most psychedelics are normally consumed orally or inhaled (vaporized), although some are also snorted:

- Orally: it is usually the slowest since the substance has to pass through the stomach and intestine to reach the bloodstream, with a first metabolism in the liver (which can partially inactivate or release certain substances), but it is one that carries the fewer risks, as long as the dose is well measured. Its speed depends a lot on the type of substance and whether the stomach is full or empty.
- Snorted: this route takes a few minutes to take effect, it reaches the blood through the nasal mucosa, but in the long run it can cause damage to the nostrils.
- Smoked/vaporized/inhaled: it is a very quick route, it reaches the blood through the lungs and takes a few seconds to take effect, although it can cause damage to the mouth, throat and lungs.

- Intravenously: the fastest and most effective, it reaches the blood directly, but carries many risks, such as the transmission of infectious diseases, damage to the veins, etc. Outside the clinical setting, it is very unusual and always inadvisable in terms of safety.

As a general rule (with several exceptions), the faster the route of administration, the lower the dose should be (because more of the substance will probably be absorbed and blood concentration will rise faster). A faster route may also usually imply the addictive potential is greater for the same substance, although in the case of psychedelics, addiction is very rare (except in the case of ketamine, or sometimes MDMA).

Mixtures and Combinations

The combination of different psychoactive substances always makes their risks and manifestations more unpredictable, usually increasing their risks.

Having said this, in the real world it is unfortunately common to find the combined use of psychoactive substances, sometimes without the person being aware of it, given that we tend to forget that substances that are very commonly consumed, such as alcohol, tobacco, caffeine, Cannabis or some medications can have a significant interaction with other psychoactive substances.

In this sense, there are psychopharmaceuticals that can be especially dangerous when combined with other drugs, such as tramadol, monoamine oxidase inhibitors (MAOIs), opioids (used to treat pain or cough), psychostimulants (used in narcolepsy or attention-deficit/hyperactivity disorder), some anxiolytics, some antidepressants, etc.

Some supplements to lose weight or improve training, as well as various medicinal plants such as hypericum (St. John's wort), black cohosh, echinacea, valerian, kava, yohimbe, ginkgo biloba, etc., may also have relevant interactions. Even some common foods such as grapefruit or certain spices can noticeably alter the metabolism of drugs and unknowingly pose a combination risk that must be taken into account.

In order to facilitate access to the scarce information available on interactions in the most common drug combinations, for some years the TripSit association[10] of risk reduction has been producing a simple chart that allows you to consult, in a quick and simplified way, the risks and effects of certain combinations of two substances. This chart has evolved into a smartphone application that, without sacrificing simplicity or speed, allows access to a little more specific information on a specific combination of substances (see https://combo.tripsit.me).

On the other hand, although cannabis does not present great physiological risks when consumed alone, it can intensify or alter the effects of the other substances with which it is combined. This is mostly at the psychological level, but also physically, and that is why mixing it with alcohol or other drugs, such as psychedelics, which some people are used to doing, does not come without harm.

---

[10] "TripSit - Harm Reduction through Education," https://tripsit.me/.

Antón Gómez-Escolar

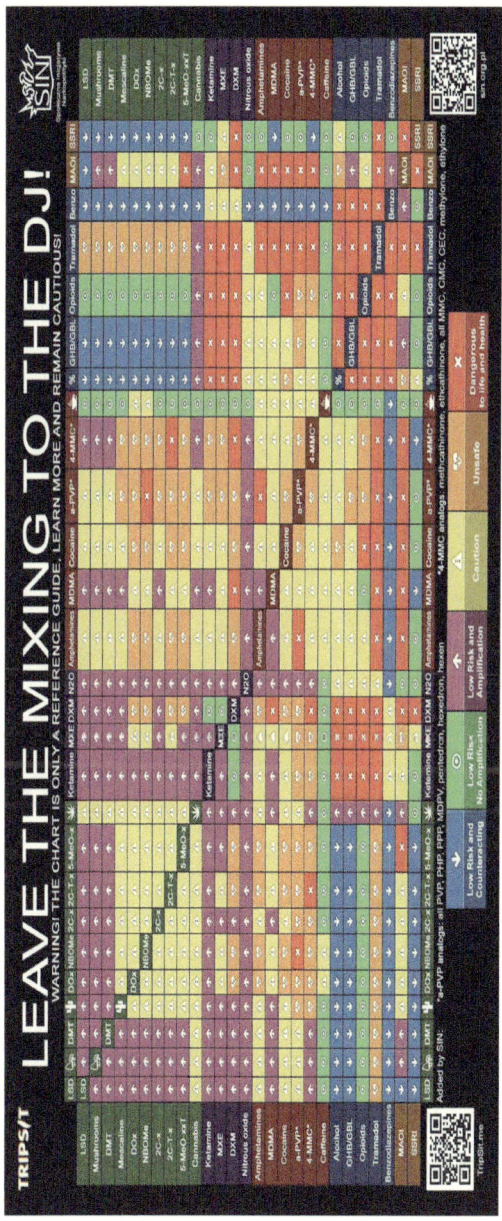

Drug combinations chart, made by TripSit (and adapted by SIN), which uses color codes to identify the risks of different combinations of two substances.

Conclusions: Looking to the Future

In these pages, I hope I have managed to give you an introductory but comprehensive picture of this exciting process of psychedelic renaissance we are experiencing, and the enormous influence it could have in the field of mental health, society and many other fields.

Just a few years ago it was unthinkable to imagine such a hopeful moment in psychedelic research, or that it would have the sociocultural and even industrial repercussions it is beginning to have, or that it would open the therapeutic paths it is opening. It Is indeed a cause for hope to the many people suffering from disorders that are so widespread in today's world, like depression, anxiety, post-traumatic stress disorder, addictions, etc. Moreover, at a time when our usual therapeutic tools are not being effective enough to tackle this epidemic of mental health disorders.

Despite the fact that, at first, it seemed that these substances were destined to revolutionize Western neuroscience and mental health therapies, ignorance about their use, together with their politicization, condemned them to the worst possible fate, their prohibition 50 years ago, taking with it any potential clinical use. But, thanks to the courage and nonconformity of many people and to the new opportunities created since the end of the 20th century, this field is now more alive than ever in the West, not only in the field of basic research, but also clinical, with several substances already in very promising clinical trials.

At the same time (even before the restart of this research), many Westerners were already exploring what the careful use of psychedelics could bring to various areas of their lives, testing them in a controlled way, in ceremonial, traditional or private contexts, with the consequent increase in their popularity, rapidly changing the social perception of these substances, even becoming a trend in various communities. Currently, activist movements are managing to carry out popular local legislative initiatives to decriminalize them or even legalize access to them for medical purposes.

But it is also not convenient to get carried away by excessive optimism regarding psychedelics just yet. Although it is true that the results of its experimental use together with psychotherapy, in controlled clinical contexts, are being very striking in many cases, we must remember that they are still, for the most part, small studies, with many limitations (trials in a few patients, with high expectations, difficult to blind[1], etc.), and it is necessary to continue with increasingly solid research before expanding its medical use or venturing into the implementation of widespread access programs. There is also not enough evidence to predict a great psychedelic future, as some would like to think, as these substances can be a powerful tool with a great impact on mental health but they will not be a

---

[1] In a blinded study, the patient does not know if they have been given the treatment or a placebo. It is very difficult to "blind" a study with psychedelics because their effects are so noticeable.

panacea. Additionally, we must not forget that its uncontrolled and uninformed use carries risks that should not be ignored. Unfortunately, although psychedelic research is becoming more accessible every day and this is allowing its clinical development to accelerate, it is still not as easy as with other substances. This desire for progress often hits a wall of prejudice and bureaucratic obstacles imposed by current drug policies, the same policies that prevented any developments in this field for decades, making it almost impossible to find financing due to scarce industrial interest.

For this reason, it is urgent to open an honest, unbiased and well-informed debate on psychedelics and how to facilitate their research, development and, most importantly, their implementation, which seems more than likely in the field of psychotherapy, but also in other possible fields. Many of these paths need a drug policy reform that eases the restrictions for research into the therapeutic applications of these substances and their mechanisms of action, as well as financing models that ensure not only quality research, but also an agile development of the implementation of these therapies if, eventually, their effectiveness and safety are solidly demonstrated. Likewise, it is crucial to prevent the problems that may arise from their popularization outside the clinical setting, through better dissemination of the knowledge of their risks and the development of risk reduction strategies by society, respecting the rights of traditional, cultural and non-clinical uses but also respecting individual freedoms, which should be considered in this debate as well.

Regarding drug policy, it seems paradoxical that psychedelics, being one of the psychoactive substances with the least addictive potential, toxicity and harm (in most cases without even reported deaths), and having enormous therapeutic potential, are de facto outlawed, being on the most restrictive international control list of substances; while other psychoactive drugs, without medicinal value, highly addictive, that cause a lot of damage and that are behind the death of millions of people every year in the world,

CLASSIFICATION OF DRUGS - LEVELS OF HARM VS LEVELS OF CONTROL

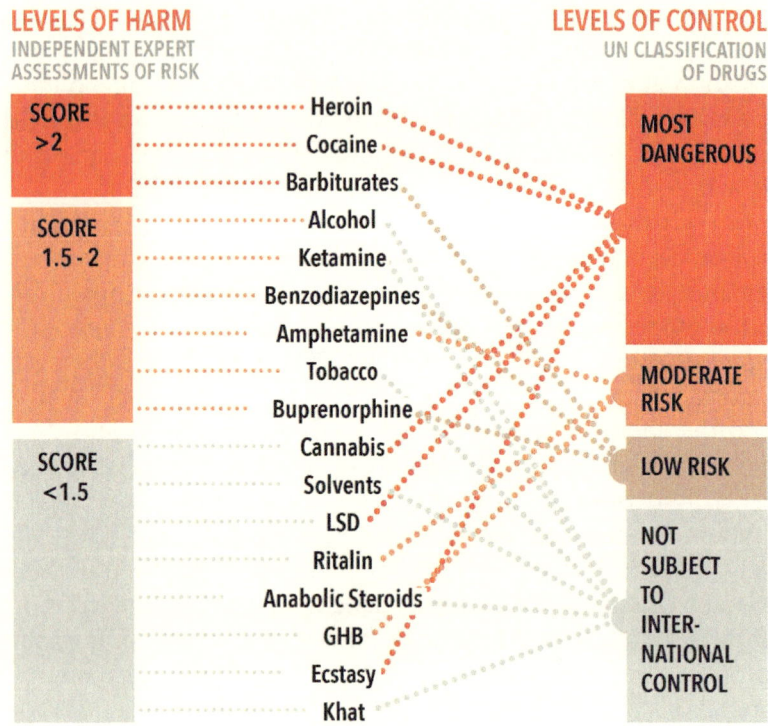

Sources: Nutt, D., King, L.A., Saulsbury, W., Blakemore, C. (2007); UNODC, Schedules of the Single Convention on Narcotic Drugs of 1961 as amended by the 1972 Protocol, as at 22 April 2017, and Schedules of the Convention on Psychotropic Substances of 1971, as at 18 October 2017.

Harm levels of different drugs, evaluated by scientists, compared to their current international legal control levels. Psychedelics such as LSD or MDMA are in the lower part of the damage, but in the category of greater legal restriction. *(David Nutt et al., "Development of a rational scale to assess the harm of drugs of potential misuse," The Lancet 369, no. 9566 (March 24, 2007): 1047-53. Nutt et al. & Gomis, Benoît. (2016). Modernizing Drug Law Enforcement. IDPC Drug Policy Guide - 3rd edition (pp. 90-96) via The Global Commission on Drug Policy).*

are fully legal and accessible to anyone of legal age, as is the case of tobacco (8 million deaths per year according to the WHO) or alcohol (3 million deaths per year according to the WHO).

In fact, most of the time, the legal status of a drug does not correspond to scientific or objective criteria of its risk, but to sociocultural and even moral criteria, and, in this sense, the case of psychedelics is especially striking if we compare its damage potential with its level of international control.

From the point of view of public health, drug policies should be based on scientific evidence and not on subjective or moral criteria. Truthful and objective information about drugs, as well as the basic principles of risk reduction, are crucial to be able to unblock this very harmful situation of social taboo that, based on misinformation, turns substances that could be very useful drugs for society into complete unknowns to the medical world, or even dangerous elements in the case of its uninformed recreational use.

In this sense, to avoid the problems that in the past accompanied the popularization of psychedelics, communication and scientific dissemination must continue to be rigorous, prudent and well contextualized, to avoid generating unrealistic expectations and a trivialization of the risks that can be associated with its poorly controlled use. This, together with a good knowledge of the substances, as well as risk reduction strategies, would largely mitigate the dangers that may be associated with their popularization, limiting the sensationalism or political instrumentalization that occurred in the past with these substances.

At the moment, we are not seeing many accidents or problems of great relevance associated with the use of psychedelics, largely thanks to the fact that, now, both researchers and society have a better understanding of the handling of these substances, but the great challenge for the future is to prevent the history of the last century from repeating itself.

In terms of financing this research, which is still so necessary, unlike other families of molecules, many of these substances are not of such direct interest to the traditional model of the private pharmaceutical industry, since they are natural substances or with an expired patent, easy to grow at home and that, in addition, are only administered on a few occasions throughout a psychotherapeutic process, producing very long-lasting results. The business opportunity is not so much in the drug itself (as it happens in daily use treatments such as antidepressants and anxiolytics) but in the delivery method and the entire therapeutic process, which would force a reformulation of the traditional pharmaceutical and therapeutic model, including a shift in the biomedical paradigm in the approach to mental health.

However, outside the current model of psychedelic-assisted psychotherapy, there are other models where a more regular use of psychedelic substances could be done, such as their speculated future use in promoting neuroplasticity or neurogenesis, in the prevention and treatment of neurodegenerative diseases through the use of microdoses or new patentable psychedelic molecules, and that could be more similar to a traditional pharmaceutical business model.

On the other hand, new organizations are also emerging around psychedelics, successfully innovating and developing different models, thereby attracting more investment and research to the field, although not all of them are viewed favorably by the psychedelic community. However, public investment in the research and development of these therapies is more necessary than ever. After all, society and the public coffers will be the main beneficiaries if this leads to advances in neuroscience and better treatments for mental health disorders in the population, especially if we take into account that these treatments could help many people with chronic disorders that do not respond to treatment, those that, in addition to the suffering that impacts them as individuals and their environment, also cope with work disabilities, which entail a large expense for health services. All things considered, investment in psychedelic research could prove to be of tremendous benefit to public health, reducing the suffering of people with chronic disorders and saving healthcare costs at the same time.

But it is also crucial to take into account the existence and expansion of its traditional uses in some cultures and the possibility that these could be restricted by their clinical use in Western medicine. These substances have been used for millennia, and it is precisely from this experience that many of the principles used today in Westernized psychedelic-assisted psychotherapy have been derived. For our culture they may be something very new, but for many others they are not at all.

In turn, this last point opens up a debate that, little by little, is becoming more evident, about whether the development of the medical use of these substances could also be extended, in the future, to "healthy" people (if we understand health only as the absence of disease) for preventive, spiritual and self-knowledge purposes, in the face of existential crises, grieving, couple conflict, etc. In short, non-medical uses, which could also be of great social value and, although today they are far from being the priority of Western clinical research, have been part of the traditional and communal use of these substances for millennia, and would represent a paradigm shift in the approach to mental and community health in our societies.

For all these reasons, just as it has been happening for some time with cannabis, disparities of opinion are also emerging within the psychedelic renaissance about what the eventual models of future access to these substances could look like and how to reach them, as well as its ethical, economic and safety considerations. In this sense, it is very likely that more and more frictions will arise between players from different sectors such as research, industry, regulation and even socio-cultural contexts, because, although they all share the same interest in the potential of psychedelic substances, they don't always share the same ends or means; something that is already becoming clear in the context of the different models that have been outlined and supported by these players. There is a disparity of opinion regarding the development of popular legislative initiatives, patents on certain elements of psychedelics, the cultural elements of their use and even in the way of presenting news about scientific advances in psychedelics or their implementation at a big scale. Many of these possible models are already developing in parallel in different places, as is the case with the combination of the popular legislative initiatives for legalization in the USA, combined with their current traditional uses, while the models of regulated medical access and pharmaceutical development keep advancing.

In the medium term, the more than probable authorization of the medical use of MDMA for the treatment of post-traumatic stress disorder (expected for 2023) and of psilocybin for depression (expected for 2025), will join that of esketamine for depression (already authorized in 2019) and will be a real litmus test of the safety and real potential of these substances, since it will probably be a great endorsement for their use outside clinical contexts. It will also test their level of acceptance in the psychotherapeutic field, in the press and with legislators. At the same time, the psychedelic industry will continue with its projected growth and innovation around such an novel business that is arousing so much interest, with growth driven by frequent good news but also very exposed to bad news.

In short, the current psychedelic panorama is made up of many different elements and, probably, there are still many more to come, so it is still early to predict the scope and future ramifications of this psychedelic renaissance, especially when more substances begin to be approved for medical use and their social popularity becomes mainstream. But, for the time being, it can be said that psychedelics are revolutionizing neuroscience. There is a lot of optimism and good prospects for their clinical use and they are garnering more interest every day at an industrial and sociocultural level. So, it does not seem risky to predict that, if the cards are played well and wisely, and research continues to show strong clinical potential, these substances could come to play an important role in the future of our societies.

We must be realistic and cautious in our optimism so as not to overestimate a phenomenon that, although it may become transcendental, at the moment is only the brilliant promise of a better future for mental health and many other aspects of our society. However, we will closely follow the exciting advances that this psychedelic renaissance may bring us.

Psychedelic Resources

Information on Psychedelics and Risk Reduction

- Psychonaut Wiki (https://psychonautwiki.org/): collaborative encyclopedia on psychoactive substances and psychonautics.
- Erowid (https://www.erowid.org/): Nonprofit harm reduction and educational resource with 60,000 pages of online information about psychoactive drugs and experiences with them.
- Tripsit (https://tripsit.me/): community focused on information on risk reduction and preparation of materials such as the Drug Combination Chart.
- RollSafe (https://rollsafe.org/): Information and risk reduction resource focused on MDMA (Ecstasy).
- TheDEA (https://thedea.org/): Information and risk reduction resource focused on MDMA (Ecstasy).

- Energy Control (https://energycontrol.org/ or https://energycontrol-international.org/): Spanish organization dedicated to risk reduction and drug analysis at a national and international level.
- Zendo Project (https://zendoproject.org/): part of MAPS, it's an organization that provides comprehensive and professional harm and risk reduction education and support to communities to help inform and transform difficult psychedelic experiences into opportunities for learning and growth.
- Kosmicare (https://kosmicare.org/): Portuguese organization dedicated to risk reduction, *trip-sitting* and drug testing.
- Drug Science (https://www.drugscience.org.uk/): independent scientific body in the United Kingdom. It works to provide clear and evidence-based information on drugs, without political or commercial interference.
- The Drugs Classroom (https://thedrugclassroom.com/)
- International Center for Ethnobotanical Education, Research, and Service ICEERS (https://www.iceers.org/): has very good information on naturally occurring psychedelics.

PSYCHEDELIC RESEARCH

- Multidisciplinary Association for Psychedelic Studies, MAPS (https://maps.org/): founded by Rick Doblin in 1986, it is a research and educational NGO that develops medical, legal, and cultural contexts for people to benefit from the careful use of psychedelics and marijuana.
- Beckley Foundation (https://www.beckleyfoundation.org/): foundation focused on psychedelic research to drive evidence-based drug policy reform. Founded and led by Amanda Feilding in 1998 as a UK-based think tank and NGO.

- International Center for Ethnobotanical Education, Research, and Service ICEERS (https://www.iceers.org/): non-profit civil organization created in 2008 with headquarters in Barcelona and dedicated to promoting scientific research on plants with medicinal properties (including psychedelics) for use in therapies and personal development.
- Heffter Research Institute (https://www.heffter.org/): NGO that promotes research with hallucinogens and classic psychedelics, predominantly psilocybin, to contribute to a greater understanding of the mind and alleviate suffering.
- Usona Institute (https://www.usonainstitute.org/): An organization that supports and conducts preclinical and clinical research to improve the understanding of the therapeutic effects of psilocybin and other consciousness-expanding substances.
- Center for Psychedelic and Consciousness Research at Johns Hopkins University (https://hopkinspsychedelic.org/)
- Center for Psychedelic Research at Imperial College London (https://www.imperial.ac.uk/psychedelic-research-centre/)
- Center for Psychedelic Therapies and Research (https://www.ciis.edu/research-centers/center-for-psychedelic-therapies-and-research)

Psychedelic Societies and Others

- Psychedelic Community (https://Psychedelic.Community): directory of psychedelic societies around the world.
- The Psychedelic Society (https://psychedelicsociety.org.uk/) in the UK.

- La Sociedad Psicodélica (https://lasociedadpsicodelica.es/) in Spain.
- Madrid's Psychedelic Society (https://www.facebook.com/MadridPsychedelicSoc/)
- PsychonautWiki Network (https://psychonautwiki.org/wiki/network): directory with a large number of websites, organizations, associations, etc. related to drugs in general and psychedelic drugs in particular.

Risk Reduction Organizations

- Energy Control (Spain https://energycontrol.org/ or international https://energycontrol-international.org/)
- DanceSafe (USA) USA) (https://dancesafe.org/)
- Zendo Project (USA) USA) (https://zendoproject.org/)
- Fireside Project (USA) USA) (https://firesideproject.org/)
- Échele Cabeza (Colombia) (https://www.echelecabeza.com/)
- Kosmicare (Portugal) (https://kosmicare.org/)
- Check!n (Portugal)
- Unity (The Netherlands) (https://www.jellinek.nl/preventie/horeca/unity/)
- Techno+ (France) (https://technoplus.org/)
- Check-it (Austria) (https://checkit.wien/) (https://www.checkyourdrugs.at/)
- Safe'n Sound (Belgium) (https://safensound.be/)
- Neurtravel (Italy)

Dug checking / Testing / Analysis

- Energy Control Spain (https://energycontrol.org/) analyze drugs at their headquarters in Spain (Barcelona, Madrid, Antequera and Mallorca) and at music festivals, nightclubs, fairs, etc.

- Energy Control International (https://energycontrol-international.org/) analyze drugs for the whole world.
- Drugs data (https://www.drugsdata.org/) (former ecstasydata.org)
- WediNos (https://wedinos.org/) (UK laboratory)
- Pill reports (https://pillreports.net/)
- Trans-European Drug Information network (TEDI) (https://www.tedinetwork.org/)

Activism

- Drug Policy Alliance (https://drugpolicy.org/): a nonprofit organization based in New York City that seeks to promote policies that "reduce the harms of both drug use and prohibition and promote people's sovereignty over their minds and bodies."
- Students for Sensitive Drug Policy (SSDP) (https://ssdp.org/): international student activist organization that fights for drug policy reform and risk reduction policies.
- International Drug Policy Consortium (IDPC) (https://idpc.net/): global network of more than 192 NGOs that promote objective and open debate on drug policies at the national, regional and international levels. IDPC supports evidence-based policies that are effective in reducing drug-related harm.
- Law Enforcement Action Partnership (LEAP) (https://lawenforcementactionpartnership.org/): formerly called Law Enforcement Against Prohibition, it is an organization that brings together police officers critical of current drug policy.

Forums

- Reddit Psychedelics (https://www.reddit.com/r/Psychedelics/): Reddit subforum focused on psychedelics.

- Bluelight (https://bluelight.org/): forum dedicated to the discussion of risk and harm reduction strategies in everything that is considered a drug, such as a substance that alters the body or mind.
- Drugs Forum (https://drugs-forum.com/): forum focused on discussion and support in addictions and risk and harm reduction.
- DMT-Nexus.me (https://www.dmt-nexus.me): forum and repository focused on DMT.
- Cannabis Cafe (https://cannabiscafe.net/): the largest Spanish-speaking forum for topics of cannabis, psychedelics and other drugs.
- Shroomery (https://www.shroomery.org/): forum specializing in psychedelics, specifically in psychedelic mushrooms, also includes information about them.
- Entheogen network (https://entheogen-network.com/): forum specialized in psychedelics.
- Mycotopia (https://mycotopia.net/): forum specialized in psychedelics.

YOUTUBE CHANNELS

- The Drug Classroom (https://www.youtube.com/user/TheDrugClassroom): Provides real education free of drug propaganda.
- Psyched Substance (https://www.youtube.com/c/PsychedSubstanceChannel): Provides education on risk reduction and drug use.
- Energy Control (https://www.youtube.com/c/EnergycontrolOrg): channel with materials related to risk reduction, prevention and information on drugs.
- Drug Science (https://www.youtube.com/c/DrugScience)

Podcasts

- Psychedelics Times (https://psychedelictimes.com/)
- Psychedelics Today (https://psychedelicstoday.com/)
- The Third Wave (https://thethirdwave.co/podcast/)
- MikeDelic (https://www.mikebranc.com/)
- Psychedelic Salon (https://psychedelicsalon.com/podcasts/)

Phone Numbers

- FireSide: helpline for psychedelic experiences (https://firesideproject.org/psychedelic-peer-support-line) tel.+16234737433

Apps

- TripSit Mobile: Risk reduction app from the TripSit association.
- TripApp (https://tripapp.org/)
- KnowDrugs (https://knowdrugs.app/)
- FireSide (https://firesideproject.org/)
- Mind Leap (https://mindleap.com/)
- Maya Health (https://www.mayahealth.com/)
- News and Current Affairs
- Sociedelic (https://www.sociedelic.com/)
- Psychedelic Spotlight (https://psychedelicspotlight.com/)
- PsilocybinAlpha (https://psilocybinalpha.com/)
- Daily Mushroom (https://news.dailymushroom.co/)
- Double Blind Magazine (https://doubleblindmag.com/)
- Lucid News (https://www.lucid.news/)
- Reset.me (https://reset.me/)

- Psymposia (https://www.psymposia.com/)
- Revista Cáñamo (https://canamo.net/)
- Revista Ulises (https://www.ulises.online/)

Documentaries about Psychedelics

- Fantastic Fungi (2019)
- Magic Medicine (2018)
- The Way of the Psychonaut: Stanislav Grof's Journey of Consciousness (2020)
- The Mind, Explained: Psychedelics (2019)
- The Substance: Albert Hofmann's LSD (2011)
- Psychedelia (2020)
- María Sabina, Woman Spirit (1979)
- Dosed (2019)
- From Shock to Awe (2018)
- Neurons to Nirvana: The Great Medicines (2013)
- A New Understanding: Science of Psilocybin (2015)
- DMT: The Spirit Molecule (2010)
- Aya: Awakenings (2013)
- The Sunshine Makers (2015)
- Dirty Pictures (2010)
- Journeys to the Edge of Consciousness (2019)
- Hamilton's Pharmacopeia (multi-season documentary series)
- The Last Shaman (2016)
- Ayahuasca: Vine of the Soul (2010)
- Entheogen: Awakening the Divine Within (2017)
- Psychonautics: A Comic's Exploration of Psychedelics (2018)
- Ibogaine: Rite of Passage (2004)
- Peyote to LSD: A Psychedelic Odyssey (2008)
- Science and Sacraments: Psychedelic Research and Mystical Experiences

Manuals and Other Publications

- Manual of Psychedelic Support (https://psychsitter.com/): The Psychedelic Support Manual is a comprehensive guide to establishing and managing support services for people who have difficult experiences with psychedelics at music festivals and similar events. The Manual grew out of the work of the Kosmicare organization in Portugal, now joined by MAPS.
- Psychedelic library (http://psychedelic-library.org/): repository of all kinds of psychedelic publications.
- Psychonaut docs (https://psychonautdocs.com/): repository of all kinds of publications for psychonauts.
- Frequently asked questions about the psychedelic experience (https://www.erowid.org/psychoactives/faqs/psychedelic_experience_faq.shtml)

Books

- How to Change Your Mind: What the New Science of Psychedelics Teaches Us About Consciousness, Dying, Addiction, Depression, and Transcendence, by Michael Pollan.
- The Psychedelic Explorer's Guide: Safe, Therapeutic and Sacred Journeys, by James Fadiman.
- The Psychedelic Experience: A Manual Based on the Tibetan Book of the Dead, by Timothy Leary
- Psychedelics Encyclopedia, by Peter Stafford.
- LSD. Cómo Descubrí el Ácido y qué Pasó Después en el Mundo, by Albert Hofmann and Jose Carlos Bouso (in Spanish).
- DMT: The Spirit Molecule: A Doctor's Revolutionary Research into the Biology of Near-Death and Mystical Experiences, by Rick Strassman.
- Pharmacotheon, by Jonathan Ott

- Historia Elemental de las Drogas, by Antonio Escohotado (in Spanish).
- Historia General de las Drogas, de Antonio Escohotado (in Spanish).
- Food of the Gods: The Search for the Original Tree of Knowledge - A Radical History of Plants, Drugs, and Human Evolution, by Terence McKenna.
- LSD Psychotherapy: The Healing Potential of Psychedelic Medicine, by Stanislav Grof.
- The Doors of Perception, by Aldous Huxley.
- Acid Dreams: The Complete Social History of LSD - The CIA, the Sixties and Beyond, by Martin A. Lee and Bruce Shlain.
- Your Psilocybin Mushroom Companion: An Informative, Easy-to-Use Guide to Understanding Magic Mushrooms—From Tips and Trips to Microdosing and Psychedelic Therapy, by Michelle Janikian.
- The Psilocybin Mushroom Bible: The Definitive Guide to Growing and Using Magic Mushrooms, by Dr. K Mandrake and Virginia Haze.
- Psilocybin Mushrooms of the World: An Identification Guide, by Paul Stamets.
- PiHKAL: A chemical love story, by Alexander & Ann Shulgin.
- TiHKAL: The continuation, by Alexander & Ann Shulgin.
- Psychedelic psychotherapy and research. Past, present and future, by Iker Puente.

Legal Information

- Release (https://www.release.org.uk/helpline)
- ICEERS Ayahuasca Defense Fund (https://www.iceers.org/es/adf/)

- Comparative resource of approximate sentences for drug crimes in Europe, by country, from the European Monitoring Center for Drugs and Drug Addiction, EMCDDA (https://www.emcdda.europa.eu/publications/topic-overviews/content/drug-law-penalties-at-a-glance_en)
- Comparative resource of approximate threshold quantities that constitute different levels of drug offenses in Europe, by country, from the European Monitoring Center for Drugs and Drug Addiction, EMCDDA (https://www.emcdda.europa.eu/publications/topic-overviews/threshold-quantities-for-drug-offences/html_en).

Other Resources

- The wheel of drugs (http://www.thedrugswheel.com/) by Mark Adley
- The drug combinations chart (https://tripsit.me/) by TripSit

GLOSSARY

Addiction: pathological search for reward or relief through the use of a substance or other actions. Usually associated with negative consequences and an inability to control behavior, as well as a dysfunctional emotional response. As for psychoactive substances, there is less and less talk of addiction and *more of a substance use disorder*.

Baseline state: state of sobriety and normal consciousness that is considered the beginning or end of the effects of a psychoactive drug.

Bomb: psychoactive substance, in a certain quantity and wrapped in a cigarette paper, for oral consumption, as a capsule.

Brain-derived neurotrophic factor, BDNF: protein that acts as a growth factor for neuronal tissue. Data have accumulated showing that BDNF has an important role in the physiological processes underlying neuroplasticity and development of the nervous system.

Default Mode Network (DMN): network of interacting brain regions that is active when a person is not focused on the outside world. It is considered a high-hierarchy network that influences and filters lower-hierarchy networks, such as sensory ones, and its appeasement under the effects of psychedelics is related to the experience of ego dissolution or "ego death."

Drug or psychoactive substance: any chemical substance that, upon entering the body via any route (buccal, nasal, oral, intravenous or others by which the substance can be absorbed), exerts a direct effect on the Central Nervous System and causes specific changes in its functions. These substances are capable of inhibiting pain, modifying mood or altering perceptions. Psychoactive substances have been used in all kinds of medical, ritual, religious or recreational contexts (examples are opium, alcohol, nicotine, caffeine, cocaine, morphine, etc.).

Harm reduction: compendium of tools that seek to reduce the harm associated with an activity, such as the use of psychoactive substances, in populations in which that activity is already causing harm. In English, there is no differentiation between risk reduction and harm reduction, and both are considered to be included within the term harm reduction.

Integration: process after a psychedelic experience in which all the content that has emerged during it is processed and worked on, emphasizing applying the abstract to real life. It is considered one of the most important parts of psychedelic-assisted psychotherapy or any other therapeutic work with psychedelics.

Microdosing: refers to the practice of using doses of psychedelics, such as LSD or psychoactive mushrooms, but below the minimum threshold to notice their psychoactive effects. People who microdose psychedelics report using them as a form of therapy, to increase creativity and intellectual performance. Given the recentness of the practice and the few number of studies, it has not been possible to scientifically verify the claims about the positive or negative impacts of this practice in the short, medium and long term. From the psychedelic community, the use of microdosing has been criticized for using psychedelics to turn a "counterculture sacrament" into one more way to engage in productivity and the consumer society. It has also been suggested that continuous use could lead to psychological addiction and increase the risk of heart disease in its users.

MK Ultra: secret CIA project. looking for military and espionage uses for various psychoactive substances (including psychedelics) and other techniques. During its years of operation (1953 - 1973), macabre secret experiments were carried out on volunteers or chosen people without their knowledge or consent, some of which ended in death.

MonoaminOxidase Inhibitor (MAOI): substance that inhibits the activity of monoamine oxidase enzymes, closely related to the degradation of neurotransmitters and psychoactive substances. They were the first antidepressants on the market.

Mystical experience: very personal introspective experience where some kind of universal unity or transcendence of time and space is described. They can occur at high doses of psychedelics, and are often associated with better long-term therapeutic outcome, so they are now often sought in psychedelic-assisted psychotherapy settings.

Neuron: main component cell of the nervous system. Its mission is to receive, process and transmit nerve impulses that come from other neurons through chemical signals (neurotransmitters) or in the form of electrical impulses. The connection between neurons or with other types of cells is called a synapse.

Neuropharmacology: study of how drugs affect cell function in the nervous system, and the neural mechanisms that influence behavior.

Neuroplasticity: ability of the neural networks of the brain (and the neurons that make them up) to modify their shape and connections (synapses) to adapt to changes in the environment or new requirements, either through learning or other adaptations.

Neuroreceptor or neurotransmitter receptor: protein complexes located in the cell membranes of neurons and that act as a lock, allowing the interaction of certain substances (neurotransmitters) with the mechanisms of cellular metabolism as well as chemical communication between cells and the synapse process.

Neuroscience: field of science that studies the nervous system and all its aspects, such as, for example, its structure, function, development, biochemistry, pharmacology and pathology, and how its different elements interact, giving rise to the biological bases of cognition and behavior.

Neurotransmitter: molecule responsible for transmitting signals from one neuron to the next, linked by a synapse. The neurotransmitter is released at the tip of the presynaptic neuron during nerve impulse propagation, crosses the synaptic gap, and acts by changing the action potential in the next neuron, called postsynaptic.

Oneironaut: explorer of altered states of consciousness produced during sleep and lucid dreaming.

Placebo: pharmacologically inert substance that is administered to a patient, as if it were a medicine, in order to compare its effect with that of a real drug, and thus rule out the effects produced by simple suggestion.

Post-traumatic stress disorder (PTSD): mental disorder classified within the group of those related to traumas and stress factors. It is characterized by the appearance of specific symptoms after exposure to a stressful event, extremely traumatic, of an extraordinarily threatening or catastrophic nature for the individual, even when the threat no longer exists.

Psychedelic: substance whose main action is to alter the cognition and perception of the mind, giving rise to non-ordinary perceptions. The term is derived from the Greek words ψυχή (psyche, "mind") and δηλείν (/dileín/, "to manifest"), which can be translated as "manifestation of the mind/soul." Normally, this effect is produced by action on the serotonin 5-HT2a neuroreceptor. Psychedelic drugs are also known by the names of hallucinogenic drugs, entheogenic drugs, visionary drugs, power drugs, psychodysleptics, psychotomimetics, eidetics, etc. Each of these names is associated with a particular worldview, is not always appropriate in all contexts, and none fully describes the psychophysiological effects.

Psychonautics/Psychonaut: from the Greek ψυχή, psyche ("mind") and ναύτης, naútēs ("sailor or navigator"), refers to the methodology for describing and explaining the subjective effects of alternate states of consciousness, including states induced by mind-altering substances, meditation. The researcher voluntarily plunges into an altered state through these techniques to explore human experience and existence.

Remission: reduction of symptoms associated with a mental disorder. Remission can be partial or complete. In mental health, the word "cure" is not often used.

Risk: probability of a negative event or damage occurring. However, it does not necessarily imply that it will occur. For example, leaning over a ledge means exposing yourself to a risk of falling, but it does not necessarily imply that it will happen (and therefore cause damage).

Risk Reduction: compendium of tools that seek to reduce the risks associated with an activity that can be dangerous, such as the consumption of psychoactive substances, when you do not want to give up said activity. Risk reduction in the use of psychoactive substances is applied to a population that has not yet suffered harm from its use and to prevent its occurrence. In English, there is no differentiation between risk reduction and harm reduction, and both are considered to be included within the term harm reduction.

Synapse: zone of approximation between two neurons, like a "connector", through which chemical signals (neurotransmitters) are sent. It allows neuronal signals to spread. Depending on the type of element that is transmitted between neurons, we can find chemical synapses (majority in our body) and electrical synapses.

Tolerance: gradual process of physiological adaptation that occurs as a result of continued exposure or administration to a substance, and that will cause the subject to be less sensitive to it. Thus, the usual dose of the substance produces progressively fewer effects, so higher doses are needed to produce them.

Trippsitter: sober person accompanying someone who is having a psychedelic experience. Their job is to take care of the person's safety and help them manage the experience if they need it.

The Legal Status of Psychedelic Drugs Psychedelics Around the World

Francisco Azorín Ortega, lawyer specialized in legislation and jurisprudence on drugs.

Introduction

In order to talk about legislation and jurisprudence on psychedelic drugs, the first thing we have to do is define the latter concept. Although depending on how broadly the term is interpreted it may have different meanings, on this occasion we will use a fairly broad definition of the term. Such definition will include all those substances such as LSD, DMT, psilocybin, mescaline, or 2C-B that have perceptible effects on consciousness through, noticeably, acting on the serotonin 2A neuroreceptors, as well as other substances with more dissociative psychedelic effects, such as ketamine, which acts mainly on NMDA glutamate neuroreceptors. There are also other substances classified as empathogenic-entactogenic, such as MDMA ("ecstasy"), with indirect interaction on 2A neuroreceptors, which many consider to be only semi-psychedelic, but which in high doses can cause considerable psychedelic effects, like those caused by its sister substance, MDA[1], or 2C-B.

It should also be noted that these psychedelic drugs can occur as isolated molecules (either extracted or synthesised), or as part of a plant or fungus (ayahuasca, psilocybe mushrooms, cacti, etc.). Or even in some animals, such as the toad Bufo alvarius from the Sonoran desert (Mexico), whose glands contain the most potent of the known psychedelics, 5-MeO-DMT. Although these toads were only recently discovered to contain this molecule, 5-MeO-DMT had already been synthesised in 1936 and isolated in 1959 from the seeds of Anadenanthera colubrina. Another drug that is also found in animals is DMT. On top of being present in many plants, this molecule is also found in small amounts in humans and other mammals. It, therefore, seems that these compounds may be far more important to the workings of nature than we could ever have imagined.

Today, the Western world has far more psychedelics at its disposal than could have been available in the psychedelic boom era of the 1960s and 1970s, as well as in the "second summer of love", which took place in Ibiza in 1987 and was exported to the UK between 1988 and 1989 with the emergence of the semi-psychedelic MDMA and "rave culture".

The explosion of the phenomenon of new designer drugs, NPS, and their sale on the internet, as well as the growing interest in shamanic cultures and their practice in Western territories, make it necessary to review and clarify the legislation and jurisprudence that tries to deal with this social reality.

---

[1] It was known in the popular slang of Spain in the 80s and 90s as "mescalinas" or "meskas" because of the similarity between its structure and some of its effects to those of mescaline, found in the San Pedro cactus and Mexican peyote.

The presence of a certain sector of the population that uses these substances on an occasional or recurrent basis to navigate their consciousness, reconcile and accept their traumas, free themselves from their blockages, relieve their stress or depression and, in short, try to live in this increasingly confrontational society more consciously and peacefully, is becoming increasingly evident in our current culture.

The legal regime for psychedelic drugs around the world is a complex subject that has always been subject to controversy and disparate interpretations, as well as constant legislative changes. In this chapter, I will attempt to provide as comprehensive and up-to-date a review as possible.

1.1 Why were Certain Psychoactive Substances Banned?

The idea of banning all "recreational" use of certain psychoactive substances was driven by the growing influence of Anglo-American Christian Puritanism and the temperance movement against alcohol in the late 19th and early 20th centuries, which in the United States also led to the prohibition of alcohol between 1920 and 1933. The campaign for prohibition was also fuelled by racist sentiments towards immigrants from China and Mexico, who used opium and cannabis[2].

In the 1960s, specifically in 1961, most countries in the world signed the Single Convention on Narcotic Drugs in New York, which banned opium, cannabis, and coca leaf, as well as their active ingredients and some derivatives (cocaine, morphine, and heroin). Later, new trends in the use of psychoactive drugs would emerge, such as the popularisation of psychedelic substances, given that, in parallel to the promising clinical research with substances like LSD, psilocybin,

---

[2] Arbour, et al. (2019). The classification of psychoactive substances. Global Commission on Drug Policy. Report 2019. Retrieved from: https://www.globalcommissionondrugs.org/.

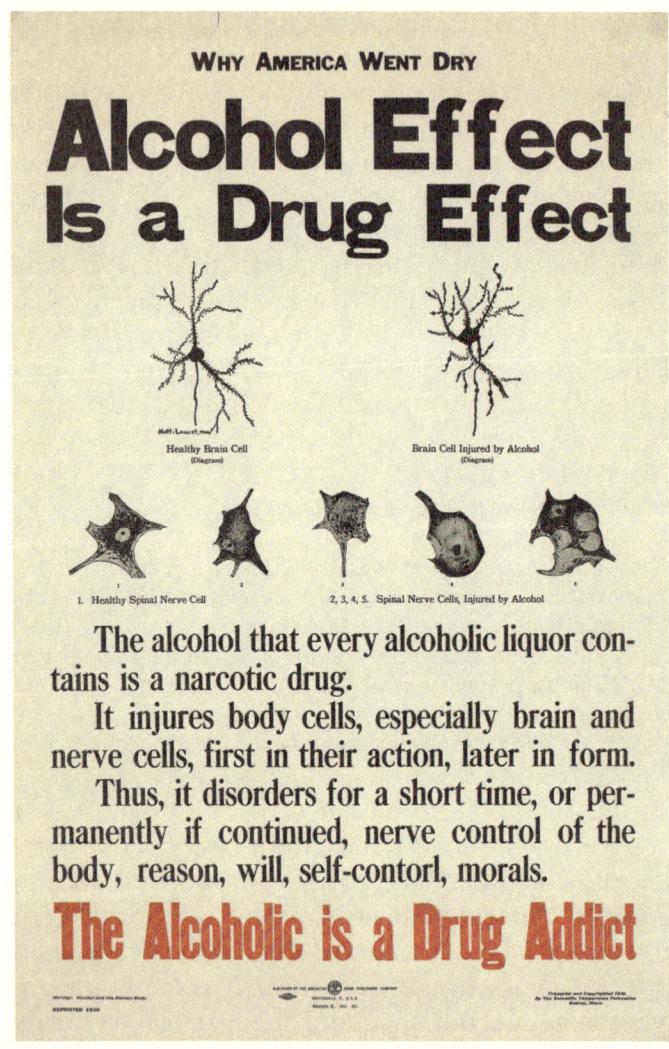

The scientific temperance movement against alcohol, which had a strong Puritan influence, enacted alcohol prohibition in the USA. The Scientific Temperance Foundation, CC BY 4.0 <https://creativecommons.org/licenses/by/4.0>, via Wikimedia Commons.

or mescaline, some university professors like Timothy Leary, writers like Ken Kesey or actors like Cary Grant, made their use fashionable in North America. This meant that the use of this category of substances quickly spread to the rest of the Western world, also playing an important role in the development of modern neuroscience.

With the upsurge of the non-clinical use of LSD, DMT, and psilocybin in the 1960s, associated with the hippie movement, the counterculture and anti-war in the context of the Vietnam War, as well as their relationship with some events reported in a very sensationalist way by the press, at the end of the decade the USA decided to ban these substances. The first to do so was the state of California in 1966 when Ronald Reagan was governor, and they were later controlled at the federal level in 1969. Subsequently, in 1971, they were included in Schedule I of the International Convention on Psychotropic Substances, signed in Vienna, when Richard Nixon, the man who declared the so-called "war on drugs", was president of the US.

In the 1980s, another of the world's most famous psychoactive substances, MDMA or ecstasy, came into vogue, described as a semi-psychedelic and known for its entactogenic-empathogenic effects. It was banned in the USA in 1985, despite an Administrative Court recommendation to include it in Schedule III given it is not very toxic and seemed to have psychotherapeutic effects. Despite pressure from some psychiatrists and other mental health professionals who used it for their treatments, the DEA (Drug Enforcement Administration) finally included it in its US Schedule I, where the most dangerous substances with no recognised therapeutic value are placed, and in 1985 it was also included in Schedule I of the International Convention on Psychotropic Substances, which lists the most toxic and harmful substances considered to have little or no therapeutic value for international control.

1.2 Criteria for Inclusion in One Control List or Another

Inclusion in one list or another does not always depend so much on the hazardousness or toxicity of the substance, or on its real therapeutic potential, but rather on a political or moral decision influenced by a given spatiotemporal context. In this regard, Nutt, King, and Phillips (2010) established a classification of the dangerousness of different drugs (legal and illegal) using a multitude of criteria, concluding that the least dangerous substances were psychedelic molecules, such as LSD and psilocybin, or semi-psychedelics, such as cannabis or MDMA[3]. These were placed way below others such as alcohol or tobacco that, despite being more harmful, are legal.

In the words of an anonymous administrator and convention participant quoted by Kleiman, ranking decisions are ultimately a consequence of the following premise: "If it's fun, it's scheduled One"[4].

1.3 The International Classification of Ketamine: A Substance With Recognised Medical Uses

The situation is different for ketamine, a substance with psychedelic and dissociative properties that was synthesised in 1962 by Calvin Stevens. Since then it has been used

---

[3] Nutt, D. J., King, L. A., and Phillips, L. D. (2010). Drug harms in the UK: a multicriteria decision analysis. The Lancet, 376(9752), 1558-1565.

[4] Arbour, et al (2019). The classification of psychoactive substances. Global Commission on Drug Policy. Report 2019. Retrieved from: https://www.globalcommissionondrugs.org/.

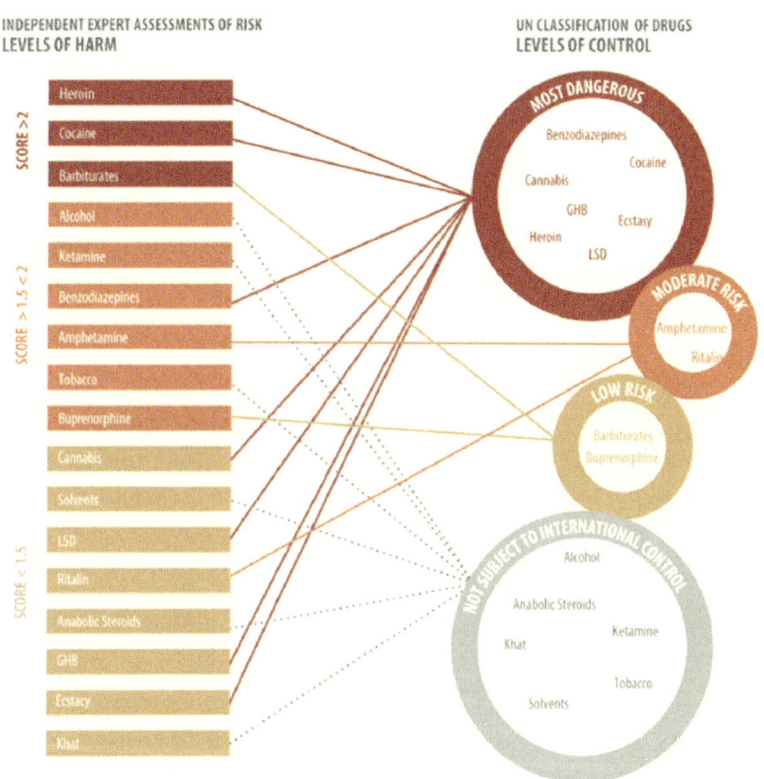

Levels of harm of different drugs as assessed by scientists, compared to their current international legal control levels. David Nutt et al., «Development of a Rational Scale to Assess the Harm of Drugs of Potential Misuse», The Lancet 369, n.o 9566 (24 de Marzo de 2007): 1047-53. & Gomis, Benoît. (2016). Modernising Drug Law Enforcement. IDPC Drug Policy Guide - 3rd edition (pp. 90-96).

therapeutically in medicine and veterinary medicine as a general anaesthetic and has also been included in the list of essential medicines of the World Health Organisation (WHO) by virtue of its usefulness and safety. Since 2019, this substance, or rather one of its purified molecular forms (esketamine), patented by the pharmaceutical company

Janssen (owned by Johnson & Johnson), has been recognised by the FDA and other drug agencies for the treatment of depression, and, likely, this therapeutic indication will also be extended to racemic (classic) ketamine.

Due to the rise of ketamine for recreational use, it was first controlled in the USA in 1999, and in 2006 it was listed by the United Nations Commission on Narcotic Drugs (CND) as a controlled substance under the 1971 Convention on Psychotropic Substances. Other states then transposed this prohibition into their national laws.

All the substances mentioned up to this point, except ketamine (which is in Schedule IV), are in Schedule I of the 1971 Convention on Psychotropic Substances where (according to the convention) the most dangerous and least valuable drugs in medicine are placed under control. Member states have also included them in the list where the most punishable substances under the respective national penal codes are to be found.

In the case of ketamine, this substance has always been recognised as having therapeutic properties as a general anaesthetic, as well as, more recently, as a psychiatric drug for the treatment of severe depression. For this reason, it has always been considered more therapeutic and less dangerous than other drugs, however, this cannot be considered scientifically correct since, for example, according to the report by Nutt et al. (2010), despite being below that of other legal drugs such as alcohol and tobacco, the harmful potential of ketamine for the individual and society is above that of LSD and psilocybin.

The WHO Expert Committee on Drug Dependence acknowledged that some concern had been expressed, stating:

Placing ketamine under international control would have a negative impact on the availability and accessibility of this substance. This, in turn, would limit access to essential and emergency surgery, leading to a public health crisis in countries where no other affordable replacement anaesthetic is available[5].

As can be seen, the case of synthetic drugs with psychedelic properties such as ketamine and MDMA, or semi-synthetic drugs such as LSD (derived from the ergot fungus), is not technically complicated when it comes to interpreting their legal status. As we will see below, legal interpretations become more complicated when dealing with plants or mushrooms that contain psychotropic controlled molecules.

The historical and legal arguments set out in this introduction require us to navigate the paradoxical legislation and jurisprudence that regulates this issue.

2. States and Cities in the USA that have decriminalised the Use of Psychedelic Substances.

2.1 US Cities that Have Pioneered the Decriminalisation of Psychedelic Substances.

Since 2012, when the US states of Colorado and Washington regulated access to cannabis for recreational use, there have been many efforts by associations advocating changes in current drug policies. To alleviate the great pandemic of mental illnesses that is increasingly present in society, such associations are seeking recognition of their therapeutic uses.

---

[5] WHO (2012) WHO Expert *Committee on Drug Dependence*, Thirty-fifth Report, WHO, Technical Report Series 973, Geneva: World Health Organization, p. 9. Retrieved from: https://apps.who.int/medicinedocs/pdf/s4898s/s4898s.pdf.

Thus, since then, not only has cannabis been regulated for recreational purposes in 20 US states and Washington DC. There have also been political and legislative movements to decriminalise the use of certain psychedelic substances in many parts of the United States, both at the state and municipal levels.

The first city to decriminalise the use of a substance other than cannabis was Denver, in the state of Colorado. In 2019 it did not quite legalise psilocybin (found in magic mushrooms) but did however prohibit wasting police and judicial efforts to prosecute its use, thus being at the forefront of decriminalising psychedelic drugs and recognising their therapeutic value.

Other West Coast cities have also joined the reform, such as Oakland (historically very familiar with the use of entheogens), which in 2019 also decriminalised the use of plants, cacti, or mushrooms containing controlled substances such as psilocybin, mescaline, or DMT; or Santa Cruz, also in the state of California, which in 2020 decriminalised the possession and cultivation of psilocybin-containing magic mushrooms, although the commercial sale of them remains illegal.

Washington D.C. followed in November 2020, and in 2021 it was the cities of Somerville, Bay State, and Cambridge in the state of Massachusetts. Hence, we are no longer talking exclusively about cities on the West Coast. The decriminalisation of psychedelics, like cannabis, has also reached the East Coast.

The latest cities to jump on the psychedelic bandwagon are Seattle (in Washington State), Arcata (in California), and Easthampton (in Massachusetts), which will not prioritise the prosecution of crimes related to entheogenic plants. It, therefore, seems that, very soon, the possession and use of cannabis and other substances such as psilocybin (magic mushrooms) or mescaline (San Pedro cactus and peyote) will not be prosecuted in most US states.

2.2 US States That Have Decriminalised or Legalised the Use Of Psychedelics

Regarding the decriminalisation of psilocybin at the state level, the state of Oregon was the first to take the big step in November 2020, recognising its use for therapeutic purposes, as it considers it useful for treating major depression or post-traumatic stress disorder (PTSD). Thus, possession of up to 5 grams of magic mushrooms, used for medicinal purposes, is legal in the state of Oregon.

The next state that seems to be getting ready to legalise the use of psilocybin for medicinal purposes is the state of California, where several proposals to legalise magic mushrooms' psychoactive molecule or other entheogenic plants for medicinal purposes have already been put forward. There are also such proposals in the states of New York and New Jersey.

2.3 Potential Problems where US Federal Law Comes into Play

Although these reforms are taking place at the local and state level, the US is a federal country, and US federal law still includes psilocybin in its Schedule I controlled substances, which are considered the most dangerous and have the least therapeutic uses. This means that, even if they are in a city or state that has already decriminalised them if a person is caught in possession of these substances by FBI agents, they can be charged with possession of illegal drugs under US federal law.

2.4 Conclusion

In summary, since some American cities don't consider them to be harmful and do instead consider them to have increasingly recognised therapeutic value, they are no longer prioritising the efforts of their local police to prosecute people who use this type of drugs. However, the only state that has legalised psilocybin for medicinal purposes is Oregon, and the US Congress, which legislates at the federal level on drug issues, is not yet in favour of legalising such substances. Therefore, the reader of this collection should take special care if in possession of a certain quantity of substances considered psychedelic, as, with a few local exceptions, they are still prohibited nationally and, of course, internationally in all countries.

3 Graduation of Penalties for Trafficking and Use of Psychedelic Substances Around the World

In order to impose a penalty on the offender, drug trafficking offences in countries that follow the rule of law are usually classified based on three basic factors: the alleged dangerousness of the substance, the quantity seized and the aggravating circumstances of the case.

3.1 Increased Penalties for the Dangerousness of the Substance

In order to assess the criminal risks that would exist in cases of arrest for possession or sale of these substances, it should first be checked whether or not the Member State in question is signed up to the 1971 UN Convention, whether or not it has also transposed the convention into national law (i.e., whether such signed international convention has been "translated" into national law) and, finally, whether those particular substances are controlled in any of the schedules of the National Drug Law of each State.

Despite this, there are countries with analogue laws: the US Analogue Substances Act, enacted in 1988, which automatically bans a substance if its structure and effects are "substantially similar" to those of an already banned drug; or the UK's Psychoactive Substances Act of 2016, which by default bans any psychoactive substance that by stimulating or depressing the person's central nervous system [...] affects the person's mental functioning or emotional state[6].

Penalties are usually imposed according to whether substances are more or less dangerous to public health. Some countries such as the UK classify them in Schedules A, B or C, with the most (officially) dangerous substances such as cocaine, heroin, LSD or psilocybin placed in Schedule A, amphetamine or cannabis in Schedule B, and tranquillisers in Schedule C7. The US also has five schedules, including in the first schedule those substances that are allegedly most abused, most toxic, and not medically licensed (LSD, psilocybin, DMT, 2CB), with ketamine, for example, being included in schedule III given it is medically licensed.

The case of Spain is, for example, more complex, having transposed the international drug conventions into domestic law by copying the same substances included in the schedules of the aforementioned international convention. Therefore, in the case of psychotropics, substances in Schedule I are officially more dangerous, and with less recognised therapeutic value, than those in Schedules II, III, and IV.

However, Article 36[8] of the Spanish Penal Code establishes a penal difference depending on whether or not the substance can cause serious damage to health. Paradoxically, however, this concept is not normative (it is not defined in the

---

[6] United Kingdom (2016) 2016 Psychoactive Substances Act. London: Crown, paragraph 2. Retrieved from: http://www.legislation.gov.uk/ukpga/2016/2/section/2/enacted.

[7] Milton Trott, D. *The Drug Users Bible. Harm Reduction*, Risk Mitigation, Personal Safety and antidote to the War on Drugs. MxZero Publishing, 2019.

law), but jurisprudential (it is applied based on what previous judgments have interpreted), because the only drug currently classified by the jurisprudence of the Spanish courts as not causing serious harm to health is cannabis, and it is in Schedule I (the most controlled and with the least therapeutic potential) of the Spanish Narcotics Law 17/1967, while amphetamine or 2CB are in Schedule II (less controlled) although they are treated by case law as causing serious harm to health. Yet, another case of nonsensical legislation.

It should be noted that this jurisprudential concept, that of serious damage to health, is subject to change through the provision of pharmacological expert evidence, i.e. what experts on the substance can say about its dangerousness in court. In fact, for example, MDMA (ecstasy) was considered by the Spanish National Court as a substance that does not cause serious damage to health in a hearing in 1994 in which the expert witness for the defence was Alexander Shulgin himself, considered the godfather or rediscoverer of this substance, as well as the mastermind behind the expansion of its use among the therapeutic community to treat post-traumatic stress disorder and other psychiatric illnesses. During the trial, the scientist compared MDMA to its chemical "big sister", MDA, to explain that MDMA is less neurotoxic than MDA and that it does not have high addictive power. Thanks to this, the court decided to consider ecstasy as a substance that does not cause serious damage to health[8] and was therefore punished with a lesser penalty than cocaine or LSD. However, later on, Spanish court jurisprudence changed, considering ecstasy (MDMA) a health hazard. This was possibly due to Leah Betts' scandal, the 18-year-old British girl who died after taking an ecstasy pill at a house party with her parents. During the days when she was in a coma, a media campaign made front pages of newspapers in the UK

---

[8] Joldi. J. *El éxtasis no causa grave daño a la salud según la Audiencia Nacional. El País*, Madrid 23 January 1994. Retrieved from: https://elpais.com/

and around the world, publishing photos of her on her deathbed and filling the streets up with pictures of her face accompanied by messages about the dangers of drugs. Later, the doctor who treated her said that she had died from over-hydration, known as hyponatremia, as she drank too much water in an attempt to quench the effect of the pill. In reality, deaths from ecstasy use are not common and occur in much smaller proportions than those related to alcohol or tobacco[9], without this resulting in the criminalisation of their possession or distribution.

3.2 Increasing Penalties for Quantity Seized

The different countries that have banned the possession and sale of different psychedelic (or other) drugs also tend to establish tables to increase penalties according to the quantity of the substance seized.

This is the case, for example, in the USA, which has tables of equivalence between substances, in which, if a certain quantity is exceeded, the minimum or maximum penalty required by federal law is increased. In the case of ecstasy, for example, there is a table of equivalence concerning cannabis, with the equivalence being 1-500. This means that 1 gram of MDMA is equivalent to the penalty for 500 grams of cannabis. This equivalence was raised in 2001 from 35-1 to 500-1, but in 2011, with the collaboration of the Multidisciplinary Association for Psychedelic Studies (MAPS), it was set by two American courts at 200-1, considering that the scientific reports provided in 2001 were based on exaggerated, and scientifically unsound, perceptions of the harmfulness of MDMA, and that MDMA was no more harmful than cocaine. In 2017, an attempt was made to re-classify the equivalence of ecstasy in a proceeding in which Dr. Rick Doblin, founder of MAPS, was an expert

---

[9] Collin, M. Estado alterado. *La historia de la cultura del éxtasis y del acid house.* Alba Editorial. Barcelona, 2002.

witness, without succeeding in having the dangerousness of MDMA reconsidered[10]. However, with the work of people like Rick and MAPS, MDMA is now in phase 3 clinical trials, and FDA recognition for the treatment of post-traumatic stress disorder and other psychiatric illnesses is expected by 2023.

3.3 Increased Penalties for Aggravating Circumstances

Penalties are also often increased for other aggravating circumstances, such as committing the crime with violence, belonging to a criminal organisation, or using minors to traffic.

Sentences for drug trafficking are typically set at between 2 and 10 years in most countries, rising to 20 years, or even life imprisonment, in countries such as the US or the UK, when there are very special and specific circumstances such as the use of criminal gangs or violence. There are regions where sentences can be particularly high, such as Africa, the Middle East, or Asia.

3.4 Tolerance in Cases of Small Quantities for Personal Use

In most European countries, some US states, Canada, and in most South American countries, drug use for personal use is tolerated, and offences for simple possession of drugs are usually punishable by a prison sentence of between 6 months to 2 years, which may be suspended if the offender is a primary offender (no previous criminal record) or undergoing drug detoxification treatment. It might also just be replaced by a fine[11].

---

[10] Multidisciplinary Association for Psychedelic Studies USSC Testimony re: MDMA March 15, 2017

[11] Cavada, J.P. *Criterios para el sancionamiento del consumo o tráfico de drogas en el derecho extranjero*. Biblioteca Nacional del Congreso de Chile. Octubre, 2020. Obtained from: https://obtienearchivo.bcn.cl/

However, the specific legislation in each country needs to be studied in detail to find out whether there is a law on minimum dose for personal use, or whether simple possession is punishable by administrative fines, etc.

3.4.1 Latin American Countries

Latin American countries such as Colombia, Uruguay, Peru, and Mexico have minimum personal dose laws, in which small quantities of various substances cannot even be punished by an administrative rule.

In Peru, for example, drug trafficking is punishable by a sentence of 8 to 15 years, and possession for trafficking is punishable by 6 to 12 years, and even life imprisonment if forced by violence or intimidation to plant drugs. However, possession for the personal use of up to five grams of cocaine base paste, two grams of cocaine hydrochloride, eight grams of marijuana and two grams of its derivatives, or two hundred and fifty milligrams of MDMA or similar substances[12] is not criminalised. Having said this, it seems that the dose is seized even if it is not sanctioned in all countries except Uruguay[13].

In Mexico and Colombia, for example, the constitutional courts have issued two rulings, on 4 November 2015 and 6 June 2019 respectively, in which, in the section on the weighing of affected fundamental rights and collective legal interests to be protected (public health and safety), it is concluded that these two collective interests should not

---

[12] Martín, A. y Muñoz, J. (2019). *El estatuto legal de la Ayahuasca en España. La relevancia penal de los comportamientos relacionados con su consumo y posesión.* Valencia: Tirant lo blanch.

[13] El Nuevo Siglo. Salvo Uruguay, dosis mínima se incauta en toda A. Latina. 6 de septiembre de 2018. Obtained from: https://www.elnuevosiglo.com.co/

prevail over the individual freedom and free development of the personality of the drug user, as long as the test of proportionality in the interpretation of these affected fundamental rights and protected legal interests is not passed. In other words, individual liberties prevail over the personal consumption of substances in the face of other considerations, such as public health and safety, allegedly threatened by personal drug consumption. However, the Colombian Constitutional Court had already declared the criminalisation of drug use unconstitutional in Ruling C-221/94. Despite this ruling almost two decades ago, subsequent governments criticised this judicial decision and attempted to re-criminalize drug use for personal consumption, generating laws that currently prohibit use but do not criminalise it. This ruling was used by academic research and by countries such as Switzerland and the Netherlands to adapt their arguments to their legislation[14].

In Argentina, penalties range from 1 month to 2 years imprisonment plus a fine for possession for personal use (art. 14, second paragraph, Law 23.737); from 1 to 6 years imprisonment plus a fine for simple possession (first paragraph of the same art.); and from 4 to 15 years imprisonment plus a fine for possession for commercial purposes (5 inc. C of the same law). The latter Article 5 also establishes penalties for trafficking of 4 to 15 years imprisonment plus a fine, and some aggravating circumstances are described in subsequent articles. Cross-border trafficking is punishable under the Customs Code (Art. 866) with penalties ranging from 4.5 months to 16 years.

3.4.2 The Spanish Case

In Spain, as long as no specific quantities of psychedelics are found that exceed what is considered usual for daily

---

[14] Uprimny, R. A 25 años de la sentencia C-221/94 en Colombia: una oportunidad perdida. Obtained from: https://idpc.net/

personal use during 3 to 5 days, and provided there are no indications of trafficking (such as having the substance divided into doses, having a precision scale, a multitude of substances, a notebook with notes, cash, etc.), the case would not be sent to a criminal court. This has been established by the National Institute of Toxicology at a maximum of 2.4gm of pure MDMA or 0.003gm of LSD[15], with a fine of between 601 and 30,000 euros[16] being imposed in these cases. However, this law is to be amended shortly, and it seems that fines for simple possession will be considered minor (the amount would be between 100 and 600 euros), and consumption on public roads will be punished with a fine of 601 euros[17]. However, perhaps because they are less prevalent in the population, substances such as psilocybin are not included in this table of quantities regarding personal consumption, nor do they appear in tables in other countries. In this case, and in order to calculate the dose that could be regarded as for personal use, and what quantities could be considered as trafficking and therefore subject to higher penalties, ad hoc expert evidence will be required. Despite exceeding the INT quantities, Spanish jurisprudence requires proof of intent to traffic the substance to convict through other evidence or indicia.

---

[15] Instituto Nacional de Toxicología (2001). Informe sobre dosis mínima psicoactiva, de 18 de octubre de 2001. Madrid: Instituto Nacional de Toxicología.

[16] Ley Orgánica 4/2015, de 30 de marzo, de protección de la seguridad ciudadana. Publicada en BOE n°77, de 31 de marzo de 2015. España.

[17] Azorín, F. *Reforma de la Ley Mordaza y cannabis: es urgente*. El Salto. 14 de diciembre 2021. Recuperado de: https://www.elsaltodiario.com/

PSYCHEDELIC'S LEGAL STATUS

Instituto Nacional de Toxicología
Cuadro de dosis mínimas psicoactivas de las principales sustancias tóxicas objeto de tráfico de drogas, actualmente vigente

Fecha de actualización: martes, 1 de diciembre de 2009 (revisado el 1 de agosto de 2021)
Archivo asociado: Cuadro de dosis mínimas psicoactivas de las principales sustancias tóxicas objeto de tráfico de drogas

	unidades peso	dosis habitual más baja	dosis habitual más alta	dosis media	Consumo diario estimado máximo	Dosis mínima psicoactiva	Previsión (3 a 5 días de consumo) en gramos
Heroína[1]	mg	50	150	100	600	0,66 mg[6]	3
Morfina	mg	10	80		2000	Intravenosa: 2 mg	
Metadona	mg	40	120		240	5 mg/3-4 horas	
Buprenorfina	mg			0,6	2,4	0,2 a 0,3 mg/8 h	
Dextropropoxifeno	mg			150	600	100 mg/hora	
Pentazocina	mg			60	360	50 mg/4 horas	
Fentanilo	mg			0,025	0,1	25 mg/hora	
Dihidrocodeína	mg			120	360	60	
Levoacetilmetadol	mg			180	180	60 mg/2 días	
Petidina	mg			100	300	50 mg/24 h	
Tramadol	mg			100	400	50 mg/8 h	
Cocaína HCl[2]	mg	100	250		1500	50 mg	7,5
Marihuana	g	1,5	2		15-20	10 mg (vía oral), 5 mg/m² de superficie	100
Haschís	g	0,3	0,5		5	10 mg (vía oral), 5 mg/m² de superficie	25
Aceite de Haschís	mg	0,03	0,06		600	10 mg (vía oral), 5 mg/m² de superficie	
LSD	mg	0,019	0,3	0,132	0,6	0,02-0,025	0,003
Anfetamina Sulfato[3]	mg	30	60		180	10	0,9
Anfepramona	mg			75	150	75	
Clobenzorex	mg			30	90	30	
Fenproporex	mg			10	30	10	
Metanfetamina	mg	2,5	15		60	-	0,3
Alprazolam	mg			1	10	0,25	
Triazolam	mg			1	3	0,125	
Flunitrazepam	mg	1	2		10	0,5	
Lorazepam	mg			5	15	1	
Clorazepato diK	mg			25	150	5	
MDA[4]	mg	20	150	80	480	20	2,4
MDMA[4]	mg	20	150	80	480	20-50	2,4
MDEA[4]	mg	20	150	80	480	20-50	2,4
Ketamina[5]	mg				200	30	

Comentarios informe INTCF 12691/03
[1] Dosis= peso total de las papelinas, con droga y resto sustancias acompañantes en base a una riqueza media del 45-50% de la sustancia psicoactiva hallada en 1997-1999.
[2] Dosis= peso medio de las papelinas en nuestro país en los años 1997-1999. Se estima que con ese peso se podrían hacer entre 2 y 4 rayas.
[3] Cantidades halladas por comprimidos en el INTCF. Los consumidores podrían llegar a tomarse entre 3 y 6 comprimidos/día.
[4] Dosis media aproximada neta de droga de abuso, según los comprimidos analizados en el INTCF.

Otros informes ampliatorios del INTCF
[5] Informe del INTCF de fecha 14/12/2011
[6] Informe del INTCF de fecha 12/01/2004

Table of doses of psychoactive substances drawn up by the Spanish National Institute of Toxicology. In the absence of evidence of trafficking, personal use is considered by the quantities estimated for 3 to 5 days' use. Source: National Plan on Drugs.

3.4.2.1 Scientific and Logical Shortcomings in Setting Doses

To further highlight the lack of solid scientific criteria when establishing penalties for drug trafficking in Spain, we can recover this excerpt from an article on the words spoken by the director of INT at the time of issuing the famous report:

> "That table was part of a technical report that was sent in 2001 to the Supreme Court, but at no point did we address whether they should be used to set sentences or not", Gómez explained. Gómez agreed with the opinions of other experts consulted, and clarified that "the effect of a toxic substance on the organism depends on the person, their size, their state and how used to it they are. It is the same as with Valium which doesn't have the same effect on everyone. Some people fall asleep with one pill, others don't feel anything when they take two"[18].

In other words, not even the authors of the report considered it fair that sentences should be passed based on said report. As historically only a summary table has been available on the internet, I requested the report via Spain's Transparency Portal. It came as a great surprise to see that there were no bibliographical references that could be refuted by other experts through contradictory expert evidence. Only a legend full of scientific and logical deficiencies could be found. For example, all substances have a range of daily doses, and to obtain the maximum amount for personal use, the highest end of the range is multiplied by 5 (in reference to 5 days of personal use). However, in the case of MDMA (ecstasy), it is stated that between 1 and 15 tablets of 80 mg can be consumed per day when, according to the report, the norm is to take 6 tablets per day (which goes against the logic of the table, which always multiplies by 5 the highest dose of the range).

---

[18] Lázaro, J.M y De Benito, E. toxicología se desmarca del baremo que utiliza el supremo para condenar a camellos. El País a 11 de abril de 2004. Obtained from: https://elpais.com/

3.4.3 Personal Use Doses for Non-Scheduled Substances

In those cases where the substance in question does not appear in the table, it is up to the police to decide whether, depending on the dose seized, a case should be dealt with under criminal or administrative law. However, as we have said, the tables are not complete and do not cover the full range of psychopharmacological drugs used by people who consume illegal substances. In fact, in the case of psilocybin mushrooms, there is an acquittal in Spain that states the following:

> In the specific case of the ruling, 670 mushrooms weighing 202.5 grams were seized. In this sense, the minimum active dose [of pure psilocybin] is around 2 milligrams, 10 to 20 milligrams is a medium dose, and a high dose is 30 milligrams or more. The effects of medium doses last for 4 to 6 hours and those of high doses for up to 8 hours. Based on these parameters, the daily dose of [pure psilocybin] consumption can be put at around 100 mg. If we multiply this amount by 1.7 mg of psilocybin per mushroom, the result is just over 1 gram of this substance [pure psilocybin]. This is an amount that guarantees consumption for about 10 days[19].

The reader will note, if experienced in the use of mushrooms, that, when it comes to psychedelics such as mushrooms or LSD, which are usually taken very infrequently, in annual or monthly doses at most, this ruling does not make much sense. However, drug jurisprudence is often constructed by people with little knowledge of the subject who assume that everyone who takes drugs is addicted and that taking a substance necessarily implies continuous use throughout the day to be under its effects 24 hours a day, every day. This flawed logic is probably derived from the problematic use of certain highly addictive opiates, such as heroin.

---

[19] Sentence from the Audiencia Provincial of Alicante nº 129/2013 of 28 February.

3.4.4 The Dutch Case

In the Netherlands, for example, possession of up to 5 grams of fresh mushrooms and 0.5 grams of dried mushrooms used to be tolerated, but in 2008 fresh mushrooms were explicitly banned. Previously, only dried mushrooms were considered to be "a preparation containing psilocybin" as defined by the 1971 Psychotropic Convention. Since 2008, the market switched from mushrooms to psilocybin-containing truffles, given that these fungal species were not explicitly controlled[20].

3.4.5 Portugal and its Risk and Harm Reduction Policy

Another country where possession of drugs for personal use is not criminalised is Portugal. Law 30/2000, adopted in November 2000 and enforced since July 2001, decriminalised the consumption, acquisition, and possession of drugs for personal use. A decree establishes the quantities that will not lead to criminal prosecution for each substance, estimating as a maximum the daily consumption of a drug throughout ten days. If someone is caught consuming in the street, they are given the option to attend an interview with a psychologist, a social worker, and a jurist so that this committee can analyse whether they present problematic consumption and, if so, offer them therapeutic help (Cavada, J.P. 2020).

3.4.6 France and Italy and their Hardline Drug Policy

France, for its part, has always been a very belligerent country on drug issues within Europe. However, penalties for simple possession are less than 1 year plus a fine and the offender is usually required to attend and pay a drug awareness course (Cavada, J.P. 2020).

---

[20] Legal situation of psilocybin mushrooms. Obtained from: https://es.abcdef.wiki/wiki

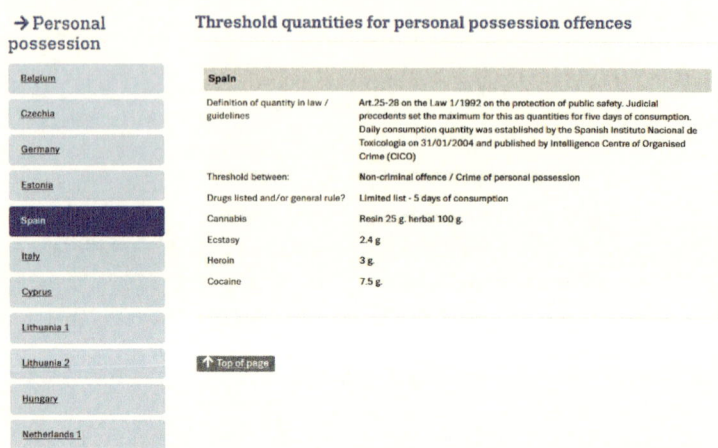

Personal consumption levels in Spain and other European countries. EMCDDA. Screenshot of the website https://www.emcdda.europa.eu/publications/topic-overviews/threshold-quantities-for-drug-offences/html_en#T1.

Italy is another country that establishes higher penalties for drug trafficking offences, especially if committed by organised mafias. In terms of penalties for simple possession, it is also a rather tough country because, even if criminal proceedings are not initiated, serious administrative sanctions, such as the loss of the driver's licence, could be established. The country also has substitution treatment for confiscations where no evidence of drug trafficking exists[21].

3.4.7 Other European Countries

Concerning the tables of doses for personal use in other European countries, the European Monitoring Centre for Drugs and

---

[21] Cavada, J.P. *Criterios para el sancionamiento del consumo o tráfico de drogas en el derecho extranjero*. Biblioteca Nacional del Congreso de Chile. Octubre, 2020. Obtained from: https://obtienearchivo.bcn.cl/

Drug Addiction produces summary tables for each country, available at: https://www.emcdda.europa.eu/publications/topic-overviews/threshold-quantities-for-drug-offences/html_en#T1.

3.4.8 Conclusion

In conclusion, in most countries that have a legal system based on the rule of law, with constitutions that protect and recognise fundamental rights of the individual, simple possession of drugs for personal use is not usually punishable by imprisonment. And if they do exist, they are usually symbolic and should be suspended if the offender is a primary offender or undergoes drug treatment. However, each factual situation can be interpreted in different ways, depending on the case, so, to minimise the legal risks of possession and use, the drug user should do his or her part to understand how the supposed tolerance of personal possession for the personal use of drugs is interpreted in the legal practice of the relevant country.

3.4.9 Special Caution in Countries with Strict Drug Laws

In some countries around the world, especially in Africa, the Middle East, or Asia, what we in the West would call a "rule of law with due process and recognition of individual rights" is not strictly enforced. Therefore, drug possession in countries such as the Philippines, China, India, Thailand, Malaysia, Qatar, Saudi Arabia, and others can lead to very serious problems with the law. Paradoxically, it seems that Thailand[22], one of these countries, intends to regulate recreational cannabis soon,

---

[22] Tailandia, primer país de Asia que despenaliza la marihuana. Diario Las Américas. 25 de enero de 2022. Obtained from: https://www.diariolasamericas.com/

having regulated access to the plant for medicinal purposes in 2020. It seems that drug policy is changing dramatically in some countries, and not necessarily only in Western ones or those with a democratic culture that, through the rule of law, recognises the individual's fundamental rights.

4. International Control of Plants Containing Molecules Classified as Psychotropic under the 1971 Convention

As mentioned above, when we encounter interceptions of plant or fungal substances containing a molecule classified as psychotropic under the 1971 Convention on Psychotropic Substances, the legal interpretation becomes quite complicated.

4.1 The International Narcotics Control Board's Interpretation of the Conventions

In this section, we will analyse the thesis of the International Narcotics Control Board (INCB) when applying the international conventions to certain psychoactive plants that are not expressly controlled but contain substances that are.

The INCB or NCBI, in its 2010 and 2012 reports, states that there are only three plants controlled by the international drug conventions. These are only the cannabis plant (Cannabis sativa), the coca leaf (Erythroxylum coca), from which cocaine is extracted, and the white poppy (Papaver somniferum), from which the opium needed to make morphine or heroin is extracted. In other words, the 1961 Convention on Narcotic Drugs only banned certain plants:

Although some active ingredients with stimulant or hallucinogenic effects contained in certain plants are controlled under the 1971 Convention, no plants are currently controlled under that Convention or the 1988 Convention. Nor are preparations (e.g. decoctions for oral consumption) made from plants containing such active ingredients under international control.

Examples of such plants or plant materials are Khat (Catha Edulis), whose active ingredients cathinone and cathine are included in Schedules I and III of the 1971 Convention; ayahuasca, a plant preparation originating in the Amazon basin, mainly Banisteriopsis Caapi (a jungle vine) and another tryptamine-rich plant (Psychotria Viridis) containing various psychoactive alkaloids such as DMT[23](...)

No plants, even those containing psychoactive ingredients, are currently controlled under the 1971 Convention, although in some cases the active ingredients they contain may be under international control. For example, cathine and DMT are psychotropic substances listed in Schedule I of the 1971 Convention, while the plants and herbal preparations containing them, namely khat and ayahuasca, respectively, are not subject to any restriction or control measures[24].

4.2 Possibility of some Countries Controlling Certain Psychoactive Plants on an Individual Basis

Despite that explained in the previous section, there may be countries that have expressly prohibited plants or parts of plants, as is the case of France with ayahuasca or the Netherlands with magic mushrooms.

However, despite the interpretations of the International Narcotics Control Board, the truth is that, in most countries, seizures of ayahuasca are indeed reported and the police do usually confiscate magic mushrooms.

In Spain, most of the judicial precedents of criminal courts and provincial courts have considered that ayahuasca is

---

[23] International Narcotics Control Board. 2010 Report. United Nations. New York, 2011.

[24] International Narcotics Control Board. 2012 Report. United Nations. New York, 2013.

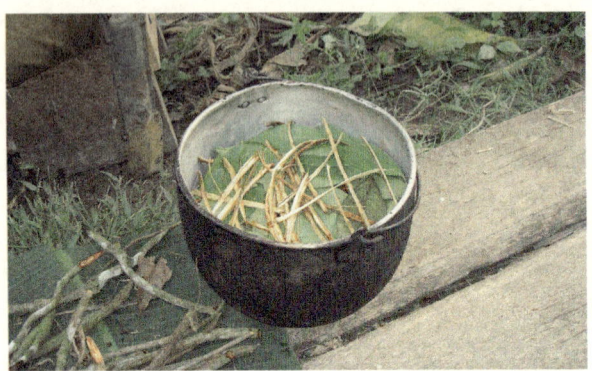

Ayahuasca, ready to be cooked.
Terpsichore, CC BY-SA 3.0 <https://creativecommons.org/licenses/by-sa/3.0>, via Wikimedia Commons.

not subject to the control regime of international treaties and that, therefore, its possession or sale is not criminally relevant.

Thus, one of the latest court rulings obtained by the author of this appendix states:

> To recapitulate, at the international level it seems clear that, either in its plant presentation or as a preparation (paradigmatically decoction for oral ingestion, which is the case here), ayahuasca cannot be understood to be included in the 1971 Convention, even though DMT is; and therefore, as a decoction or in its plant presentation (the plants from which it is obtained), it is not subject to international control.

As a conclusion of this absence of specific mention at the national level and the lack of legal coverage in the 1971 Convention for its inclusion, we, therefore, understand that this preparation is not subject to special control in Spain, nor can it, therefore, be included in the definition of Article 368 of the Criminal Code[25].

---

[25] Sentence from the Audiencia Provincial of Málaga (Sección 1ª) n° 86/2021, March 10.

4.3 PRE-TRIAL DETENTION FOR FALSE-POSITIVE METHAMPHETAMINE TESTS

A person who was acquitted for receiving a package with ayahuasca from Peru spent three months in prison because the substance showed a false positive for methamphetamine in the presumptive colourimetric test carried out by the police (something that usually happens with these plants). Therefore, until the substance was analysed by the laboratory, with a confirmatory test, and until the corresponding appeals were filed because ayahuasca is not controlled, the investigated prisoner could not be released. Despite this, the Anti-Drugs Prosecutor's Office charged him with a crime against public health and asked for four years in prison.

There are also cases in which the investigating courts have ordered provisional imprisonment for the seizure of tobacco snuffs called rapé, which are sometimes containing DMT, are showing a false positive for amphetamine or MDMA in the presumptive colourimetric tests carried out at customs. Even though a document from the Spanish Customs and Excise Department states that, as almost all proceedings end in a file or acquittal and that, normally, people who travel with suitcases loaded with ayahuasca from Colombia or Peru are no longer sent to provisional prison, controlled deliveries of ayahuasca should not be carried out, the truth is that, as the appearance of these is that of a substance in greyish powder form that gives a false positive for MDMA, there have been provisional prison admissions for such rapés. In other words, if 3 or 4 kilos of it are seized and produce a false positive, it is easy to enter prison until the Health Department determines, in a confirmatory manner, the substance in question and its quantification. An injustice that confirms the deficiencies of the system, the lack of public resources and knowledge when it comes to the state exercising its greatest power, the punitive power, or what the Romans called ultima ratio or the ultimate reason of state: criminal law. In this case, in the form of pre-trial detention, a legal institution that renowned penalists such as Gerardo Landrobe have criticised in a multitude of works and labelled as "legalised injustice".

5. Countries that Have Recognised or Banned Certain Plants with Controlled Molecules As Psychotropic

5.1 Lack of Clarity in the Wording of International Conventions

As mentioned above, the legal interpretation of the international fiscalisation of plants containing molecules controlled as psychotropic by the 1971 Convention has never been simple or peaceful and has always generated controversy.

All this controversy stems from the wording of the international conventions and their official commentaries.

Sánchez and Bouso (2015) state in a report:

> What does not seem to be so clear is whether, in order to continue allowing the traditional use of these psychoactive plants, a State Party to the convention must formulate a reservation or not. Reading the text of the treaty, one would say yes. But the Commentary introduces a statement that, in a way, creates a paradox concerning what the convention itself establishes: when it says that "[...] Continued tolerance of the use of the hallucinogenic substances mentioned at the 1971 Conference does not require the formulation of a reservation under paragraph 4" of Article 32 since, following the traditional way of dealing with this issue in the framework of international drug control, the commentators consider that "the inclusion in Schedule I of the active ingredient of a substance does not mean that the substance itself is also included in the Schedule if it is a substance clearly distinct from the substance which constitutes its active ingredient".

There, therefore, exists a disparity between the text of the Convention and its official commentary signed by the UN Secretary-General. This discrepancy was clarified by the INCB in the above-mentioned reports of 2010 and 2012, which stated that these plants are not subject to international control[26].

5.2 COUNTRIES THAT HAVE MADE RESERVATIONS TO INTERNATIONAL CONVENTIONS AND RULINGS CLARIFYING THIS ISSUE

Only Mexico, Peru, the United States, and Canada have indeed made reservations to the 1971 international treaty to allow certain traditional uses of these substances by native communities in the Amazon basin or indigenous reservations in the USA or Canada[27].

In Chile, for example, a judgment was handed down in 2012 (Manto Wasi case) in which an ayahuasca ceremony where a police officer had infiltrated was judged. It was considered that ayahuasca could not be identified with DMT controlled by the 1971 international convention and Decree n° 867 of 2007 of the Andean country controlling DMT, but that P.Viridis, or B. Cappi, plant components used to prepare ayahuasca, could be. The ruling stated that ayahuasca did not pose a danger to public health and following the case, the Director of

---

[26] Constanza Sánchez y José Carlos Bouso, *Ayahuasca: de la Amazonía a la aldea global*, International Center for Ethnobotanical Education, 2015, https://www.tni.org/files/publication-downloads/dpb_43_spanish_web_19122015.pdf.

[27] Sánchez, C y Bouso, J.C. (2015). *Ayahuasca: de la Amazonía a la aldea global*. TNI. Obtained from: https://www.tni.org/

Public Health requested the Ministry of the Interior to control ayahuasca. The initiative did not go ahead[28].

France, however, does follow a prohibitionist model. In 1999, a controversy arose over a complaint by a mother of a member of a daimist group who claimed that her son had lost touch with reality. The case resulted in a conviction by the Paris Court of First Instance on 15 January 2004. The ruling was appealed on appeal to the Paris Court of Appeal, which ruled on 13 January 2015 that, although ayahuasca has hallucinogenic effects, it can be distinguished from synthetic DMT, which is what is undoubtedly subject to the prohibition under French law. Furthermore, it was not possible to speak of a preparation in the technical and legal sense, as this would require the existence of a pure substance. As a result, the court ruled in favour of acquittal (Martín and Muñoz, 2019). This pronouncement caused alarm among the authorities who, in order to avoid the situation highlighted in the ruling, decided to include all plants that are used or usually used in ayahuasca decoctions in the Decree of 20 April 2005, thus prohibiting the uses of this plant in France (Martín and Muñoz, 2019).

5.3 Religious Uses and Cultural Heritage

In Brazil, a country with a strong "ayahuasca" culture, religious uses are recognised. Moreover, Brazil has not made a reservation to the 1971 Convention, and in 1985 the Ministry of Health included B. Cappi and P. Viridis as controlled substances. However, the "ayahuasca church", the UDV, fought a legal battle which led to a study being carried out in communities that use ayahuasca in order to show that it had a significant positive effect (absence of alcoholism, lower infant mortality, and malnutrition, crime rates close to zero, absence of violence, etc.). As a result of

---

[28] Martín, A. y Muñoz, J. *El estatuto legal de la ayahuasca en España. La relevancia penal de los comportamientos relacionados con su consumo y posesión.* Tirant Lo Blanch. Valencia, 2019.

Ayahuasca ceremony at the Takiwasi Centre (Perú)
Takiwasi, CC BY-SA 4.0 <https://creativecommons.org/licenses/by-sa/4.0>, via Wikimedia Commons.

this report, the exclusion of plant species used in the preparation of ayahuasca was declared by Resolution No. 6 of 4 February 1986 (Martín and Muñoz, 2019).

Subsequently, Resolution No. 1 of 25 May 2010 of CONAD (Council on Narcotic Drugs) ratified the legitimacy of the religious use of ayahuasca in one of the most detailed documents to date regulating the uses of ayahuasca in religious practices, prohibiting its commercialisation for profit, emphasising the avoidance of the offering of tourist packages, etc. (Martín and Muñoz, 2019).

Peru, for its part, was the only country to make a reservation, under Article 32 of the 1971 Convention, regarding plants containing Schedule I psychotropic substances that have been traditionally used by certain small, clearly defined groups in religious ceremonies. This happened in 2008 when they declared ayahuasca a national cultural heritage. However, in contrast to Brazil, there is no detailed regulation, but rather a set of customs and practices.

Canada, the USA, and Colombia also allow religious uses of ayahuasca and, the first two, allow peyote cacti too.

In the Netherlands, religious uses of ayahuasca were allowed, but a Supreme Court ruling in 2019 changed the criteria and considered that the right to health prevails over religious freedom, declaring such use illegal29.

5.4 Attempts to Ban a Multitude of Medicinal Plants by the Spanish State

In 2004, an attempt was made in Spain to ban by ministerial order a list of 197 plants that were considered toxic or dangerous by the government at the time. The case was appealed before the National Audience, which, as well as the Supreme Court in its ruling of 9 July 2008, nullified the Ministerial Order of 28 January 2004 on the grounds of formal errors in the order. The prohibition of these plants was not attempted again in this country, so they are not subject to national control nor, as we saw earlier, to international control.

5.5 The Case of Peyote: Countries that made Reservations and Those that Consider It Illegal

Regarding peyote, a report by the ICEERS Foundation states:

> There are more than 40 North American Indian tribes in many parts of the United States and Canada that use peyote as a religious sacrament.

The psychoactive alkaloid in peyote, mescaline, is a controlled substance under the 1971 Vienna Convention and

---

[29] Ferrer, I. (2019) El Supremo holandés prohíbe la importación de ayahuasca. El País, 2 de octubre de 2019. Obtained from: https://elpais.com/sociedad/2019/10/01/actualidad/1569948785_005223.html

is included in Schedule I. Its use, sale, and manufacture are therefore prohibited. However, the peyote plant is not included in the schedules of the conventions, and its regulation depends on the legislation of each country. Thus, in Canada mescaline is in Schedule III, and peyote is explicitly exempted from regulation if it is not prepared for ingestion, while in Brazil, France, Italy, and other countries peyote is considered illegal. Other countries, such as Spain, do not mention peyote in the lists of controlled plants, although this does not imply that the sale of peyote cannot be considered an illegal act.

In the case of US legislation, the use of peyote is permitted only in ceremonial contexts for persons belonging to the Native American Church.

> *The Mexican government was one of the countries that, when adhering to the 1971 Convention and ratifying it on 20 February 1975, made an express reservation about its application, as there are certain indigenous ethnic groups on its territory that traditionally use wild plants containing Schedule I psychotropic substances, including peyote. Within Mexican legislation, peyote cactus is not properly prohibited or regulated, as it is not included in any section of the General Health Law. Its use is permitted to the Huicholes. Even so, peyote is considered an endangered plant, so, with exception of traditional use by indigenous peoples, its collection is prohibited[30].*

6. Differences between Criminal Significance and Administrative Regulation of Plants Containing Molecules Classified as Psychotropic

To be fully aware of the legality surrounding these substances, it is necessary to differentiate between criminal and administrative legality. The truth is that the uses of ayahuasca and other plants are not authorised at the administrative level in almost any

---

[30] Peyote: Basic information. Obtained from: https://www.iceers.org/

country in the world. Only certain religious uses exist, as we have pointed out in the previous section. In other words, plants with controlled substances cannot be sold as food or medicine, even if they are not expressly prohibited by international conventions or national laws transposing these conventions into national law.

6.1 Projections for Recognition of Medical Use of Psychedelics in the Short Term

This lack of administrative recognition will be short-lived. Clinical trials with psilocybin, MDMA, LSD, ibogaine and DMT are well advanced, and it is expected that the use of these substances will soon be authorised by the US, Canadian, European, and worldwide drug agencies for the treatment of depression, PTSD, anxiety, addictions, etc,

6.2 The Canadian Case

Even though they are controlled, due to scientific advances in the recognition of the therapeutic properties of these molecules, their advanced clinical research stage into phases 2 and 3, the safety shown so far and the need for new drugs in this field given the delicate mental health situation exacerbated by the pandemic, the Canadian Health Agency (Health Canada) has just authorised doctors' access to psychedelic substances for mental health treatment.

In practice, this means that, in cases where other therapies have failed, are inadequate, or unavailable in Canada, physicians could, on behalf of patients with serious or life-threatening conditions, apply for access to restricted medicines through Canada's Health Special Access Program (SAP)[31].

---

[31] Canada Gazette, Par I, Volume 154, Number 50: Government Notices. December, 12, 2020.

The proposed amendments are not intended to promote or encourage the early use of unapproved drugs, nor to circumvent well-established clinical trial or drug review and approval processes. However, these amendments could provide an additional potential option for physicians treating patients with serious or life-threatening conditions where other therapies have failed, are not suitable, or are not available.

As mentioned above, for the time being, ketamine or its isolate, esketamine, is the only substance that is currently fully administratively recognized. But very soon there will be more. Not only will cannabis be an administratively recognised medicine, but other no less important substances (MDMA, psilocybin, DMT, etc.) are also knocking on the door to have their therapeutic properties recognised. One can already hear them: Knock, knock!

In conclusion, the past and present research driven by people like Alexander Shulgin, Rick Doblin, Claudio Naranjo, David Nutt, Jordi Riba, Roland Griffiths, Amanda Fielding, Jose Carlos Bouso, Robin Carhart-Harris or the authors of this book collection and many others, will soon allow new substances, substances that have been unjustly stigmatised, demonised, abandoned and banned for more than 60 years, to be authorised in order to deal more effectively with the pandemic of mental illness that plagues our societies.

7. Historical, Ecological and Cultural Reasons why Plants with Molecules Classified as Psychotropic were not Banned

7.1 Historical and Cultural Reasons

The historical, ecological, and cultural reasons for this choice are varied, but we could say that plants containing the alkaloid dimethyltryptamine (DMT) and mushrooms containing psilocybin are very numerous and are found all over the world. This means that legislators would have to be controlling substances that could grow naturally in any field or garden patch.

One of the most important books ever written on psychedelics, TiKHAL, authored by two of the world's most influential people in the study of psychedelics, Alexander and Ann Shulgin (1997)[32], contains a chapter titled DMT is everywhere.

This chapter can be found within the third part of the book titled Botany of tryptamines and at its beginning, we can read the following:

> *What is at the top of the pyramid? N, N-dimethyltryptamine, or DMT, of course. I think this is the right time to talk about the substance and the Drug Law, as 1966 is an interesting time when both stories converge. Manske first synthesised DMT in 1931. It was then independently isolated from two different plants: in 1946 by Goncalves de Lima (from Mimosa hostilis) and in 1955 by Fish, Johnson, and Horning (from Piptadenia peregrina). In 1956 Szára reported its activity in humans as a synthetic entity. The first legal restrictions on its research came in 1966 in response to the growing popularity it gained through the literature of Burroughs, Metzner, Leary, and others in the early 1960s; and in 1976, Christian noted its involvement as a component of the healthy human brain (and perhaps as a neurotransmitter). The year 1965 marked the beginning of the use of initials, both as to substance and organisation names, in Federal Law Enforcement. It was then that, largely motivated by the psychedelic hippie movement of the younger generation at the time, the Drug Abuse Control amendments were passed and came into force. This led to the founding of the BDAC (Bureau of Drug Abuse Control), which became part of the FDA. These amendments were drafted to try to control non-narcotic substances (so-called dangerous substances) such as DMT, LSD, DET, ibogaine, bufotenine, DOM, MDA, MDMA, and TMA. BDAC was an agency that acted in parallel, but not in contact, with the already existing FBN (Federal Bureau of Narcotics), which was exclusively dedicated to the control of the three known narcotic substances: heroin, cocaine, and marijuana. (...) (Shulgin, A. & Shulgin, A. 1997).*

---

[32] Shulgin y Shulgin, *Tihkal: The Continuation*

Therefore, the origin of the control of DMT as a pure substance comes from factors such as its popularisation, in both its pure and crystallised form, given it was synthesised even before it was discovered within countless plants, as well as to the fact that it is even found in the human brain, something that should not be so surprising given its similarity to the serotonin molecule and hence its metabolic proximity.

7.2 ECOLOGICAL REASONS

A little further on, Shulgin and Shulgin (1997) continue: The answer to the second question is that DMT is simply almost everywhere you look. It is in this flower here, in that tree there, and in those animals further away.

The book's chapter is divided into sections to indicate where DMT can be found: Marine world (S. ehina, S. auria, etc.); Toads (Bufo); Herbs (Birdseed or Phalaris species, etc.); Legumes (Acacia, Mimosa, Illinois flower, Sophora secundiflora seed or mescal bean, etc.); Psychotria (Psychotria viridis); Limes, lemons and Angostura bitters (Zanthoxylum arborescens and Z. procerum). (Shulgin, A. & Shulgin, A. 1997).

Different species of psilocybe mushrooms also grow wild around the world, as can be seen in various books. Many sources can be consulted to accredit the large number of mushrooms containing molecules that are controlled under international law (psilocin and psilocybin), but some notable ones are the following ones: Psilocybin Mushrooms of the World[33], Psilocibes (the mushrooms)[34], Teonanácatl[35]

---

[33] Stamets, P (1996) *Psilocybin Mushrooms of the World: An Identification Guide.*

[34] Bouso, JC. (Ed.). (2013). *Psilocibes. The mushrooms.* Motril: Ultraradio

[35] Ott, J. Bigwood, J. Wasson G. Belmonte, D. Hoffmann, A. Weil, A. Evans. R. (1985). *Teonanácatl. Hongos alucinógenos de Europa y América del Norte.* Madrid: Swan.

Psilocybe mexicana photographed in Veracruz, Mexico Alan Rockefeller, CC BY-SA 4.0 <https://creativecommons.org/licenses/by-sa/4.0>, via Wikimedia Commons.

and Pharmakhoteon[36]. Almost all varieties of psilocybin mushrooms discovered up to the time of publication can be consulted here.

In the book Psilocibes, we find a chapter IV, authored by Òscar Parés, which lists some of the existing varieties of mushrooms that contain psilocybin: Cubensis, Panaeolus/Copelandia cynescens, and Panaeolus/Copelandia tropicalis.

The author continues below:

> There is a third grouping of psilocybin fungi that is worth considering. It is not distinguished from the previous two by its genetic family but by its form or presentation. Called truffle (Latin: sclerotium, plural: sclerotia), it is a hardened compact mass of mycelium containing psilocybin. It is produced when the environmental conditions are not favourable for the flower, or reproductive apparatus (read: the fungus) to sprout from the long underground mycelium. Under this heading, we would include the most widespread Psilocybe tampanensis, but sclerotia of Psilocybe mexicana and Psilocybe Atlantis are also commercially available. (...)

---

[36] Ott, J. (1999). Pharmakoteon: Cogniciones

7.2.1 Psilocybe Fungi found on the Iberian Peninsula

Following the quotation in the previous section:

> (...) *Psilocybe cyanescens and Copelandia cyanescens are also known to have been found in open fields on the Iberian Peninsula.* (...)
> (...) *We now turn to two other psilocybe fungi of special interest that occur in the Iberian context. The first of these is Psilocybe hispanica. This fungus was discovered in the Huesca Pyrenees.*

In Galicia, we find the Psilocybe gallaeciae, which according to Guzmán, one of the most prestigious mycologists in the world, belongs to the variety. P. mexicana. There are indications that two other mushrooms with psilocybin content can be found in Catalonia: Psilocybe subbalteatus and Panaelus cyanescens.

The book we have just quoted also contains chapter VII entitled Visionary Fungi in the Iberian Peninsula, written by Ignacio Seral Bozal.

To get an idea of the number of psychoactive mushrooms that are not legally controlled and exist in the Iberian Peninsula, we will cite the different sections into which this chapter is divided such as we previously did with the TiHKAL chapter (Shulgin & Shulgin, 1997).

Amanita muscaria[37]. Species: Amanita phantherina and Amanita gemmata.

- Genus Panaeolus. Species: P. cyanescens,
- Genus Pluteus. Species: P. salicinus. P. antricapillus.
- Genus Inocybe. Species: I. aemacta, I. corydalina, I. coelestium and I. aeruginascens.
- Genus Gymnopilus. Species: G. spectabilis.
- Genus Psilocybe. Species: P. hispanicae, P. galicae, P. cyanescens, P. semilanceata.

---

[37] Psychoactive but not psychedelic mushroom.

As we can see, the argument put forward to defend the non-control of plants with DMT content is also applicable in the case of psilocybe mushrooms. There are many genera and species of psychoactive mushrooms in the world. Some of them, such as Amanita muscaria, do not even contain controlled molecules. Ibotenic acid and muscimol (the psychoactive principles of this species) are not subject to international control, therefore, in this case, it would not even raise the doubts regarding varieties of mushrooms that contain controlled molecules that we are trying to solve. Despite this lack of regulation, the consumption of this mushroom does not produce classic psychedelic effects and actually poses far more health risks than any other psilocybin-containing fungal species.

Bearing this in mind, in case of a hypothetical control of these mushrooms, one could present the exception of the international convention that states that, if the organism wildly grows in that territory and there is a traditional use, reservations to the convention could be accepted.

Mescaline-containing cacti are also present not only in American countries but also in Spain and other southern European countries.

7.3 Reasons given in the 2014 TNI report

To understand a little more about how these international Conventions were put together, let us quote a paragraph from a TNI report (Trans National Institute, 2014) which reads as follows:

> The problem regarding how to deal with the traditional uses of certain plants arose again at the 1971 conference, especially concerning psilocybin-containing mushrooms and the mescaline-containing peyote cactus, both hallucinogenic substances listed in the 1971 Convention schedules. Then, as of now, mushrooms and peyote were used in religious and healing ceremonies by Mexican and North American indigenous groups. Unlike the position they took during the 1961 negotiations, this time the US authorities accepted the "consensus that it is not worth

trying to impose control measures on biological substances from which psychotropic substances can be obtained (...) North American Indians in the United States and Mexico use peyote in religious rites and the misuse of this substance is considered sacrilege".

By excluding plants from which alkaloids could be extracted from the scheduled lists, the 1971 Convention deviated, with good reason, from the prevailing zero-tolerance rule that had been applied in the Single Convention. The very concept of "psychotropic substances" was a distortion of the logic underpinning the control framework, as the term lacks scientific credentials and was originally invented, in effect, as an excuse to avoid the much stricter controls of the Single Convention being applied to the wide range of psychoactive, mostly synthetic, drugs included in the 1971 Convention[38].

7.4 Conclusion

There may be several reasons as to why no plants are controlled under the 1971 Convention on Psychotropes. One of the most likely reasons is the fact that if all plants containing any active substances categorised as a psychotropic were to be banned, a large part of the world's flora would be illegal. Given that in some other instances some plants are indeed controlled, it may also be that the conventions understand that it is not desirable to control plants that are not considered extremely dangerous. After all, unlike controlled plants such as the opium poppy or the coca plant, which could kill in high doses, psychedelic plant sources rarely pose a direct risk to physical health.

In conclusion, it seems that solid arguments exist such as mental health, risk and harm reduction, and what is known as the "management of risks and pleasures", and not only on a scientific but also on a historical, legal, cultural, and ecological level. These arguments can and should be, taken into account by both the readers and public authorities when, with the greatest legal guarantees, facilitating access to psychedelic therapy.

---

[38] Anthony Henman* and Pien Metaal (2014). *Hora de abrir los ojos.* Trans National Institute. Recuperado de http://fileserver.idpc.net/library/TNi-publication-plants-spa.pdf

LEGAL GLOSSARY

Alkaloids: secondary plant metabolites, usually synthesised from amino acids, which have in common their water solubility at acidic pH and their solubility in organic solvents at alkaline pH. True alkaloids are derived from an amino acid and are therefore nitrogenous. All those with the amine or imine functional group are basic. Many psychoactive substances are alkaloids.

Ayahuasca church UDV (Unión Do Vegetal): together with Santo Daime, another of the great ayahuasca churches in the world.

Criminal significance: when an alleged offence is covered by an article of the Criminal Code of a given State and the consequence is a legal measure consisting of a custodial sentence, a financial penalty, or the deprivation of a fundamental right, such as disqualification from holding public office, disqualification from participating in elections or disqualification from association with the victim. There are also security measures consisting of the internment of persons who are not criminally liable, such as those who have committed the offence because of a psychiatric illness.

Daimista: parishioner of the Church of Santo Daime (ayahuasca church).

DEA: Stands for Drug Enforcement Administration. It is the agency of the US Department of Justice dedicated to combating the smuggling and use of illegal drugs in the United States, as well as money laundering. Although it shares jurisdiction with the FBI domestically, it is the sole agency responsible for coordinating and prosecuting anti-drug investigations abroad.

Designer drug: engineering in the synthesis of new drugs whose mission is to create substances that mimic other substances under international or national control. The classic example of a designer drug would be fentanyl, which mimics controlled opiates. And the paradigm of a psychedelic designer drug would be 2CB, synthesised by A. Shulgin in 1974 in an attempt to find a molecule similar to mescaline. Terms such as NPS (New Psychoactive Substance) or RC (Research Chemicals) are also used to define these when they are very new and not yet internationally controlled.

Detoxification treatment: a measure imposed by a court as a substitute for a prison sentence for drug-related offences. The convicted person must complete the treatment under the warning that, if he/she fails to attend the appointments, or fails to pass the treatment, the benefit of the suspended sentence will be revoked.

European Monitoring Centre for Drugs and Drug Addiction (EMCDDA): a European public agency set up to monitor and publish reports on the prevalence of drug use in the states of the European Union, and to assess and advise on drug policy.

Federal law: laws passed in the US Congress. They differ from the laws of individual states in that they affect all American citizens, and can only deal with certain very important competencies attributed by the US Constitution to the US Congress, located on Capitol Hill in Washington D.C. The FBI (Federal Bureau of Investigation) is responsible for investigating offences covered by and punishable under federal law.

ICEERS Foundation: a non-profit foundation based in the Netherlands and Spain dedicated to the research of applications of plants containing psychoactive molecules, controlled or not, for the treatment of different diseases, as well as to the protection of the cultures that use them in a traditional way. They have ECOSOC status at the United Nations Commission on Narcotic Drugs.

International Convention on Psychotropic Substances: Together with the 1961 Single Convention on Narcotic Drugs and the 1988 United Nations Convention against Illicit Traffic in Narcotic Drugs and Psychotropic Substances, the 1971 Convention forms the current international drug control system. It was prompted by the rise in the use of hallucinogenic or psychedelic drugs and to control non-narcotic substances, such as those included in the 1961 convention.

International Narcotics Control Board, INCB (NCBI): an independent, quasi-judicial body of experts established under the 1961 Single Convention on Narcotic Drugs by the merger of two bodies, namely the Central Standing Committee on Narcotic Drugs, established under the 1925 International Opium Convention, and the Narcotics Control Bureau, established under the 1931 Convention for Limiting the Manufacture and Regulating the Distribution of Narcotic Drugs. INCB consists of 13 members, each elected to serve for a term of five years by the Economic and Social Council.

Jurisprudence: doctrine established repeatedly by the Supreme Court or the Constitutional Court, when interpreting the Constitution and laws.

Legislation: a set of rules and laws that regulate the relations between people in a country or a particular sector. The legislation makes it possible to organise a given sector and a country as a whole.

PSYCHEDELIC'S LEGAL STATUS

MAPS (Multidisciplinary Association for Psychedelic Studies): a non-profit organisation founded in 1984 by Rick Doblin to research the medical and cultural uses of psychedelic substances.

Ministerial Order: a legal instrument of Spanish law that is not strictly speaking a law, decree, or regulation, and which serves, in this case, to include substances in one or another list of the different national drug laws that transpose international conventions into domestic law.

Narcotic substances: these are the substances included in the 1971 Convention. This would be a legal or juridical term as they are those included in Schedules I and II of the 1961 Convention on Narcotic Drugs. Moreover, many of those included here could not be defined as narcotic drugs, but cannabis would also be defined as hallucinogenic, or semi-psychedelic. Or cocaine, which is not a narcotic in the strict sense, but can be considered as a local anesthetic with stimulant properties.

National Institute of Toxicology (INT): an official Spanish agency composed of pharmacologists, physicians, and toxicologists whose role is to provide technical advice and reports to inform governments and judges when enacting laws or passing judgements.

New York Single Convention on Narcotic Drugs of 1961: international treaty signed on 30 March 1961 in New York, which forms the international legal framework for drug control. The Convention defined narcotic drug as: "any of the substances in Schedules I and II, natural or synthetic", and recognises in its preamble that the medical use of narcotic drugs is indispensable for the relief of pain and that States signatories to the treaty should take "the necessary measures to ensure the availability of narcotic drugs for such purposes".

Presumptive colourimetric test: a field test performed by the police to provide a quick indication that a particular substance may be classified as a narcotic or psychotropic substance. It differs from confirmatory tests in that, in presumptive tests, there is a possibility of false positives and negatives, and it is not possible to quantify the purity of the substance seized and, therefore, whether it exceeds the minimum psychoactive dose, or whether it is a toxic dose. Example of a presumptive test: Duquenois or Marquis.

Proportionality test: legal doctrine for the interpretation of conflicting fundamental rights in a legal relationship, whether these concern two fundamental rights of the individual, or a right of the individual as opposed to collective legal goods, such as public health or collective security.

Psychotropic substances: are those included in the 1971 Convention. As with narcotic drugs, this is a legal term, as it includes substances that can be classified as stimulants (amphetamine) or hallucinogens (LSD).

Regulation: a rule that develops the content of a law.

Reservation to an international treaty: a unilateral act by which a party expresses, with regard to the conclusion of an international treaty, its intention to exclude or modify an obligation arising therefrom. Reservations are a means of promoting the conclusion of treaties.

Second Summer of Love: the period between 1988 and 1989 in the UK during which acid house developed, providing the soundtrack for the emergence of rave culture, a synergistic combination of a drug (namely ecstasy, which came to England, where it was also known as "E", together with another way of understanding music recreationally and the social component of dance) and rhythms.

The United Nations Commission on Narcotic Drugs (CND) was established by the Economic and Social Council (ECOSOC) of the United Nations by Resolution 9 of 17 February 1946 as the governing body of the international drug control treaties. It is a functional commission of ECOSOC. The CND meets annually in Vienna, Austria, to examine and adopt a series of decisions and resolutions related to the implementation of the drug treaties and policies about narcotic drugs and psychotropic substances.

Transparency Portal of Spain: public agency created in the Spanish State to ensure that citizens can consult important documents, the knowledge of which is necessary to respect the principles of publicity, justice, and information owed by the State to its citizens.

War on Drugs: a policy promoted by the US government aimed at the prosecution of the production, trade, and consumption of certain psychoactive substances. The term was popularised by the media shortly after a press conference held on 18 June 1971 by US President Richard Nixon.